Survive to Thrive

Survive to Thrive

Sustaining Yourself, Your Brand and Your Business

from Recession to Recovery

by

Philip H. Geier, Jr.

For Information, address The Geier Group,
70 E 55th Street, 15th Floor, New York, New York 10022.
Library of Congress Control Number 2009904733
10 DIGIT ISBN: 1-4392-4129-5
13 DIGIT EAN: 978-1-4392-4129-5

To my family, without whose support I would not be where I am today.

And to my parents, Philip and Jane Geier, who I miss everyday.

Introduction

WHEN I BEGAN working on this book in the spring of 2008, the question of whether or not America was entering a recession had not been answered. At the start of the year, one prominent survey of CEOs had predicted a flat economy with the Dow ending the year about where it started: above 13,000. U.S. ad spending had slowed in 2007. But '08 was an Olympic and Election year. Hopes were high that spending would rebound and grow about four percent.

Don't worry. This is not a book filled with predictions.

I'm writing these words in February 2009, just days after the inauguration of President Barack Obama. His historic election ushers in a new political era. But no one—no president, CEO, investor, economist, journalist, or academic—can predict with any certainty what comes next.

The global financial meltdown has plunged us into a new era of uncertainty. Whole nations and industries are being transformed. And every day produces new headlines that only add to the uncertainty.

The world has changed dramatically. But my reasons for writing this book have not. From the outset, this book has been about change. In these pages, I describe how great companies, great brands and their advertising agencies have responded to everything the world has thrown at them for the past hundred years.

This book covers the history of global marketing and advertising—from the Great Depression and World War II to the eight recessions I have lived through since entering the business world in the late '50s. My timeline spans many decades—from the growth of radio, to the advent of television, to the emergence of the internet. The stories in these pages illustrate how global advertising has evolved from the days when American brands, creativity and optimism were the dominant forces in the marketing world, to the world we live in today, where globalization connects us all—from Moscow to Mumbai, Beijing to Buenos Aires, Sydney to San Francisco.

My hope is that this book will give you valuable lessons in dealing with change and delivering continuous improvement as you approach all your marketing and management decisions.

How to manage change

Just a generation ago, the globalized, high-tech, information-saturated world we live in today was unimaginable. My career in global advertising began at a time when there was no CNN or MTV. No Microsoft or Intel. No Nokia or Samsung. No Google. No iPod. No YouTube. No Facebook. No Wikipedia. No Twitter. Russia was part of the Soviet Union. China didn't allow advertising. The fax machine was a novelty. Research was done in the library. Records came on vinyl. Air travel was an enjoyable luxury for the privileged few.

Yes, indeed, times have changed.

But one thing hasn't changed. Now, as then, the world's most valuable global brand is Coca-Cola.

That's right. Through all the technological, political, economic, and marketing transformations we have seen over the past few decades, the brand that pioneered global advertising—and introduced the "One Sight, One Sound" campaign concept back in 1963—remains the world's most valuable and powerful brand.

How brands like Coke, Esso (Exxon), and L'Oreal conquered the world

In writing this book, my aim is to offer you an insider's view of the history of globalization and show you how to apply many of the lessons of globalization to your own marketing and business challenges. I'll illustrate why some brands endure and grow stronger, while others fade away. And I'll show you how younger brands can use new technologies and marketing techniques to leapfrog their competitors in the global marketplace.

I'll present cases studies—like Coca-Cola's—that offer indispensable lessons for any business leader or marketing professional looking to expand to new and emerging markets. After all, Coke isn't number one simply because of its "first mover advantage." Throughout the years, it has demonstrated many of the traits that are essential for *all* global brands looking to succeed in a competitive and changing marketplace: Sound strategic planning; cultural awareness and sensitivity; a commitment to creative excellence; plus disciplined and agile execution.

I know first-hand how tirelessly the company and its people have worked to succeed as global marketers. And I know how hard Coke's agencies, especially McCann-Erickson, Interpublic Group's largest agency, have labored to make sure Coke's messaging has connected with consumers in every language and every corner of the world.

I'll tell you what many of global advertising's pioneers—from Coca-Cola, to Exxon, to L'Oreal, to Nestlé, to Unilever—discovered about advertising across borders and cultures. The right way to approach new markets. The best way to execute. And many of the mistakes you'll want to avoid.

How the advertising industry evolved to meet the challenges of globalization…and the problems that followed

This book is the not just the story of global brands. It's also a history of how the advertising industry as a whole and Interpublic in particular, evolved to meet the challenges of globalization.

It's a story I can tell from a highly personal perspective spanning more than four decades.

I began my career at the McCann-Erickson agency in 1958 and retired as the Chairman and CEO of Interpublic Group, McCann's parent company, in 2000. Throughout this time, Interpublic and McCann-Erickson acted as multinational or global partners to an expanding list of major clients. Our client-centric focus meant we followed and often led our clients in many new directions.

When I became CEO and Chairman of Interpublic Group in 1980, the company had 8,000 employees, revenue of $500 million, net income of $21 million, and a market capitalization of $500 million. When I left at the end of 2000, Interpublic had grown to 50,000 employees in 650 offices in 127 countries, with revenue of $5.6 billion, net income of $473 million, and a market cap of more than $12 billion.

Throughout the '80s and '90s, I charted a new course for the company, a course that allowed us to expand in many new directions and take on aggressive competitors in the advertising industry, such as WPP and Omnicom. As the company expanded and grew, we added new agency networks (including great agencies such as Lowe, Lintas, Deutsch, Mullen and The Martin Agency) to manage client conflicts, we expanded the range of services we offered, and we integrated every aspect of the global communications effort.

Over that 20-year period, Interpublic's stock had a compounded annual growth rate of 22% and the company was the #1 management holding company in advertising for many of those years.

There are a lot of lessons to be learned from that experience. And again, I'll point out the kind of mistakes you should avoid.

Because in addition to telling you how to *Survive and Thrive* in today's challenging economic times, I'll also use this book to explain how a very successful company ended up with the kind of problems from which every global business can and should learn.

How to ensure your brand connects with today's and tomorrow's consumers

Ultimately, my goal with this book is to give you the insights and tools you need to better navigate through today's difficult times and achieve long-term success in the global marketplace.

For today's consumers, global brands are seldom more than an arm's length or a mouse click away. Our global, 24/7 culture gives consumers access to a virtually unrestricted diet of news, entertainment, sports, fashion and marketing messages. And unlike old media, which "push" content and advertising to consumers on fixed timetables, new media technologies allow consumers to "pull" the content exactly when and where they want it.

This combination of globalized communications and consumer control creates fundamental challenges for multinational businesses and brand marketers everywhere, whether they compete on a global, national or local level.

Times are hard. But I hope you're motivated by the challenge ahead and by the advice you'll find in these pages.

CHAPTER ONE

Know What You're Selling

How to find your brand's essence and connect it with
consumers in every market and every medium

"We are not here to sell a parcel of boilers and vats, but the potentiality of growing rich beyond the dreams of avarice."
                    —Samuel Johnson, conducting the sale of Thrales brewery, London, 1781

Understand the brand

IN TODAY'S CUT-THROAT, globally competitive world, it's tougher than ever to differentiate your brand. But do it effectively and the potentiality of great riches still remains.

Thinking like Samuel Johnson helps. He knew that dramatizing the benefits of a brand is far more effective than simply describing its features.

No matter how complicated or how feature-packed your *product* may be, you must be able to articulate the essence of your *brand* in a way that gives your customers something they can understand, relate to and believe in.

The Coca-Cola Company discovered early on that while its main product was syrup, its brand essence was *refreshment*.

Microsoft made people comfortable with computers not by explaining the intricate workings of computer software, but by promising *information at your fingertips*.

For Exxon and its international Esso brand, success was built not on the me-too nature of its gasoline, but on the memorable ways it delivered images of *power and reliability*.

By uncovering, dramatizing and promoting your own brand's essence, you will develop a platform from which all your marketing efforts will flow.

Samuel Johnson, by the way, convinced David Barclay (founder of Barclays Bank) that his "parcel of boilers and vats" was worth 135,000 pounds—$22.5 million in today's dollars. Clearly, that was neither the first nor the last instance of a financial wizard overpaying for some well-marketed assets!

In this chapter, I'll explain the success of the world's first global brand campaigns and highlight why the branding principles behind them are still applicable today.

"One Sight, One Sound"

1963 was an unforgettable, inspirational and, ultimately, tragic year. It was a year filled with sights and sounds that still resonate in the world's collective consciousness.

Martin Luther King made his "I have a dream" speech in Washington, DC and created unstoppable momentum for civil rights legislation. Beatlemania swept the U.K. and began its relentless global march. Elizabeth Taylor starred in *Cleopatra*, the most expensive Hollywood movie of the 20th century. In November, the world was stunned when President Kennedy was assassinated in Dallas.

1963 was also the year in which global advertising came of age. Not with a cacophony of sights and sounds, but with a single—and simple—strategic shift by The Coca-Cola Company.

The campaign Coke introduced that year, created by the McCann-Erickson agency, had the theme "Things Go Better With Coke." But more important than the slogan was the strategy behind it.

The campaign marked the launch of what Coke under its marketing leader Donald Keough called the "One Sight, One Sound" concept, an approach designed to ensure that, whatever the medium, whatever the language, all of Coke's marketing communications would be instantly recognizable—both visually and aurally—in every corner of the world. "One Sight" meant that all ads would keep the same family look, with certain basic and universally repeated elements. "One Sound" meant that the consistent use of music would give Coca-Cola advertising "a familiar ring no matter where it meets the ear."

"One Sight, One Sound" allowed Coca-Cola to connect with consumers on a gut level entertaining the senses, touching the emotions and, at the same time, selling real product benefits. It was also a key component of Keough's broader vision: ensuring the Coke brand was always just "an arm's length away," whether that meant a supermarket's refrigerated cabinet or a small Coca-Cola stand in the rice fields of Thailand.

The success of "Things Go Better With Coke" was immediate and lasting. The campaign would eventually feature many of the most famous musicians and singers of the day – including Roy Orbison, Ray Charles, and The Supremes.

By the end of the 1960s, Coca-Cola's commitment to global branding extended not just to advertising but to every consumer touchpoint with design consistency evident in everything from its uniforms and truck designs to its vending machines and point-of-sale displays.

Today, of course, the concept of global branding and the use of central creative ideas to drive global campaigns is so embedded in our culture that it's hard to remember that it wasn't always this way. But if you're looking to succeed in today's communications world, you'll be following in the footsteps of some highly creative and successful marketers. It will help you to understand how global advertising evolved, which principles of branding, consumer motivation, and advertising effectiveness still apply and how to avoid repeating the mistakes that have already been made.

What Coke discovered in the 1960s

1. Global brand consistency touches all the senses and every aspect of the consumer experience.

2. Creative campaigns built on a strong central idea, once published, can win over non-believers.

3. Senior management plays a key role in communicating and supporting global brand strategy.

These same principles continue to be used effectively by global brands as varied as Starbucks, Samsung, HSBC, The Gap, and Google.

Advertising history: From prehistory to 1950

Advertising has been around since man first painted on cave walls. In ancient Egypt, papyrus was the medium of choice.

The printing press and the growth of newspapers in the 17th and 18th centuries allowed for advertisements to be more widely distributed and for mail-order advertising to take off. It was also an era in which consumers grew increasingly cynical of the hucksterism of many marketers, especially those promoting unproven medical cures.

It wasn't until the last decades of the 19th century that the notion of nationally distributed products, and the modern concept of branded advertising, created by a professional agency, truly took hold.

New manufacturing techniques made it possible to produce and package identical products and distribute them nationally. Department stores appeared in fast-growing cities such as New York, Chicago, and Philadelphia. Catalogues for companies like Sears Roebuck and Montgomery Ward became "must-haves" even in rural communities. At last, consumers could start buying from a wide selection of recognizable brands and do so with confidence in what they were buying.

At the same time, previously elitist magazine publishers adapted their own business models and began slashing prices to make their products more available to an eager reading public. In the process they created a dynamic new medium for the marketers of everything from soaps to cigarettes to canned foods.

The first modern advertising agency—N. W. Ayer & Son—opened its doors in Philadelphia in 1869. And, as the client population exploded, the agency business soon became a crowded field.

The agency I was to join in 1958—McCann-Erickson—dated back to 1902 and 1912, the years when: a) Alfred Erickson launched The Erickson Company to serve clients such as Fiat Automobiles and Bon Ami cleansers; and b) the H. K. McCann agency opened with the credo "Truth Well Told," working for clients such as Chesebrough (Vaseline) and multiple ex-units of Standard Oil Company.

Early in the 20th century, the advent of radio led to further rapid growth in marketing communications and the advertising agency business. Between

1923 and 1930, 60% of American households acquired a radio and, for the first time ever, advertising could speak directly to consumers in their homes, using the power of the human voice to convey emotion and spark listeners' imaginations. While other countries adopted a publicly funded approach to radio broadcasting, America's commercial-friendly approach meant that single-sponsored, advertiser-funded programming was commonplace. The line between programming and advertising was often blurred, giving advertisers and their agencies a huge role in the creation of a shared American culture.

The rapid growth of radio, combined with the economic boom of the 1920s, contributed to the continued success and complementary strengths of the McCann and Erickson agencies. When the two agencies merged in 1930, the new McCann-Erickson agency, with a combined $15 million in billings, represented the largest merger the advertising business had ever seen.

In the 1930s, McCann-Erickson emerged as a leader in radio innovations being the first to deliver shortwave broadcasts from a ship in mid-ocean, creating a live show from a transcontinental flight to help inaugurate new Boeing planes and leading the way with programming innovations like adapting full-length books such as *Charlie Chan* for serial broadcasts. McCann-Erickson brought Benny Goodman to the air with *Let's Dance*, a program produced for National Biscuit Company (Nabisco); created *Believe-It-or-Not Ripley* for Standard Oil Co. of New Jersey; and launched the careers of the Marx Brothers on an ambitious, five-night-a-week show called *Five Star Theatre*.

At the same time, in the age of talking pictures, on-screen advertising became a hot new medium both in movie theaters and at trade shows. McCann-Erickson dived right in. In 1931, the agency produced one of the first sponsored sound films using animation by Dr Seuss in a movie for Flit insecticide.

Throughout the '30s and '40s, an era that saw the Great Depression, World War II, as well as Hollywood's "Golden Age"—radio, magazines, and newspapers remained the dominant mass media. Outdoor advertising was also extremely important, both in the big cities and along the nation's and the world's increasingly populated highways.

Television, though introduced in the 1940s, didn't become a mass medium until the 1950s. McCann-Erickson presented its first television show, a 10-minute sketch sponsored by Flit and called *India Summer*, on NBC-TV on April 19, 1940.

The agency began weekly programming and sponsorships two weeks later.

Like the internet's first banner ads a half-century later, these efforts, while pioneering, were not seen by the masses. In 1946, there were still only 7,000 TV sets in the United States. In 1948, there were one million. By 1950, there were 50 million and the stage was set for the next stage of advertising's evolution.

The evolution of advertising

1. Product advertising has been with us since the beginning of time.
2. The creation of nationally branded products in the late 19th century allowed consumers to buy with confidence and develop specific brand preferences.
3. "New media" have consistently emerged to transform the advertising business.
4. Advertising agencies played a key role in developing the advertising and the programming that shaped modern culture.

   Advertising agencies and marketers continue to find new ways to integrate branded content into the emerging platforms of today and tomorrow including video games, social networks and mobile media.

"The care and feeding of ideas"—and tigers

In 1948, a 32-year-old research guru named Marion Harper succeeded H.K. McCann as CEO of McCann-Erickson. Shortly after taking over the agency, Harper made a speech entitled "The Care and Feeding of Ideas." It gave an early look into how Harper planned to challenge his agency, his clients, and his industry to embrace a steady stream of creative, structural, and media innovations.

Said Harper:

> Of all businesses, this is the business of *ideas.*
> Always has been. Always must be.
> For *ideas* are what people buy.
> So *ideas* are what sellers must sell.
> *Ideas* are what line the shelves of our pantries and refrigerators.

Ideas are what we brush our teeth with, shave with, bathe with, dress in.

Ideas are what we eat, where our children go to college.

An *idea* is whom you marry, where you live, what you do to earn your living.

Ideas are what people buy – *ideas* are what sellers must sell.

As McCann-Erickson continued to develop new ideas for clients, one idea demanded more care and feeding than any other: the Esso Tiger, the global symbol of Exxon's gasoline brand.

Esso was perhaps the first true global account. Back in the 1920s, the H.K. McCann agency had "followed the flag" of Standard Oil ("Esso") to Europe. By the mid-'30s, McCann-Erickson expanded into Latin America, opening offices in Buenos Aires and Rio de Janeiro after winning the advertising business for Standard Oil's Latin American subsidiary.

Esso had used an image of a tiger in various markets since the early part of the 20th century. The tiger first appeared in Norway. It was spotted in the U.K. in the 1930s, but the campaign was halted by World War II.

In 1959, the tiger was reborn in America when Emery Smith, a copywriter in McCann's Chicago office, penned the famous line: "Put a Tiger in Your Tank." The campaign's success meant that it was soon extended to Esso's European affiliates.

Research showed the potency of the Esso Tiger, a symbol of power that consumers could relate to on an emotional level. Plus, it was adaptable. From market to market, using the Tiger still allowed Esso clients to create their own product-specific messages and incorporate competitive information about quality and additives.

By 1964, McCann-Erickson, fresh from its global creative success with Coke, convinced Exxon that the Esso Tiger should be the focus of a single, centrally created, global brand campaign.

Built around Bob Jones' memorable illustrations, the campaign's global rollout was executed with tremendous fanfare.

As *Time Magazine* noted in May 1965, "Esso's frisky, whimsical tiger with the high-octane tail has become a roaring success all over Europe…Though most U.S. ad campaigns are sharply revised and toned down for export, the tiger was crated and shipped with only minor changes, such as substituting the word 'motor' for the untranslatable 'tank' in the wording of French and Italian slogans...In just the month since it was introduced with unprecedented hoopla...the (campaign) has spread to 14 countries, leaving a trail of 1,000,000 tiger tails and such gimmickry as tiger T-shirts, balloons, pencils, coloring books, key rings, windshield decals and jigsaw puzzles." Most important, *Time* also pointed out: "Riding on the tiger tale, Esso stations in Europe are pumping record volumes."

The new creative appeared on every continent and was soon hailed by *Advertising Age* columnist Harry W. McMahon as "my nomination for the most important advertising campaign in the entire history of international advertising." Nearly 50 years later, Esso's "Put a Tiger in Your Tank" campaign remains one of the most famous and successful in advertising history.

The campaign demonstrated the power of a central creative idea to elevate a brand above "me-too" product status. It also showed the possibilities that occur when a client and an agency share a successful history, understand and adapt the key elements of a brand's heritage, and appreciate how symbolism can communicate simply and powerfully in ways that transcend language and cultural barriers.

Then world events intervened. The severity of the 1973 oil crisis made the use of a cartoon tiger suddenly inappropriate. It was dropped from Esso's advertising.

That might have been the end for the Esso Tiger, but two years later, McCann's U.K. agency found a way to turn a problem into an opportunity. The agency updated the campaign by shooting new TV commercials that used new graphic techniques to show a live tiger prowling through everyday environments. The symbolic power of the tiger remained, but the realism was more in keeping with the mood of the times. These dramatic new ads were so powerful that they, along with a new "Rely on the Tiger" slogan, were quickly embraced and adapted by Esso clients in other international markets. In a time of upheaval in the oil markets, the campaign was a great way to reinforce Esso's leadership image and the consistency of its product.

Still, the U.S. client, having moved on to a more promotional campaign, wanted nothing to do with the new creative. But maybe there were some ego issues too. After all, Exxon's home office was in the habit of *exporting* creative, not *importing* it.

I was in Europe at that time and had just been named a vice-chairman of Interpublic Group. Working with my McCann-Erickson colleagues on both sides of the Atlantic, we presented a review of the new international campaign to Exxon's Chairman, Clifton Garvin.

Garvin was interested in one thing: Results. When he saw how well the live tiger was doing around the world, he insisted that the U.S. division test the creative and use it if was shown to be more effective. In those days, Exxon was run in a similar way to the U.S. Army. Once a decision was made, it was moved forward and executed.

Needless to say, in consumer testing, the live tiger destroyed the U.S. ads. It was the first time I witnessed something that has since become commonplace: the importation by an established global brand of internationally produced creative to the U.S. market.

Tiger takeaways

1. Symbolism is an effective and flexible way to communicate product benefits in ways that transcend language and cultural barriers.

2. Promoting everyday products with a sense of humor and showmanship is a great way to connect with consumers.

3. Once consumers start identifying with your brand, sales follow.

   Combining symbolism and showmanship still works—just look at the best-loved brands in your supermarket aisle and the popular campaigns for brands such as Apple's iPod, Nike and MasterCard.

My own first steps in the advertising business

Before I entered the advertising business, I was the mastermind behind three of the greatest product innovations of the 1950s. Truly fantastic ideas. Surefire hits with consumers. Each with incredible money-making potential.

Or so I thought at the time.

Here's the story of how I became an enthusiastic and over-confident entrepreneur, why I failed, and how the advertising agency business came to my rescue.

I grew up in Cleveland. The oldest of six boys. I was reasonably smart, reasonably athletic, and reasonably adventurous, too. When my teenage girlfriend Gail Ryan went to Briarcliffe College, I applied to Colgate and followed her to New York, commuting to the city to see her on weekends. I didn't last long on the tennis team because of those trips to New York. (I didn't last long on the football team either. But that was because I was a too-slow tight end.) Eventually, Gail and I went our separate ways. But while at Colgate, I made three lifelong friends—Charles Garivaltis, Rocky Stoner, and Larry Bossidy. To this day, we still get together once a year. I also earned the nickname "Deals," which grew out of my association with that buddy Larry (the future Vice Chairman of GE and Chairman of Honeywell). Larry had the franchise for the soda and cigarette machines along fraternity row. I saw the money he was making, so got into the business, too. I picked up a couple of the other fraternities and started offering another essential: late-night sandwiches, the demand for which peaked way after the kitchens were closed. Before long, I was running a car service to New York City, too.

"Deals" Geier was on his way.

During my various trips into New York, I fell for another young lady. Her name was Joan Bennett, a striking blonde. Though Joan would end up marrying a much better catch by the name of Ted Kennedy, before the end of junior year she was wearing my pin. Many evenings, as I sat in her living room waiting to take her out, I'd hear her father upstairs talking to himself. Was he crazy? No. Just in the ad business. Mr. Bennett worked on Nestlé's Nescafe account and on the nights before a big presentation, he practiced in front of a mirror. It seemed like almost every time I was there, I could hear him rehearsing his lines. I said to myself, "Well, this may not be a bad business to be in." Selling strategic and creative packages and all you needed was a mirror in which to practice. This might be an interesting field; these are multi-million dollar accounts! This was my first exposure to the advertising possibility. And I can thank Joan Bennett Kennedy for that.

But I didn't jump in immediately. My next stop was business school. When my grandfather had passed away during my junior year, he left me $20,000, which I invested in Litton Industries. It turned out to be a good pick and I doubled my money. Suddenly I had enough to finance myself through Columbia Business School. In those days, you could go to business school right out of college and, if you carried certain credits from the college, they counted for your first year at business school. So, I loaded up on economic and business-related courses in Colgate and was able to get through Columbia Business School in one year, going through the summer and Saturdays.

Columbia proved to be a tough experience. One of the major requirements was a course in Statistics. The professor, an unusual grader, usually flunked 12% of the class automatically; that was the bar. To clear it, I needed help. I went to my professor and asked if I could get a tutor. For a bottle of scotch a session, he took me on himself. After the final exam, which I thought I did reasonably well on, we all gathered to see how the scores went and – lo and behold – his 12% mark went down to 10%. A breakthrough! Luckily, I was above the 10% mark. I think my scotch sessions probably made eight or nine other students very happy as well. But truth be told, I know it wasn't because of the scotch. It was because I was willing to ask for help and learn.

What I taught myself at Columbia Business School

1. Forget your ego – Focus on the task at hand and the best way to achieve the end result.

2. Ask for help – You've got nothing to lose and it goes a long in way in helping you succeed.

3. Give it your best shot – Put in the effort and demonstrate your commitment.

4. Make your own luck when you can – I may not have been the greatest statistician, but I knew how to shift the odds in my favor.

In the aftermath of the global financial crisis, these basic lessons are more pertinent than ever. Hard work, authenticity, and collaboration are back in favor.

Big plans

After my Columbia graduation, I went back to Cleveland and entered the National Guard, which was a six-month program plus some weekly meetings. The time had come to start my business career.

"Deals" Geier, with his newly minted MBA, was all set to conquer the world.

I knew from my studies, as well as my own observations, that new and innovative products that improved consumers' lives were gaining rapid acceptance in the booming U.S. economy. I had some ideas of my own—and I intended to make a killing. I started a new product development company, living off my small National Guard check and a little I had leftover from college. The experience made a difference in my life.

The first product I developed was a toothbrush with toothpaste in the handle. I had a design for an injection molding machine and I went to Hilton Hotels and got a test market package agreement. I didn't have the wherewithal to fund the whole project myself, so I negotiated with the company that owned the only available molding machine for the design. They were willing to work with me on the basis of taking a percentage of the profit, not the revenue. Looking back, this was a good deal. However, these were the early days of venture capital, and I was more interested in owning all of it myself. I decided to back off and move directly to my next foolproof idea.

I went back to Hilton and made my pitch. Imagine this: glycerin soap with advertising in the center. Every time you washed your hands during your stay, you'd continue to see the Hilton Hotels logo. It was a great form of extended branding, too. After all, I reminded them, everybody takes the soap out of the hotels. Again, however, a special machine was needed and, again, after pricing it out, I couldn't carry it off.

Fear not! My third idea was sure to be a winner. I grew up fishing and enjoyed sailing, and I knew that wherever humans went to find water and sun, they would also find mosquitoes. Why not invent suntan lotion with an insect repellent? I went to the head chemist at Bonnebell Cosmetics to develop the formula. I then went to a distribution company that works with boating and sports shops, Tempo Products, and got a packer who liked the product and provided me a 60-day payment plan. Being the business-school genius that I was, I looked for ways to reduce costs and maximize my profits. I discovered I could save a few cents in manufacturing costs if I silk-screened the plastic bottles. Brilliant idea. Except that doing so caused problems with the bottle tops. In many of the boxes, one or two were not screwed tight enough, causing the product to leak and ruin the labels. My lotion instantly became repellent to my distributors, who, seeing even the slightest damage, sent the whole case back.

Three strikes and I was out.

As I licked my wounds, I considered the pitfalls of my go-it-alone approach. In trying to develop and launch my three products, I had refused to go out and get additional capital because I didn't want to give up any part of my ownership. I was too greedy.

What I learned from my entrepreneurial errors

1. Seek feedback on your vision – Always listen to others—and be open to the advice of experts.

2. Get the financing you need – Giving up an ownership stake is far better than retaining 100% of nothing.

3. Don't scrimp – You may have only one chance to succeed, so invest in doing it right first time.

In my new career in venture capital, I make sure that the people I invest in are clear on and comfortable with these foundations for success.

The career decision that changed my life

"Now what?" I asked myself.

After my failed product launches, I needed to get a real job – and a new start in business. I wasn't looking too far into the future, but I figured I should give advertising a try.

Advertising was a glamorous profession in the late '50s and about to enter its "golden age." Remembering Joan Bennett's father presenting to a mirror, I figured I had the necessary skills. Equally important, I sensed I could have a lot of fun.

But the main reason I felt I should go to work for an agency was that, although I would need to start at the bottom, I could get into a training program and work with clients in different industries, which would give me some insight on what kind of career I really wanted to be pursue. I didn't think of staying with an ad agency long-term; I thought I'd end up on the client-side perhaps even at Procter & Gamble in Cincinnatti. So, I applied for a training program with McCann-Erickson which, at that time, had a Cleveland office. I had a choice of two companies, J. Walter Thompson in New York or staying in Cleveland with McCann-Erickson, with the possibility of eventually moving to New York.

I chose McCann because I realized I would work with multiple clients and gain exposure to different types of businesses; whereas, JWT in New York would likely assign me to just one or two accounts. It was probably the best decision because it gave me an understanding of the breadth of the different businesses. Best of all, because I was dealing with a smaller agency, I was able to work closely with clients and be involved with them at mostly a higher-level than I normally would have in New York.

The Cleveland office was the perfect launching pad for my career in advertising. Though at that time, I had no clue that I was to become a McCann and Interpublic "lifer."

I finished my National Guard duty and shortly afterwards moved to New York. Funny enough, I began as a Junior Account Executive on the Nestlé account for little chocolate Morsels. I was working on the account that Joan Bennett's father was pitching to in the mirror years before.

In New York, I lived in a small hotel called the Pickwick Arms, in an 8'x10' room with a shared bathroom. Even with my great MBA degree, I was making a little better than a secretary's wage. However, in my second year in New York, I finally learned something about M&A. The first merger I worked on was marrying my wife, Faith. Faith was a beautiful brunette for whom I happily gave up blondes. She was particularly lively and full of fun; she loved football and the beach. She turned out to be a great partner and finally taught me to share. Luckily, she was particularly good with clients, too.

CHAPTER TWO

Challenge the Status Quo

*How to strengthen your business through
reinvention—even when the world won't listen*

"There is nothing wrong with change if it is in the right direction."
—*Winston Churchill*

Built-in obsolescence

IF WE'VE LEARNED anything in the past two years, it's that no brand, no company and no industry comes with a long-term guarantee.

Once-mighty newspapers, automotive brands and financial firms have disappeared. And industries that have failed to reinvent themselves satisfactorily are now facing the prospect of having their future activities monitored or regulated by the government.

More changes are coming to many industries. And the world I know best—global marketing communications—will not be immune.

But it's interesting to note that, over the past few decades at least, advertising agencies and marketing companies have found ways to evolve in many ways—large and small—that have helped the industry survive every downturn and embrace every change the world has thrown at them.

Change in the advertising business may not always move in the "right direction," or even be readily embraced, but the lessons to be learned can be applied in many fields beyond marketing. In this chapter, I'll look at how the industry has evolved, how it looks today and some of the mistakes that were made along the way.

The Big Four

Anyone who has entered the advertising business in the past 20 years has stepped into an industry dominated by a handful of global holding companies.

The "big four" – Interpublic, WPP, Omnicom, and Publicis – are publicly traded corporations that own hundreds of individual companies (including most of the major global agency networks), employ tens of thousands of people, and generate billions of dollars in income each year. Their main competitors – Havas, Aegis, and the Asian-based giants Dentsu and Hakuhodo – employ the same holding company model, as do smaller rivals such as MDC in Canada and Chime Communications in the U.K.

In the same way that media conglomerates such as NewsCorp and Time Warner create news and entertainment content that touches consumers around the world, the advertising holding companies are responsible for the lion's share of the branded marketing communications that reach consumers in every language, every medium and every market.

It wasn't always this way.

When I became CEO of the Interpublic Group in 1980, there was no "big four." At that time, Publicis was a successful French agency with an international (though less than global) network. Omnicom was still six years away from the "Big Bang" merger between BBDO and DDB Needham that would create it. And WPP? Back in 1980, it was a small English manufacturer of shopping baskets, then known as Wire and Plastic Products, plc. It was not until 1985 that Martin Sorrell began acquiring shares of the company that would in 1987 be relaunched as WPP Group, a company whose own shopping basket would soon be filled with such venerable agencies as J. Walter Thompson, the Ogilvy Group, and Grey.

In later chapters, I will talk more about the explosive growth of the global holding companies that occurred in the 1990s and the successes and failures that followed.

In this chapter, I will look at how the holding-company model first emerged in the 1950s, the uproar it created, as well as the benefits the new "agency-within-an-agency" concept delivered to clients and the agencies themselves. I'll also explain how and why Interpublic's holding-company model became the model for the industry and why today's holding companies are well-positioned to succeed in today's increasingly digital and "media-neutral" world.

Innovation and uproar

In 1954, America was in the midst of a baby boom, an economic boom and a TV boom. By the time *The Tonight Show* debuted with Steve Allen as host, 56% of U.S. households had a TV set. Some businesses were even closing early on Mondays so people could get home in time for *I Love Lucy*. Advertisers were investing unprecedented amounts in the new medium. Advertising agencies were growing rapidly. And McCann-Erickson, under the leadership of Marion Harper, was growing fastest of all.

Having assumed control at the age of 32, Harper was pushing his agency to excel creatively and in new research techniques and also in new business growth. Harper grew the agency's billings from $47 million in 1948, when McCann ranked fifth among U.S. agencies, to $167 million in 1956, second only to J. Walter Thompson.

But in the midst of this stunning growth, Harper saw one problem.

In the 1950s, one of the main restrictions on an ad agency's growth potential was its inability to handle conflicting accounts.

The limitation that an agency could only handle one account in each product category at a time was one thing. Even worse, from Harper's viewpoint, was the fact that an agency could actually lose an account as a result of a big client making an acquisition that brought them into a category where the agency already had an existing account.

Harper decided to change all that—with an innovation that would spark uproar throughout the industry.

In 1954, McCann-Erickson acquired Marschalk & Pratt, an agency that had handled radio (and later TV) work for Standard Oil since 1934. Marschalk's involvement with Standard Oil had long been a source of irritation for Harper's chairman, Harrison McCann, so the acquisition was a great way to bring all the pieces of the Standard Oil account back into McCann-Erickson's expanding global network.

But Harper was thinking beyond one account. He decided to use the Marschalk acquisition to fire the opening shot in a new campaign to reshape not just McCann-Erickson, but the whole industry.

Harper moved the Standard Oil business over to McCann. But unlike any of the agency's previous acquisitions, he didn't rename his newly purchased agency. He left the Marschalk name hanging on the door.

His reasoning was simple. He needed to respond to a changing world and open a new avenue for business growth. Harper knew that consolidation on the client side was becoming a fact of life and that it was something he could not control. His solution: manage Marschalk as a separate "agency-within-an-agency." Because of its size, Marschalk would be able to handle smaller accounts than McCann on a profitable basis, but also, since it operated under a different name, Harper announced it could also handle competitive accounts.

The idea was, to say the least, controversial. Competitors in the industry spoke out against it. Two major clients—American Mutual Life and Fuller Paints—quit McCann. And Tile-Tex severed its ties with Marschalk.

Despite the loud opposition and initial setbacks, Harper stuck with his plan. Always the champion of ideas, he promoted his new parent company idea as no different than GM's. If Buick, Chevrolet, and Oldsmobile dealers could compete against each other despite being owned by the same company, why couldn't agencies?

Harper proved they could. Even as McCann-Erickson continued its rapid growth through the 1950s, Marschalk also flourished. By 1960, the smaller agency had expanded to ten offices, with billings up fivefold, from $6.4 million to $34 million.

Most important, Harper was soon able to deliver high-profile proof that his holding company could successfully manage competitive accounts. As the airline industry expanded rapidly, Marschalk pitched and won the Sabena account despite the fact that another McCann-owned agency, Pritchard-Wood, handled BOAC. McCann agencies now represented two highly competitive airlines, which were then locked in a battle with Pan-Am for the highly competitive transatlantic tourism market.

Harper's idea evolved into the formal establishment of Interpublic Group of Companies, Inc., in 1961. Half a century later, it remains the same basic model for the industry's global holding companies.

> **What Marion Harper taught the advertising world**
>
> 1. To find new growth opportunities, think big and challenge the obstacles others accept.
>
> 2. Look to other industries for solutions that might apply to you.
>
> 3. The more transformational the idea, the more resistance it generates and the more long-term change it creates.
>
> *Harper made himself temporarily unpopular by taking on his own industry but in the long-term that mattered little; he was proven right.*

What a holding company should—and shouldn't—do

Despite the success of his new holding company, Marion Harper didn't get everything right.

Harper was committed to making Interpublic a center for excellence in the industry. He saw early the need for agencies to offer "total marketing communications" and launched a public relations agency, a sales promotion unit, and a marketing research operation, dubbed Market Planning Corporation (later Marplan). In the early 1960s, he bundled these units into a central group called Communications Affiliations, Inc. In building this group, he sought to hire the best minds in the business, including top talent from ABC Radio, CBS TV, General Foods, and *Sports Illustrated*. He brought in Emerson Foote, the high-profile co-founder of the Foote, Cone, and Belding agency. He also hired the TV visionary Sylvester (Pat) Weaver, the former chairman of NBC who, among other things, created *The Tonight Show* and was father of the actress Sigourney Weaver.

Soon, Interpublic possessed many of most talented players in the world of advertising and communications—part of a centralized marketing and planning organization designed to help Interpublic win new clients by applying the best strategic, research, creative, and sales talent to the new business process.

It was a team that looked great, not only on paper but also in clients' boardrooms as Interpublic's new business pitches were being made.

The only problem: The Interpublic all-stars were *not* an agency and clients realized quickly that the team that was trying to win their business wouldn't be actually working on their account.

I saw this dilemma first-hand in my Cleveland days, when Emerson Foote flew in to help pitch a new account. Even beyond his industry-wide reputation, Foote was a tall, distinguished-looking executive. He could have been sent straight from central casting. He stepped off the plane and directly led a rehearsal of the presentation. Obviously exhausted, he then disappeared for a nap, asking to be woken in time for the client meeting. Foote gave a great presentation, detailing all the ways that Interpublic would support the client's activities through the Cleveland office. But the client said no choosing instead to work with an agency whose principals would be available day-to-day and directly involved with the strategy and creative.

On a larger scale, it soon became apparent that Harper's centralized new business process wasn't working. The "star system" was not dazzling clients as Harper expected it would. Meanwhile, the individual agencies were sitting back, neglecting their own new business efforts on the assumption that head office was doing all the heavy lifting.

Harper's early vision clearly needed some refining. Foote left Interpublic and the agency business in 1964, a year after Pat Weaver quit the firm. (Interestingly, Weaver was then recruited by a good friend of my family, John Brooks, who headed Lear-Siegler. Brooks, a person I admired tremendously, wanted Weaver to help launch a bold new venture in which his company was investing: Subscription Television, Inc. This would have been the first provider of pay-cable in the U.S.. Unfortunately for both of them, TV broadcasters banded together and helped block the company with a ballot initiative in 1964. Even though the Supreme Court later found the initiative unconstitutional, STV had already gone out of business.)

One of the reasons Harper's idea for a centralized new business operation failed was because it infringed on the autonomy and accountability of the individual agency chiefs. And the same was true when it came to delivering additional client services in a centralized manner.

In hindsight, its easy to see that the system had two built-in problems: First, centralizing services such as sales promotion encouraged agencies to de-emphasize areas of expertise in which they needed to excel simply to stay competitive. Second, a system in which agencies randomly funneled requests to a centralized department made it impossible to guarantee that workers in the central department would not be given access to confidential information from two competing accounts.

The structural mistakes of these early days were soon corrected, and Interpublic moved to a system designed to push all relevant client services inside the agency to avoid conflict issues, while centralizing only the corporate and back-office functions that would support the agencies' client-focused efforts.

At least twenty years before companies such as Omnicom, WPP and Publicis embraced a similar business model, Interpublic had developed a clear understanding of what such a holding company should and shouldn't do.

In other industries, holding companies have learned lessons the hard way. ITT, which sought to drive earnings by buying companies outside its range of expertise, soon lost its leverage of size by consolidating too much decision-making in the headquarters office. In 1995, the company split itself in three. General Electric had similar problems, but remedied them successfully when it pushed operating decisions back down to the divisions.

What the holding company should do:
1. Set corporate strategy and financial objectives.
2. Establish fiscal management and operational controls.
3. Guide personnel policy.
4. Incubate new programs and project for implementation by the operating units.
5. Initiate, manage, and approve mergers and acquisitions.
6. Provide centralized functions: legal, real estate, travel services, recruitment aid, employee benefits, and executive compensation management.

What the holding company should NOT do:
1. Pitch new business.
2. Compete with agencies in offering creative or other client services.
3. Manage day-to-day client relationships.
4. Discourage agencies from developing the skills they need to stay competitive—internally and externally.
5. Limit the autonomy or accountability of agency management.

The birth of the creative boutique

Marion Harper didn't just create the concept of the modern holding company. He also established what was perhaps the first creative boutique to be housed inside a global agency network.

Jack Tinker & Partners was Harper's internal "firefighting squad" called to action to deal with the "three-alarm" creative and marketing problems wherever they appeared in the Interpublic network.

Tinker himself was a legendary McCann-Erickson art director who had won the industry's Art Director of the Year Award in 1952. His "partners" were copywriter Don Calhoun; Myron McDonald in account service; and Dr. Herta Hertzog, the famed Austrian researcher whom Harper had recruited in 1943 to help him revolutionize the industry's research techniques. (Most viewers of the TV show *Mad Men* are probably unaware of the striking resemblance the show's fictional Austrian researcher "Greta Guttman" bears to the real Herta Hertzog. Any similarities are, of course, purely coincidental.)

Housed in the Dorset Hotel in New York, Jack Tinker & Partners had no assigned clients, but the small boutique quickly became recognized for its abilities to save the day on a myriad of problem accounts.

Quickly, the boutique became a breeding ground for some of the industry's best creative talent. Among them, copywriter Mary Wells, who gained a reputation for tremendous, strategically-sound creative work, often built around a product's physical benefits. When she worked on Alka-Seltzer, all of a sudden two effervescent pills were popped into the glass instead of one – not only doubling product usage, but also creating an unforgettable sight and sound commercial.

Whatever she learned at Tinker, Wells put to good use throughout her career. She went on to great fame as the cofounder of the highly successful Wells Rich Greene agency. I know from first-hand experience that as well as being a great creative thinker, she was a great account person too—a unique talent. One time, McCann-Erickson went head-to-head with Wells in a new business pitch to Philip Morris chairman Joe Cullman and his Marketing Director Jack Landry. The McCann team was comprised of Paul Foley and Bill Backer—two of the agency's best-ever creative talents—and me. Thankfully, we did enough to win the two Philip Morris coupon brands we pitched. But Mary Wells didn't walk out empty-handed either. Joe Cullman was impressed enough to give her the "consolation prize" of Benson & Hedges. It was a brand with a high price and high-quality image but still perceived as a lesser piece of business. In working with Philip Morris, Wells helped relaunch Benson & Hedges in a new longer (100mm) size at a new popular price. The brand took off. And so did her agency.

Jack Tinker & Partners, the boutique that Marion Harper set up in the Dorset Hotel, eventually spun off as an agency in its own right and was credited with helping lead the "creative revolution" that transformed advertising in the 1960s. When Tinker was inducted into the Art Directors Hall of Fame in 1973, Mary Wells said, "some people run agencies like banks or religious organizations or like Bellevue Hospital. Jack ran his like a Scott Fitzgerald novel. He created a witty, glamorous atmosphere that was intensely personal and tremendously productive."

Marion Harper—best known for his research skills, his emphasis on his client's business results, and the introduction of the advertising holding company—was never a champion of creativity for creativity's sake. But he knew he needed to create a space inside Interpublic in which creativity would flourish. Like many of the seeds Harper planted in his time as Interpublic CEO, the concept of the creative boutique is one that continues to bloom a half-century later, in an industry where "the care and feeding of ideas" is still as important as ever.

From success to excess

In the early days of Interpublic, Harper was driven by an intense rivalry with—and desire to overtake—the largest agency of the day, J. Walter Thompson. Some might call it an obsession. To keep the company's executives focused on the drive to be number one, he held a large annual meeting each year, where his keynote speech would focus on the company's "thrust for growth." As a relative newcomer to the McCann agency, I was impressed to watch Harper read through his script, pencil in his changes, then take the stage and speak at length without referring once to his notes. The man not only had vision, he also had a photographic memory.

Harper's "thrust for growth" led to rapid expansion in the '60s. He made a total of 38 acquisitions between 1958 and 1965, helping him surpass the J. Walter Thompson agency. By 1963, Interpublic was officially the biggest marketing and advertising company in the world. An *Advertising Age* editorial heralded his achievement, saying Harper was "first to realize the significance and potential of internal competition in the advertising field" and had success-fully demonstrated that the problem of serving competitive accounts "can be licked by having separately housed and separately operated agencies operating under the general corporate umbrella of a holding-management company."

But by 1964, questions were emerging as to whether the global expansion had gone too far, too fast. An article in *Fortune* magazine that year was headlined "Marion Harper's Big Tent." Perhaps prophetically, the text was illustrated with cartoons showing a variety of high-wire acts.

The circus atmosphere continued even as the revenue projections in Interpublic's "Forward Plans" were not being met.

By the mid-60s, Harper's management style had become increasingly autocratic, resulting in the departure of several key lieutenants. He also allowed his corporate and personal spending to get out of control.

On the corporate side, Harper purchased a DC-7 from KLM, hired a full-time crew and steward, and had the plane retrofitted to create a lavish "flying palace," with bronze lamps, artworks hanging from silk panels, deep, gold-pile carpet, and more. It was the most extravagant corporate jet of its day and he used it frequently.

In the continued rush for new business, Harper would load the plane with big thinkers like Paul Foley and Jack Tinker and develop presentation concepts in mid-air, en route to a client meeting. Often, Harper instructed the pilot to circle above its destination, not letting the plane land until he was satisfied with the quality of his team's presentation ideas.

Harper even used the DC-7 to skip the country and fly to Geneva with his second wife Valerie on the day he was due in court to face tax evasion charges, stemming from his ill-fated investments in the pure-bred cattle business. Harper had got into the business as a tax write-off, but became obsessed with the cattle game, paying top prices for bulls at auction and devising plans to revamp the industry with a cattle-leasing scheme he thought could make him #1 in the cattle industry, just as he had become #1 in the ad world. As tax laws changed, though, his accountant didn't stay on top of the new regulations, and Harper was indicted for tax evasion. When he missed his day in court, the IRS won a default judgment and seized all his cattle holdings.

Executives inside Interpublic and McCann-Erickson were growing increas-ingly alarmed. While the established agencies in the group were generating record revenues, not only were corporate expenses getting out of hand, but many of Harper's new acquisitions were not meeting their financial targets. Harper raised more eyebrows when he gave his wife Valerie the greenlight to launch her own Interpublic unit, a fashion agency in Paris. Meanwhile, Harper was becoming increasingly negligent in regard to the cost of his own lavish lifestyle and had started borrowing heavily from the company to meet his personal obligations.

By 1967, Marion Harper, the ringmaster who had put together the greatest show in advertising, was looking more like a juggler running out of hands. That November, faced with an unanticipated corporate loss that threatened Interpublic with bankruptcy, the board voted to remove Harper as CEO.

To the outside world, accustomed to reading glowing portraits of Harper in publications such as *Time*, *Newsweek*, *Fortune* and *The Wall Street Journal*, Harper's fall was sudden and surprising. Insiders, especially those who had witnessed the changes in his behavior over two or more years, were less surprised. But the board had acted in time and under new CEO, Robert Healy, Interpublic's finances were put back in order. The company was profitable again within a year and went public on the New York Stock Exchange in 1971.

Marion Harper's mammoth contributions to the advertising industry were acknowledged somewhat belatedly. He was inducted into the Advertising Hall of Fame in 1998. In 2000, *Advertising Age* hailed him as #2 on its list of the 100 most important advertising people of the 20th century (second only to Bill Bernbach). It was well-deserved recognition, but I've no doubt that Marion Harper would have preferred to be listed at #1.

Lessons from a downfall

1. **Keep your ego in check**: A corporation is never a one-person show.

2. **Be smart about acquisitions**: Growth at any cost isn't always worth the cost.

3. **Spend on your clients not yourself**: Always keep corporate expenditures under control.

4. **Care about your people**: Pay attention to issues of executive retention and employee morale.

5. **Enjoy your success wisely**: Don't let a lavish lifestyle interfere with your business judgment.

6. **Business is about tomorrow, not yesterday**: Look forward.

Unfortunately, this book was not published three years ago. I could have sent a copy to the CEOs at Bear Stearns, Lehman Brothers, Merrill Lynch, and all the big commercial banks.

Why the holding-company system works

Marion Harper's holding company concept was a simple solution to ensure growth for his company and to anticipate clients' changing needs in an era of corporate consolidation. The model continues to work because of the benefits it offers for clients, for agencies, for investors and for the holding companies themselves.

For clients: Working with a holding company allows clients to market their brands consistently, effectively, and efficiently across a full range of marketing disciplines. The holding company relationship also offers a high degree of flexibility for clients such as packaged goods marketers that operate in a variety of product categories and may wish to move assignments between agencies for creative or account-conflict reasons. Holding companies also offer clients:

- Access to independent local agencies capable of producing in-country creative
- The ability to try alternative agency resources without major publicity or upheaval
- A global system to support international rollouts
- Consistent methodologies to measure effectiveness in multiple markets
- Allocate resources, people and money.

In an era of globalized communications, rapidly changing media options and intense competition between brands, the holding company relationship delivers both the strategic and executional flexibility that many marketers need to succeed.

For agencies: Working within a holding company gives individual agencies all the advantages of being part of a global organization. The agency draws upon centralized back-office support in key areas such as employee benefits, accounting, legal services, real estate, travel services, and executive compensation management. The services provided by the holding company allow agency managers to invest more time in serving their existing clients and in concentrating on their own new business development. Agencies within the network can compete with each other to win new accounts and take on accounts that are competitive with those in their sister agencies, as long as strict confidentiality of information is maintained. In addition, agencies can collaborate with one another when appropriate, across marketing disciplines and geographies, providing additional services to clients whose agency-of-record relationships are maintained elsewhere in the network. To maintain client confidentiality, Interpublic and other holding companies require that:

- No employee can transfer from one company-owned agency to another if he or she has worked on a competitive account without signed approval from the client and management.
- No client information can be transferred from one agency to another, on penalty of dismissal.
- Agency personnel must sign non-compete clauses when given privileged information on specific accounts.

Despite these necessary restrictions, holding companies offer individuals many opportunities to create varied career paths within the same corporation, while retaining and transferring the benefits of long-term employment at the same company (e.g., vesting in 401(k) plans and stock option programs).

For the holding company: Owning a broad portfolio of specialized advertising and marketing companies creates a scale that allows for strategic planning and investment on a global basis, while allowing management to insulate itself from downturns in a specific discipline or geography. Providing shared services from a central office in areas such as basic accounting and reporting, legal, tax, real estate, and travel services, helps reduce operating costs within each agency, improving margins and profitability. While the holding company is certainly not a bank that individual agencies can dip into as needed, it does have the deep pockets to implement programs and practices that enhance the entire network, whether in support of capabilities that directly benefit clients (e.g., research) or company-wide training programs.

As the Interpublic website states, "the role of the holding company is to provide resources and support to ensure that our agencies can best meet our clients' needs."

In other words, if it makes sense for a function to be centralized, that's what happens. Otherwise, that function stays at the agency.

For Wall Street: The major advertising holding companies serve as a proxy for the global marketing communications industry. These companies offer investors a way to participate in the growth of the global consumer economy, separate from the major media and entertainment players, such as NewsCorp and Time Warner.

In fact, at a time when traditional media companies are facing an enormous challenge in migrating their advertising dollars to new digital platforms, *Advertising Age* recently noted that holding companies are benefiting from their "success in diversifying into marketing disciplines that aren't dependent on the selling of ad time – such as digital, customer relationship management and public relations – and (from their) heavy investment in international markets that remain fast-growing even in tough times."

Clearly, Marion Harper's holding company idea has not only stood the test of time, it still gives companies like Interpublic, WPP, Omnicom and Publicis the flexibility they need to both serve their clients and respond strategically to ever-changing market conditions.

CHAPTER THREE

Put the Right People in Place

How to import, export and home-grow the talent you need to succeed anywhere

"Our inventory goes down the elevator every night."
—*Fairfax Cone, co-founder of the Foote, Cone and Belding agency*

The knowledge economy

IT HAS BEEN 50 years since Peter Drucker first coined the term "knowledge worker," but in today's world the concept is truer than ever.

For companies in many industries—marketing communications among them—success or failure is driven by the ability of employees to apply brainpower, creativity, and teamwork to the tasks at hand.

But what are the best ways to recruit and retain talent, to integrate new ways of thinking into an organization, and to nurture the right kind of corporate culture?

In this chapter, I'll tell you how McCann-Erickson and Interpublic have approached the talent issue over the last few decades, how "transferable power" can transform an organization and the many ways in which investing in people can create greater success for both the individual and the business.

A different world

The 2008 Beijing Olympics were viewed by 4.7 billion people in more than

200 countries around the world.

The worldwide sponsors of the Games—instantly recognizable brands such as Coca-Cola, GE, Johnson & Johnson, Kodak, Lenovo, McDonalds, Omega, Panasonic, Samsung, and Visa—surrounded this global spectacle with integrated messaging on TV, the Internet, mobile media, in print, and outdoor and with all manner of sales promotions and marketing tie-ins.

Like the Games themselves, these global marketing efforts were executed with a remarkable combination of flair and control. Throughout the world, the agencies supporting these clients worked together to ensure that key brand attributes and strategic messages were relayed consistently and effectively to every corner of the globe and without a single baton drop.

The Beijing Olympics were a clear example of how the world has changed advertising and how advertising has changed the world.

Just a generation ago—until the 1970s—advertising was banned in China. And right through the '70s most global clients and agencies were still trying to figure out how to overcome the ego differences, language barriers and culture clashes that stood in the way of truly effective global communications.

Running a successful global agency means embracing all the personalities, styles and opinions that are drawn to any highly creative business. But it's not just about talent, it's also about training. It's not just about ideas, it's also about disciplined execution.

The fact that today's global agencies perform as effectively as they do is a tribute to the vision of global agency network's early pioneers—most particularly McCann-Erickson and J. Walter Thompson—and the commitment they showed in staying true to that vision, serving their clients, and developing their people.

A people business

Way back in 1947—more than six decades before the global spectacle of the Beijing Olympics—Harrison McCann thought he'd just about seen it all. After founding the H.K. McCann agency in 1912, the head of McCann-Erickson had invested in the expansion of his global agency network throughout the Roaring Twenties and the Great Depression, and despite years of international turmoil that had culminated in the devastation of World War II.

He didn't do it for the money.

McCann wrote in a 1947 memo: "This foreign business has always been a headache and, on the whole, unprofitable. Over the years, we are pretty heavily in red ink on our foreign operations. If the world was in the process of settling down, and we could see an era when trade would flow freely between the United States and other countries of the world, we could capitalize on these facilities of ours, and our foreign operations would be a distinct asset. However, with the bad economic conditions in Europe, and with jealousies and rivalries and oppressive legislation in the various countries of South America, the outlook for our foreign operations is not encouraging."

McCann-Erickson announced it had no plans to open any further international offices.

At that time, McCann-Erickson and J. Walter Thompson were the only two advertising agencies that had developed far-flung international agency networks. McCann had pioneered the networked office approach and ensured that his clients benefited from the best possible multi-office and multinational coordination.

But McCann's European and Latin American expansion had always been costly. Turnover in international offices was high. Even in the best of times, the cost of supporting these networks had threatened to collapse them. And these were not the best of times.

Through it all, McCann knew that running an advertising agency was, above all, an investment in people. Even if he couldn't quite figure out how to make his international network profitable, McCann wasn't about to abandon the people who held it together.

People like Neil Godber, the novelist who kept McCann-Erickson London operational continuously throughout World War II, delivering regular reports to head office, such as this one from April 1941: "… dashing to roof to put out incendiary bombs whenever necessary…offices have suffered no damage from bombings, but we have helped other agencies whose quarters have been bombed…recently secured a new account."

People like Charles Blondel who ran the Paris office until it was liquidated in 1940 following the fall of France, then started his own independent French agency. The agency became the new McCann-Erickson France in 1945 when McCann bought back an 81% controlling interest.

People like Max Pauli, the longtime agency head in Germany, who was released from a POW camp in 1946 to reestablish the company and quickly started adding new accounts. Within four years, McCann-Erickson was Germany's #1 agency.

By 1948, the same year the Marshall Plan was launched to help rebuild European economies, McCann recommitted the agency to its investment in international expansion. It was a commitment that would ensure McCann-Erickson's future status as a major global agency. But clearly, it wasn't made purely for financial reasons.

As Marion Harper said in his eulogy for H.K, McCann following his death in a car accident in 1962, McCann could have invested his money in ways that would have made him "many times wealthier," but in staying true to his pioneering vision and to the people who had stayed true to him, he had made "an epoch-making decision."

Sharing expertise

As Chairman of the agency throughout the 1950s, McCann lived to see many of the ways Harper, who became CEO in 1948, would make his long-term vision pay off.

Harper approached the international challenge with the same relish and competitiveness he brought to all aspects of the business. And he recognized early the way multiple forces were reshaping the ways his clients did business:

- *Improved communications*, particularly television, were revolutionizing the ways products could be marketed to a mass consumer audience.
- *Product standardization* was expanding the opportunities for multinational brand marketing.
- *Heightened competition* among international and local manufacturers was expanding the overall client universe.
- *Rising disposable incomes* were creating new opportunities for a wide range of products in both established and emerging markets.

Harper had inherited an international network and an agency with a proven track record with global and multinational advertisers. For him, the route to continued international growth lay in selling clients on the benefits of McCann-Erickson's state-of-the-art research techniques and effective multinational brand coordination.

To do that, Harper needed to make sure his worldwide employees knew, understood and embraced the expertise and methodologies that separated McCann from other agencies.

In those days, employee training was a major challenge. As late as 1956, even as McCann-Erickson employed 1,300 people in 24 offices outside the U.S., only about a dozen of these employees were Americans. The vast majority of Harper's international team had no experience in the U.S. market.

Harper committed his agency to the kind of internal meetings and training programs that would build relationships and transfer knowledge throughout the network. Bringing people together face-to-face had a big impact. McCann-Erickson's first worldwide meeting of agency managers happened in 1951. Another took place in 1956, followed by additional training programs in the U.S., and regional meetings in Europe and Latin America.

Harper's approach helped create an environment in which international offices combined well and supported each other, while continuing to receive consistent support from the head office. By the 1960s, it wasn't unusual for agencies in continental Europe to have creative teams collaborating on multinational accounts. In 1968, the new McCann-Erickson Hakuhodo agency in Japan benefited from the work of a global creative and marketing team, which developed Nescafe's famous "Cities of the World" campaign, which ran successfully in Japan for more than 15 years.

More than anything, Harper was driven by a desire to help his clients achieve business success. Especially in international markets, he understood that clients would be attracted to agencies that could give them a competitive edge.

He was right.

By emphasizing training for his agencies and consistent research techniques for his clients, Harper grew his non-U.S. client base from 142 accounts in 1950 to more than 500 by 1960.

By 1968, *Advertising Age* reported that McCann-Erickson's international training program had helped develop "a new young breed" of international executives with the skills required to move throughout the global network.

And the agency's emphasis on executive and creative training continues to this day, including programs developed with leading business schools to upgrade executive skills and promote the continual transfer of knowledge to all parts of the network.

> **Harper's approach to knowledge management**
> 1. **Bring people together**: Give your team the opportunity to meet and get to know each other
> 2. **Provide training in standardized techniques**: Educate your people in the areas where consistency is essential
> 3. **Encourage future cooperation**: Communicate guidelines for cross-market coordination and problem-solving
>
> *Key lesson: Ideas can be executed most successfully when people have a shared knowledge base and are working within established parameters*

Recognizing the global opportunity

On February 14, 1958, the ad world was rocked by a stunning development. Marion Harper, McCann-Erickson's CEO, had resigned the $26 million Chrysler account in favor of the much smaller Buick assignment.

The *New York Times* headline (on a story that bore the byline of future Interpublic vice chairman Carl Spielvogel) read: "Ad Men Are Surprised: Winner Had Not Been Listed Among Candidates—Shift Called Biggest of Kind."

The news was surprising for three reasons. First, in those days it was unheard of for agencies to fire clients, especially one as big as Chrysler, which McCann had served since 1943, and was at the time enjoying record sales. Second, as the *Times* reported, McCann had not even been in the running for Buick, whose general manager Edward Ragsdale had visited 12 other New York agencies during the very public review process. Third, unlike all the work that had gone into winning the Coke account a couple of years earlier, neither Harper nor the McCann team had put together a major pitch to win the business. In fact, all that Harper had done was ask his research head Don

Armstrong and creative director Paul Foley to show Ragsdale some of the McCann research that had correctly predicted Chrysler's sales success and the simultaneous slump that was hitting Buick.

Ragsdale was already well aware of the work that Paul Foley—the creative star who joined the agency in Detroit in 1955—and his team were producing for Chrysler. Now, understanding how McCann's sophisticated research methods were used to underpin each Chrysler campaign, he knew all he needed to know.

He wanted McCann and Paul Foley on his account.

While the finalists in the pitch were awaiting word from Buick, Ragsdale quietly called Harper and offered him the account. Harper asked for a little time to think.

In weighing his options, Harper recognized the long-term global possibilities offered by Buick and the rest of the GM organization. He also knew that, despite the success seen by the outside world, there were many frictions on the Chrysler account. Among the problems: the Chrysler client was continually second-guessing himself and making excessive requests for changes to the creative work.

Still, in choosing to resign a major client in such a public way, Harper did something unheard of in the industry at that time. The reaction was predictably negative. "Where's the loyalty?" people asked.

The Chrysler client was incensed. Instead of accepting Harper's resignation letter serving 90 days' notice, he insisted on firing McCann-Erickson immediately.

But while the rest of the industry was focused on Detroit, Harper knew that General Motors, which McCann had served internationally on the Opel account since 1929, was a client that would grow with his agency in all parts of the world. He was willing to take a short-term hit on his U.S. business and endure some bad publicity in order to strengthen a partnership that had significantly more long-term, global potential. Soon after taking on Buick, McCann's U.S. agency also won the GMC Truck and Coach Division.

Foley was quick to switch gears and start producing great work for Buick. He was a curmudgeon but also a great leader, becoming the chairman of McCann-Erickson U.S. in 1964, president and CEO of the agency in 1968, and then Chairman and CEO of Interpublic in 1971, remaining chief executive until the end of 1979.

> **Lessons in resigning Chrysler**
> 1. Think strategically: Sometimes it's better to take a short-term hit to achieve substantial long-term gains.
> 2. Think globally: Make the best decision for the overall business—even at the expense of your largest market.
> 3. Think about loyalty: There may be times to walk away from a souring client relationship, but don't do it lightly.

Localizing the business

By the 1960s, McCann-Erickson was an agency with a truly global scope, expanding into all the major markets of Western Europe and the Asia-Pacific region, and augmenting its comprehensive Latin American network.

As Marion Harper had predicted correctly, major U.S. and European brand marketers were now pursuing multinational and global strategies and facing increasing competition from local marketers.

Harper had positioned McCann-Erickson to exploit the growth of global campaigns. In addition to working for global pioneers, such as Esso and Coke, major global efforts were underway for clients such as Gillette, Goodyear and Nestlé.

McCann had successfully built a network and exported the results-oriented advertising expertise that would make it, by 1971, the number one agency in international billings, finally supplanting the longtime leader J. Walter Thompson.

In the face of this international success, the concerns of managing a global agency network—the "unprofitable headache" that Harrison McCann had described many years before—had diminished substantially.

But the headache could still be felt in certain markets.

The fact remained that, as successful as it was on a global basis, in many countries, McCann-Erickson was still regarded as only an international agency for international clients. Even in major markets like the U.K., where McCann had a long-established presence, the agency ranked a lowly #18 in the market. The same held true in many other countries, where the agency lacked a credible reputation for handling local accounts.

In many of McCann's non-U.S. offices, it was common for the agency to rely on a handful of global clients for 75% or more of its local billings, leaving the office's fate at the mercy of a handful of central decision-makers in far-off markets.

By the end of the 1960s, it was obvious that many of the agency's worldwide offices needed to be more competitive in their own local markets and find a way to move their business mix more to a 50/50 balance between international and local.

This was a challenge that McCann-Erickson addressed strategically and effectively in the 1970s and '80s with a concerted effort to send executives overseas in key assignments. By personally exporting the U.S. agency's culture, attitudes and methodologies, McCann was finally able to solidify its reputation with local clients and translate global expertise into local business.

Overcoming the local challenge

1. The perception problem: Clients assume international agencies only work for international clients.

2. The reality problem: You can't gain a credible in-market reputation if you don't work for local clients.

3. The solution: Deliver something local agencies can't match. For McCann, aggressive new business efforts were combined with a focus on achieving what clients value most: measurable results.

How "Mad Men" went global

Despite the international successes McCann-Erickson enjoyed through the '50s and '60s, one fact remained: The U.S. agency, and the New York office in particular, was still the dominant part of the network.

In 1963, the New York office billed more than all other U.S. offices combined. And other offices in the U.S. network, such as Chicago, Detroit, San Francisco, Los Angeles, and Houston, were themselves bigger than most individual country operations.

Madison Avenue was the heart of the world's most sophisticated and developed advertising industry, and American agencies possessed skills and expertise more advanced than any other nation. The reasons for this were simple:

- **Continuity**: The American advertising industry had been least affected by the disruptions of two world wars and had operated continuously since the late 19th century.
- **Budgets**: In the world's largest consumer market, U.S. advertisers had a long history of investing heavily in mass media to support nationally distributed brands.
- **Competition**: In the U.S., with the stakes higher and competition fiercer, marketers and agencies were continually refining all aspects of the communications mix to gain a competitive edge.

By the 1960s, Marion Harper had established both McCann-Erickson and the new Interpublic head office as centers of excellence in all aspects of advertising and marketing. McCann and Interpublic led the industry in all aspects of research, from consumer motivation to creative testing to the most effective uses of media. Harper had also expanded McCann-Erickson's global network to better serve an increasingly multinational roster of clients.

McCann's international agencies benefited greatly from Harper's emphasis on training and knowledge management. But it took Eugene Kummel, president of McCann-Erickson International, to recognize the final part of the equation.

Kummel realized that for all Harper's emphasis on increasing his employee's brain power, advertising remained at heart a people business. If McCann-Erickson wanted to truly export its culture and its best practices, it also needed to export one more thing: its people.

Harper's own efforts in this area had met with limited success. One of his last big executive hires was Marvin Corwin, whom Harper lured to Interpublic from DDB. He was later sent to London with the idea that Corwin could run McCann's European operations. Like many of Harper's final decisions, this one was ill thought out. Corwin had no experience with McCann, Interpublic, or any of the company's major clients. He also hated socializing, a big detriment especially in the fun-loving U.K. market. The fit was all wrong, and Corwin didn't last long in Europe or at Interpublic.

Kummel had a better approach. With a concept he called "transferable power," he began relocating experienced U.S. executives into international offices around the world, specifically to help the agency develop a coherent global culture in which "internationalized individuals" would help strengthen the agency's business and professional reputation.

One example was the expatriate Kummel sent to Frankfurt where GM's Opel division was headquartered. Harper had understood the global potential of GM. But it wasn't until Kummel put the right person in Germany that McCann's GM relationship went into overdrive. By 1972, the agency was working with GM in 50 countries.

"Transferable power" was Kummel's way of physically transporting the agency's key strengths on behalf of its global clients:

- **Category expertise:** McCann's U.S. executives had deep knowledge of fastest-growing global categories, such as automobiles, food, beverages and packaged goods.
- **Research knowledge:** The U.S. team had a highly developed understanding of the latest effectiveness techniques—and the need for consistently applied methodologies.
- **Account coordination:** Working within McCann's U.S. network meant executives understood the need for—and benefits of—multi-office cooperation.

In 1968, I became one of the executives to whom Kummel offered an international assignment. Having moved from Cleveland to become an account executive in the New York office in 1960, I stayed there for most of the '60s. I had soaked up the McCann culture working on high-profile, big-budget accounts such as American Home Products, Nabisco, Nestlé and Philip Morris. Now, not quite sure what I was getting myself into, I boarded a plane to London.

CHAPTER FOUR

Sell Yourself—And Your Ideas

*How to market yourself and your business to
colleagues, clients and governments*

"If you want to gather honey, don't kick over the beehive."

—*Dale Carnegie*

Play to your personal strengths

IF YOU WANT to get people to work with you or for you, they first have to believe in you.

Let's assume you possess a few fundamental characteristics, such as intelligence, integrity, hard work, dedication, plus a tolerance for innovation and calculated risk-taking.

But beyond that, who are you? What defines you? How do others perceive you? What about you should people believe in?

Your personal strengths—and how you demonstrate them and adapt them over time—are crucial to your long-term business success.

Consider this list of ten of the most famous and successful business personalities of recent years: Michael Bloomberg, Richard Branson, Warren Buffett, Bill Gates, Steve Jobs, Rupert Murdoch, Sam Walton, Jack Welch, Meg Whitman, Oprah Winfrey.

Each one of these people has inspired employees, investors, business partners, and customers over many years. But their personalities and the methods they have used to inspire are very different.

To succeed in business, you don't need a charismatic personality. You don't need to be the world's greatest analyst or investor. You don't need to be a technological visionary. (Though if you are any one of these things, use it!)

You do need to be able to use your own personal strengths in a wide variety of situations. You need to be able to listen as well as to make yourself heard. You need to earn people's trust. You need to be able to make the right impression on people in a way that's always true to yourself.

In this chapter, I'll look back on some of the situations I faced in my own career. I'll take you back to specific places and times, but the lessons are timeless: How to overcome suspicion within your own organization. How to adapt to a new business and social culture. How to succeed in getting your own ideas across in ways that benefit yourself, your clients and your business.

A chilly reception.

September 1968. I stepped out of a black London cab at 9:15 am on a chilly Monday morning. My wife Faith was back at the hotel enjoying breakfast with our two young daughters. Hope was five years old and Johanna just eight months. If I had any lingering doubts about transplanting my young family from New York to London, I pushed them out of my mind. It was my first day at McCann-Erickson's U.K. headquarters on Howland Street and I needed to get to work.

"Good morning, sir," said a gray-suited, gray-haired gentleman perched behind the lobby desk. I introduced myself to Charlie Johnson. A retired Air Force man, he'd been a fixture at the agency for more than fifteen years.

Charlie knew I was coming. He told me I was welcome to take "the lift" to the management offices on the fifth floor.

I stepped out of the elevator into a dark vestibule. I double-checked the illuminated button above the now-closing elevator doors. This was 5, all right. My eyes adjusted. I fumbled for the light switch, and the lights flickered on, all the way down the empty, silent corridors.

I walked once around the floor and, seeing no signs of life or freshly brewed coffee, headed back to the elevator. I stopped at floors 4, 3, 2 and 1 on my way back to the ground floor. All of them were equally dark and deserted.

"Is this one of those British bank holidays?" I asked Charlie.

"No, sir," he said.

"Well, what the hell time do people start work around here?"

Charlie laughed and told me I'd have to wait at least another half-hour. I took his advice and headed to the café down the street for an extra cup of coffee.

I'd learned my first lesson in how British advertising was practiced at the tail-end of the "swinging sixties." Unlike in New York, where the suits were at their desks by nine, U.K. management sauntered in around ten. In New York, creatives were expected at ten. In the U.K., they were rarely sighted before 10:30 or 11.

An hour later, I was back on McCann's 5th floor, sitting with four other men and one woman in Jack Powers' chairman's conference room.

Jack and I were the only two Americans. And based on the looks I was getting from the four Brits, they felt there was one too many Yanks in the room.

Clearly, these new colleagues—managing director, creative director, research director, and financial director—formed a tight-knit, hostile group. They were people who would like nothing more than to see me fail.

I had arrived at a time of transition. While still overseeing the U.K. agency, Jack Powers was moving up to head all of McCann's European operations. Jack was a forceful, dynamic, no-nonsense operator who had worked on the Esso account for many years. His personality and business savvy made him a big hit with clients and he clearly had won the respect of the London agency team.

Jack would be a very tough act to follow. But that didn't mean the locals didn't feel ready to assume command. The British managing director had set his sights on the top job. What he didn't know was that I had moved to the London agency with the understanding that I would soon be taking Jack's place.

The chill in the room told me all I needed to know about the internal challenge I faced.

I realized at once that the temporary role I had accepted—my title was chairman of the strategic committee—was not structured in a way that would help me succeed in all the ways I needed to. After more than ten years working for the U.S. agency, I knew there were four major areas that could define and shape your ability to lead:

1) *Authority to make decisions*: It's crucial to have a clearly defined role that combines authority and accountability if you are going to manage successfully.
2) *Direct involvement with clients*: Building relationships—and focusing your efforts on helping your clients succeed—gives you the leverage to succeed inside the agency.
3) *Ability to win new business*: This is the clearest demonstration of your capability to move things forward.
4) *Financial responsibility*: The ability to take accountability for meeting revenue targets and driving overall performance is the ultimate measure of any agency leader.

I saw my problem clearly enough. I had walked into a situation where none of these things would be handed to me on a plate. For the next twelve months, my challenge would be to learn all I could about the U.K. market while proving myself to a team over whom I had no direct authority, or professional or financial accountability.

Notwithstanding the chilly reception, this was a team that in twelve months time I would be expected to lead.

Four keys to agency leadership
1. Authority to make decisions
2. Direct involvement with clients
3. Ability to win new business
4. Financial responsibility

Warming to the challenge

Despite the lack of authority offered by my "strategic" role, I realized that there were two key areas where I could make an impact on the agency's fortunes.

First, was the Esso account. This had been Jack's purview for years and he was well respected by the U.K. client. But with Jack moving on to a regional role it was clear that Esso would need its own U.K. contact on the account.

Second, was in the area of new business development. In those days, McCann-Erickson London had a less-than-stellar reputation for attracting local clients. Known as a U.S. shop that worked almost exclusively on global clients and brands, the agency ranked a disappointing #18 in the U.K. market. I wanted to change that—and fast.

Focusing on both Esso and new client pitches had clear advantages for me. It would allow me to win influence within the agency even without authority. If I did both things well, I would prove to the internal team I could deliver on their behalf. Equally important: While I would report to the Managing Director on new business, I would report directly to Jack on the Esso account, which was a great protection against the agency's internal politics.

Working with Esso gave me my first insights into the similarities and differences of working in the U.K. market. Esso was a global brand and the U.K. client was highly receptive to the U.S. expertise I could bring to the account. My experience on Nabisco and Philip Morris came into play, along with my respect for the strategy and research-based approach for which McCann-Erickson was world-renowned.

Having direct client contact also gave me new insights into why the London office kept such different hours than the U.S. agency. The work day may have started later but it invariably carried on late into the night.

At the end of the sixties, three-martini lunches were still common in New York. In London, the agency and client relationship called for a similar approach to "liquid lunches."

But in London it didn't stop there.

Cocktails in the agency started at five, after which the creatives invariably headed to the nearest pub, and the account guys took clients out for dinners that usually stretched past 11pm.

As they say, it was a tough job, but somebody had to do it.

Breaking a sweat for the home heat account

One of the best ways to grow your business is to add more work from existing clients. Through my Esso gasoline client, I had an early line into a separate Esso account: the U.K. home heating campaign was being considered for a review. We had been doing a great job on the main account, and both Esso's Managing Director and Marketing Director were in favor of giving us a shot at this new piece of business.

The Advertising Director in charge of the account was Terry Bray, a fitness fanatic from Wales. Everyone involved made sure to let me know that it was Terry's decision whether or not we got the account.

He listened patiently to my pitch: The history and success of the existing global partnership between Esso and McCann-Erickson. The many ways we had customized Esso's creative for the U.K. market. The credentials of the local creative and media team that would focus on his account. And how McCann-Erickson's strategic and research expertise would be applied to his own local account.

As the meeting came to an end, Terry stood up and shook my hand. He was a few inches taller than me, with the lean, athletic look of a distance runner.

"OK, Phil," he said. "I'll race you for the business. How about a twelve-mile run this Sunday? I'll even give you a three-mile head start."

I couldn't help feeling I was getting set up, but, after negotiating an extra week to prepare, I accepted his challenge.

With less than two weeks to get myself into shape, I jogged each evening around the West London streets. As I huffed and puffed in my running shorts, I could feel just how much the British diet and advertising lifestyle had taken their toll. But Terry was giving me a three-mile start, I told myself. How could I possibly lose?

The day of the race came. We stood at our starting lines, three miles apart. Terry had assured me he was "Welsh by birth and not by nature." But in order to keep each other honest, we had each sent our own car and driver to accompany our opponent along the course.

I had nine miles to cover. He had twelve. I didn't care how I did it. Winning was all that mattered. I set out strong and charged through the first mile. Then I slowed down into a more manageable trot for a couple of miles more. Then I degenerated into an alternating walk-run-jog that I hoped would see me to the finish line. Five miles into the run, the heavens opened and hailstones the size of golf balls began raining down on me. Those suckers were big! I headed for the cover of the nearest bus shelter and waited for the storm to blow over.

As soon as the storm eased, I plodded on. With a mile to go, I was still out front. There was no sign of Terry. I pressed on toward the finish line, which was the car park of Terry's local pub, the Queen Adelaide in Putney.

Half a mile to go. In one of my increasingly desperate glances over my shoulder, I saw a solitary runner in the distance.

With quarter of a mile to go, I could hear the steady beat of his footsteps behind me. By now the colorful pub sign was already in view. As I got closer, I could see the face of that long-deceased monarch after which the pub was named. A crowd from the agency had gathered in the parking lot to cheer me on.

But the cheers weren't enough. Thirty yards from the finish, Terry breezed past me.

I staggered despondently into the parking lot. Terry was hardly out of breath. We shook hands. He congratulated me on my effort and offered to buy me a pint.

Best of all, as we headed to the bar he told me that, even though I'd lost the race, I'd impressed him enough to win his business.

Understanding the local challenge

The key challenge McCann-Erickson London faced was building our local client roster. I knew that winning a solid base of local clients was crucial for the agency's stability and growth. I also knew that bringing in new, primarily local accounts would be the quickest way to gain the support of the senior people inside the agency.

At that time, British clients were keenly interested in the U.S. way of doing business. They had great respect for the expertise that American advertisers and agencies such as McCann had developed. But they didn't like the actual "hard sell" approach when it was executed in their own market.

British advertising was already known for its subtlety, sense of humor and its ability to entertain. Creative "hot shops" led by Collett Dickenson Pearce were generating buzz and winning awards. Clients loved their work. Plus, the U.K. had only one commercial TV channel. Any advertiser who put his product on television could expect to see positive results, even if the product was hardly featured in the ad itself.

My dilemma was simple. British advertising was not only fun, it worked. For most clients, there was no downside to giving their business to a smart, local agency.

To succeed, I needed to show clients how their advertising could and would work even better. I had to convince them that a new approach combining better strategic positioning with a British advertising sensibility was worth trying.

If I did that, I knew the agency could really take off.

Three basics of client satisfaction
1. Know his industry and his business problems
2. Provide solutions beyond advertising
3. Deliver measurable results

You can't sell anything if you can't sell yourself

In advertising, as in many industries, acceptance starts on a personal level. Getting things done means making connections. Likeability is an important, often under-rated asset. On the account side, sociability is a crucial step in building relationships based on trust and respect.

In my early days in London, I decided my charm offensive would be best waged outside the agency. At the very least, my "outsider" status was no threat to the clients who held the purse strings. Even if they had no intention of giving me their business, they could afford to be polite. It didn't cost them anything to take a meeting. They might even learn from me.

In addition to my "day job" on Esso, my "night job" became focusing on new business. I met marketers for drinks or dinner. I asked them for their views on the state of British advertising and how they approached their own marketing and competitive challenges. I took notes. I researched their companies and industries. In doing all this work, I took a systematic approach to identifying the client prospects most likely to be considering a change of agencies.

Key factors I looked for included:

1. Declining market share for one or more of their brands.
2. Bad press on the advertising they were running.
3. Changes at the top, at the marketing director or senior management level.

Before approaching any new prospect, I also took care to develop specific suggestions to discuss and gather relevant case histories that showed how McCann had addressed similar marketing challenges in other markets.

In Europe, relationships take longer to develop than they do in America. But once established, these relationships are even more solid. Unlike their U.S. counterparts, who are quick to shift agencies in the face of short-term performance factors, European clients are far more likely to take a longer term view. When problems arise—as they invariably do—a European client's first instinct is to work with the agency to resolve the issues, rather than severing ties with a business partner he trusts and enjoys working with.

One man with whom I developed a particularly good rapport was Sir Richard Trehane, chairman of the Milk Marketing Board. This was the archetypal local account—a cooperative association of dairy farmers who were used to thoroughly British, down-to-earth marketing campaigns.

A dairy farmer himself, Sir Richard had long championed the need for a national marketing effort. For several years, the MMB had been using the slogan "Drinka pinta milka day." The campaign had worked well. But Sir Richard was ready for a fresh approach.

How to get considered for a new business pitch
1. Focus on long-term relationship building within the industry.
2. Systematically identify potential "in-play" accounts.
3. Position your agency as a "top three" contender ahead of the review.

Putting art before science

The Milk Marketing Board was one of the U.K.'s biggest accounts. I knew that winning it would represent a huge breakthrough for my "American" agency.

Through my conversations with Sir Richard Trehane, I also knew that, while he was acknowledged as a marketing visionary, he approached business challenges with a highly scientific mind. But when it came to creative decisions, he paid great attention to his wife, Lady Elizabeth.

David Ogilvy once said, "the consumer is not a moron, she is your wife." Sir Richard took that even further. He was known for inviting Lady Elizabeth a highly opinionated woman with a passion for contemporary art to sit in on agency presentations.

Knowing how influential Lady Elizabeth would be during any future account review, I invited her to curate an art show inside the agency. The event would give McCann-Erickson a great entrée into the London art scene and would allow Lady Elizabeth to showcase her creative contemporaries and her own specific tastes.

She approached the challenge with relish. And we at the agency responded in kind, with a promotion and PR effort that generated tremendous buzz for the show and the artists on display.

Following the indisputable success of the event, the McCann team was naturally invited to pitch for the business when the Milk campaign was put into formal review. We put on a great presentation. Lady Elizabeth was highly vocal in her support.

And, with a wink and a nod, Sir Richard awarded us the account.

1969: A transition year

As the "swinging sixties" came to an end, there was change in the air in London. The Beatles made their last public performance on the rooftop of the Apple Records building, an event that was broken up by the Metropolitan Police. Throughout the country, amid growing resentment about striking unions and the social changes of the "permissive society," the mood was turning against Harold Wilson's Labour government.

Of course, the United States was going through an even more tumultuous era. As Nixon was sworn in as President, opposition to the Vietnam War was approaching fever pitch and the country was heading toward a recession.

1969 was the start of a difficult period for McCann-Erickson in the U.S.; it was a time when Interpublic management would be thankful for the global strength of the McCann network. In 1969, McCann's International billings surpassed those of the U.S. for the first time. It was also a time of transition at our largest international office: In mid-year I became Chairman of the U.K. agency.

Right around the time Neil Armstrong was taking "one small step for (a) man, one giant leap for mankind," I was making a leap of my own.

In succeeding Jack Powers, I knew it was important to have a team in place that I could trust and that shared my vision. After nearly a year in London, I had delivered a series of "wins" to the agency that had earned most people's respect. It was clear that Ann Burdus, who headed research, and Nigel Grandfield, who ran the account service department would have big roles to play in our future. But it was also obvious that the Managing Director who had preceded me in London was not willing to continue in a number two role. After conversations with me and Jack, we crafted the right kind of exit package for him and he was able to announce his retirement in the most proper way.

Meanwhile, Ronnie Kirkland, the agency's Creative Director signaled that, as soon as I could announce his replacement, he was planning to down-shift his career and spend more time with his horses while starting up a small boutique agency.

Reaching for the stars

With space exploration on everybody's minds, I was particularly aware of Leo Burnett's famous words: "When you reach for the stars you may not quite get one, but you won't come up with a handful of mud either."

As the new head of McCann-Erickson U.K., I intended to reach for the stars. But I knew I couldn't do it alone. I also needed to *hire* some stars as quickly as possible.

Finding a new Creative Director represented my first real test as agency chief. I knew that if I was to truly grow the agency, I needed someone who not only possessed tremendous intellect and creative skills, but also had extensive packaged-goods experience.

Most important, I was looking to elevate the position to a partner level within the agency. I believed—and subsequently pushed throughout the agency—that the Creative Director should be a true partner in the business. That included having him be involved in the agency's business planning process and with the review meetings with McCann's and Interpublic's management.

This was a key change for our company and our industry. It paid off big time when I hired Barry Day with Jack Powers' support.

Barry came to us from Lintas, the Unilever agency. In his interviews with me and Jack, it was obvious that he had both the intellectual capacity and the creative skills to succeed in the role we had imagined. And being British helped, too.

Barry was a creative leader who fully embraced the challenge of winning new business and growing our U.K. market share. He energized the creative team, brought in new talent and before long we were impressing clients not only with strategy and research, but also with the quality of our creative execution.

Barry also encouraged us to find a creative way around McCann's policy of not handling political clients.

Yes, Prime Minister!

In early 1970, Harold Wilson and the Labour Party found themselves back in favor with voters and comfortably ahead in the opinion polls. Wilson seized the chance to call a snap election.

Barry Day pitched me on the idea of handling the advertising for Britain's Conservative Party, headed by Edward Heath.

It was a nice idea. But it had one big problem. A few years earlier, McCann-Erickson had instituted a worldwide policy of not accepting political parties as clients. (Back in 1959, McCann had bought Australia's third-largest agency, Hansen-Rubensohn, which was run by the legendary Sim Rubensohn. Sim was an adman whose passion for socialist politics often ran contrary to the interests of the agency's mostly conservative clients.)

I knew, however, that the opportunity for McCann-Erickson to somehow get involved with the U.K.'s national election campaign was too good to pass up. It would add to our credibility in the market. Best of all, if Heath did somehow win the election, it would really establish us as a U.K. agency.

Given the U.K.'s short election cycle, Barry and I quickly hatched a plan whereby he would work on the election campaign—which included speeches for Ted Heath as well as Conservative Party commercials—but only in his spare time. This was approved by Interpublic management and clearly laid out in a document signed by both parties. (This soon became the model for how most senior agency people work on U.S. political campaigns.)

Barry threw himself into his challenge and worked closely with Heath and the Party leaders on all aspects of the messaging. It was a valiant effort. But, if you believed the opinion polls, it looked like a lost cause. The final numbers before the election showed Wilson's Labour Party ahead by 12%.

But you can't always trust the pollsters. On election day, the voters told a different story. Heath won the popular vote by a 3% margin along with a clear Parliamentary majority.

After the election of 1970, Barry Day's and McCann-Erickson's stars were clearly rising. We had a true friend in the man who was now Prime Minister. And in the 12 months after the election, Ted Heath helped cement our reputation with clients by attending four VIP dinners in the agency's dining room. It was the kind of "local acceptance" that truly stamped us as a major player in the U.K. market.

Taking it to the top

One of the great balancing acts in the agency business is choosing how and when to approach the "boss of bosses" at any client company.

Especially within international companies, there are sensitivities at every level. Going over a local client's head to pitch directly to the big boss can often do more harm than good. Even if you win the business, it's not wise to make an enemy of the guy who holds the local budget.

In 1972, when Dr. Anton Rupert, the South African head of the Rembrandt Group (now Compagnie Financier Richemont AG), created Rothmans International—a single global organization to reduce duplication in his tobacco businesses—I saw an opportunity.

Dr. Rupert was a huge admirer of Joe Cullman, the Philip Morris chairman, so my background on Philip Morris was of interest to him. That made it easy to get the appointment. At the same time, I suggested their U.K. Managing Director join the meeting. Smart move. Dr. Rupert was a big believer in partnerships. He wasn't about to award the account to my agency over the head of his local decision maker. The U.K. client appreciated the fact we didn't go over his head and that he was part of the meeting. And he was also smart enough to see that his boss was heavily in favor of his newly globalized company working with McCann-Erickson: a truly global agency with highly relevant tobacco expertise.

Rothmans was a big win for the U.K. agency. Dr. Rupert had a strong belief in a consistent brand image. Once he approved a campaign, he liked to stick with it. We understood him well. In turn, he appreciated that we didn't push for big creative changes when small ones would do. Some years the biggest change in a campaign was nothing more than a four-inch adjustment of the hand holding the cigarette. With media commissions still at 15%, the account became a powerful annuity, underpinning the agency's finances for years to come.

When dealing with smaller companies, it often makes sense to cultivate a relationship with the boss. One such client was Bowyers Sausages. This was a private company, run by a colorful character named Newton Clair. He and his wife were East-Enders by birth and marvelous company, but I sensed that they both craved a higher degree of social acceptance. (In the class-conscious society of Britain in the early '70s, being the nation's #2 sausage maker wasn't enough to overcome the "wrong" accent.)

To remedy that situation, my wife and I hosted a costume party for a large group of friends. Costume parties were a rare occurrence in London and our themed event, at which Mr. and Mrs. Newton Clair were introduced as honored guests, was a great way for people to interact with an element of play-acting that helped eliminate any real or perceived class barriers.

It certainly helped reinforce my own personal relationship with Newton Clair. When the account came up for review several months later, the chemistry we had established with the client clearly played a role in McCann pitching the account.

> **How to win the pitch**
> 1. Demonstrate a superior understanding of the client's business challenges.
> 2. Combine strategic thinking with creative excellence.
> 3. Outline how you will deliver—and measure—results.

A harmonic convergence

The period of 1967-72 was a terrible time for U.S. advertising in general and McCann-Erickson in particular. In that period, U.S. billings actually shrank 25% and, by 1973, the agency was no longer in the U.S. top 10. Amid the agency's other troubles, the nearly-10 week GM strike of 1970 hit McCann hard. As Stewart Alter notes in *Truth Well Told*, most shops suffered in that period, but "none of the U.S. agency declines were as dramatic as McCann-Erickson's."

Overseas, the picture was the complete opposite. International billings grew 114% between 1967 and 1972, and in 1971, *Advertising Age* reported than McCann had overtaken J. Walter Thompson as the world's largest agency in non-U.S. billings.

In the U.K., the agency was going from strength to strength. We were the people who had helped the government get elected. We were keeping milk fresh. For the first time ever, we were creating advertising that truly "clicked" with the British consumer sensibilities and delivered results that clients could take to the bank. At the same time, a new song featuring our most famous global brand was being sung around the world and reinvigorating the agency's international reputation.

Shot on a hillside near Rome, the "I'd Like to Buy the World a Coke" commercial became a global phenomenon in 1971 and 1972. The spot had its origins at Shannon Airport in Ireland, where hundreds of people got stranded one night due to heavy fog in London. Among them was Bill Backer, McCann's New York-based Creative Director. As Backer watched people bonding over a Coke in the airport cafeteria, he pulled out a napkin and scribbled the words: "I'd like to buy the world a Coke and keep it company." Those words fed into a catchy and evocative song, written in collaboration with U.K. songwriters Roger Cook and Roger Greenaway, that became a bestselling single recorded by the New Seekers. It remains one the U.K.'s top 100 bestselling singles of all time.

The "hillside" commercial featured a multicultural gathering of young people from around the world—all singing in perfect harmony—and is credited with helping Coke regain and retain its status as America's most-popular soft drink. The spirit of the ad was even felt in apartheid-era South Africa. After Coke and McCann resisted a request for an all-white version of the ad, the commercial was accepted without changes by the state-run TV network.

Putting it all together

As the British economy slowed in the early '70s, McCann's emphasis on results became especially important to U.K. advertisers facing sales pressures and budget cuts. Ted Heath's government was beset by the same kinds of union troubles that had damaged Wilson's reputation. Then the global oil crisis of 1973 sent Western economies into chaos.

In the midst of a recessionary environment, McCann-Erickson London focused on the "nuts and bolts" solutions clients needed.

We restructured the agency to offer Europe's first-ever fully integrated communications package. Along with the advertising agency, we established direct response, PR and sales promotions agencies all working together under the McCann umbrella.

The first client to take advantage of this new offering was Spar, a retail food distribution franchise client. With Spar stores scattered throughout the country, the client was eager to test and measure different creative and promotional offers. Each week, retail results were fed by the client to the agency, and we worked to refine the offers and promotions for the coming week. The success of the Spar campaign reinforced McCann's reputation with retail clients.

Our integrated agency also tried to launch a new innovation with the potential to revolutionize the U.K. market. Adapting the successful green stamps formula from the U.S., where consumers earned stamps for retail purchases and used them to purchase gifts from a catalogue, we proposed a new kind of coupon that consumers would collect and redeem in a similar way. The coupon would be built into the packaging of the product and limited to one brand per category. This idea—a forerunner of the many marketing "rewards" programs that are so common today—had particular appeal to companies such as Procter & Gamble with brands in multiple categories. And the built-in exclusivity of the program meant that every client wanted to hear about it and consider it as either as an offensive or defensive marketing strategy. The out-of-the-box thinking behind the concept allowed us to present to top management at every major consumer product and cemented our reputation as a top-flight, forward-thinking marketing agency. Ultimately, though, enough manufacturers were able to band together to kill the proposal, convincing the members of their advertising association that its exclusivity provisions would deliver an unfair competitive advantage.

Despite this minor setback, McCann-Erickson U.K. continued rising through the ranks of British agencies.

It would be nice to say we did it all with great people, great work, and a great team spirit. But compensation policy also had a lot to with it.

In the U.K. in the '70s, our integrated agency had a straightforward incentive plan designed to motivate staff, incentivize cooperation, and reward performance. It's a compensation policy that I tried unsuccessfully to impose on other Interpublic agencies for many years, but it never really took hold until the concept of integrated services became established worldwide in the early '90s.

Simply put, each of the McCann divisions—advertising, direct response, PR and sales promotion—had a bonus target that was 50% based on individual division performance, and 50% on overall agency performance. The only way to get the maximum payout was to cooperate with your colleagues!

Four basics to agency performance
1. Create the right structure.
2. Hire and develop the best talent.
3. Incentivize cooperation and performance.
4. Encourage out-of-the-box thinking.

Window dressing

One of the challenges of managing a fast-growing agency is ensuring that your most established clients still enjoy the same level of service and attention they expect and deserve.

There are times, of course, when this is not exactly possible and you must either pray for their indulgence or distract them from your inattentiveness.

After I had been in charge a year or so, I was very happy with the growth the agency was achieving. There was a new energy inside the agency. We were starting our workdays at a regular hour. We were making frequent new business pitches. Our management team had gelled to the degree that we could finish each other's sentences. If one of us missed a presentation, we had no problem trusting a colleague to step into our customary role.

On the downside, because of the sheer volume of our new business pitches, some of our oldest clients were grumbling that they were being kept waiting in the reception area for longer and longer periods.

I pondered this problem one weekend as I took my regular Sunday afternoon stroll down the King's Road with my young daughters. This being the early '70s, hot pants and tight T-shirts were all the rage. I put myself in the shoes of my mostly male clients and imagined being stuck in a waiting area for twenty or thirty minutes with only Charlie Johnson for company.

By the following week, I had given Charlie a new assignment, handling the lift and managing the internal traffic flow.

In his place, a glamorous young lady was stationed in the reception area, wearing a figure-hugging T-shirt and bright red hot pants. Her job was to greet clients and offer them tea, coffee, or simply eye candy.

She did her job well. All grumbling stopped. The new business pitches continued apace. And later, the hot pants look proved equally popular with clients all over Europe. (The only exception was Germany.)

And that's the final secret as to how McCann-Erickson moved from #18 to #2 in the U.K. market. We did it with great people, great work, a great team spirit, and a great compensation policy. But the hot pants helped too.

CHAPTER FIVE

Maintain Your Agility

*How to anticipate and respond to disruptive change
while retaining your competitive edge*

"Be prepared."

—*Boy Scout motto*

Respond and adapt

"Be prepared for what?" someone once asked Robert Baden-Powell, the founder of the Boy Scout movement.

"Why, for any old thing," he replied.

These days, you need to be prepared for all kinds of events that might impact your company, your industry and the markets in which you operate.

Thinking narrowly, you must be prepared for changes within your industry, such as new competitive challenges and changing consumer tastes and expectations.

Thinking broadly, you must be prepared for the all kinds of external events from natural disasters to terrorist threats, from the long-term effects of climate change to the potential disruption of global pandemics.

In this new political and economic climate, you must also be prepared for the kind of sweeping legislative changes that can happen with the stroke of the pen.

In this chapter, I'll discuss the challenges my company faced in the 1970s including recessions, pricing pressures, reshaped political maps, and more. And I'll highlight the lessons that you can apply to similar conditions today.

The new world order

In 1971, Interpublic Group (IPG) became a publicly listed company on the New York Stock Exchange, an event that confirmed a remarkable turnaround in the holding company's fortunes over the previous three years.

But while the company itself was on a firmer financial footing, tectonic shifts were taking place in the world of advertising. A recession was decimating the U.S. advertising market (and McCann-Erickson in particular). At the same time, European companies and brands were expanding into the U.S. and International markets. Meanwhile, in every major country, the dominance of American advertising agencies was being challenged by a new breed of confident, creative, and culturally savvy agencies who were more locally rooted and "spoke the language" of their local consumers.

Particularly in Europe, the NIH syndrome—Not Invented Here—created an immediate barrier. Local clients and agencies were increasingly confident in their own abilities and were always looking to control their own budgets and creative destinies.

In 1971, I stepped into a new role, as EVP-regional director for McCann-Erickson in Europe, still based in London. I had experienced the NIH syndrome first-hand in the U.K. market. Along with everything I had learned from Barry Day, Ann Burdus and Nigel Grandfield and their teams, my years working with clients at McCann U.K. had shown me many ways to use creativity, science, and occasional theatricality to win over local clients.

Now I had to take these lessons onto the regional stage to countries as culturally distinct as France, West Germany, the Netherlands, Italy, Sweden, Denmark, Spain, and Portugal.

Up until the early '70s, while there were certainly worldwide assignments, most international business at global agencies was won on a country-by-country, assignment-by-assignment basis.

At McCann, we had two great global accounts—Esso and Coke—which illustrated how successful a single strategy and creative platform could be.

Competitively, J. Walter Thompson was still the number one worldwide agency and was known for its work on Ford and its Unilever packaged goods accounts. Meanwhile, Ogilvy & Mather was establishing its global reputation with its own Unilever assignments and powerful clients such as IBM. But elsewhere, multinational assignments were frequently patchwork affairs, with some local clients buying into international campaigns and others doing their own work locally.

Up till then, the advertising debate had focused primarily on the effectiveness of global vs. local strategies. But in the early '70s, as Europe's Common Market expanded and European-based clients looked to grow their international presence, regional communications strategies became a new imperative.

My job was to position McCann-Erickson for growth in the new Europe, a challenge made especially urgent given the continued weakness at the U.S. agency.

Forever changes

It's a truism that nothing is as constant as change. But when change happens at the highest level of a company or country, new leaders often chart new courses, reverse old policies, and create change that can be transformational.

Two changes that occurred in the late '60s were to have a big impact on how Europe—and European advertising—evolved throughout the '70s.

The first leadership change altered the future of a company. It happened in the Interpublic boardroom in New York City on November 9, 1967.

A special board meeting had been called to address an urgent financial crisis that threatened the entire firm. Following a spate of acquisitions and a reckless rise in expenses, Interpublic found itself facing an unanticipated annual loss of $3 million. Such a loss would put Interpublic in violation of the company's loan agreements and possibly plunge it into receivership. The board needed to act and fast. They voted to remove Marion Harper from the CEO position. In Harper's place, they elected Robert Healy president and CEO. Healy wanted to move as quickly as the situation demanded. But the bankers who had forced the change of leadership wanted to put some very tough restrictions on Healey and his CFO, Bill Casey. Things came to a head in one passionate meeting when Casey (who had already cleared the move with Healy) threw a set of keys across the table at a senior banker from Chase Manhattan.

"If you think you can run the place any better, go ahead!"

By the end of the meeting, Healy and Casey had obtained $10.2 million in revolving credit from Chase. Healy then prevailed on three major clients—Coca-Cola, Heublein and Carnation—to pay their media commissions in advance. And he followed that by undertaking a painful but necessary restructuring, closing and merging units and reducing staff.

By pushing decision-making down into the operating companies, Healy succeeded in returning Interpublic to profitability as soon as the following year a recovery *Advertising Age* described as "bordering on the miraculous," given that it was achieved in such a short time. Then in 1971, having put the company back on solid footing, he retired, handing the Interpublic reins over to Paul Foley, the long-time creative leader of McCann-Erickson.

Twenty-two years later, in September 1993, I was quoted in Robert Healy's *New York Times* obituary saying, "he was instrumental in pulling the company back from a financial precipice, and set Interpublic firmly on the path toward professional and financial growth."

The second leadership change altered the future of a continent. When French President Charles de Gaulle retired from office in April 1969, the way was opened for the future expansion of the European Economic Community (EEC). While in office, de Gaulle had sought always to limit American and British influence in continental Europe. To that end, he had used his veto power to prevent the United Kingdom from joining the EEC whose founding members, France, West Germany, Italy, Belgium, the Netherlands, and Luxembourg had abolished many internal EEC trade tariffs in 1968.

De Gaulle's successor, Georges Pompidou, was more pragmatic. He withdrew France's opposition to the expansion of the EEC. In 1972, a new accession treaty was signed and, on January 1, 1973, the "Common Market" expanded to include the U.K., Ireland and Denmark. (Today's European Union includes 27 member states, 16 of which share the Euro as a common currency.)

> **The realities of change**
>
> 1. Expect change to be constant—but be prepared for times when it's sudden, surprising, and transformational.
>
> 2. A change of leadership—or strategy—can quickly send companies or countries in new directions—and create new business opportunities.
>
> 3. In times of rapid change, size and strength are usually less important than agility and adaptability.
>
> *Be prepared. Be ready to respond and adapt to events you cannot control. In today's world, "any old thing" can happen.*

A whole new ballgame

Regional advertising was fast becoming a reality and I knew that being first to exploit the opportunities could put McCann-Erickson in a powerful position.

While the notion of pitching—and winning—business on a pan-regional basis was still fairly new, I also knew McCann-Erickson had a number of strengths that would serve us well.

Global expertise. In the early '70s, consumers and clients across the planet could recognize and quote McCann's creative work. With Coke, we were teaching the world to sing. With Esso, we were putting a tiger in the tank for drivers in thirty-four countries.

Local reputation. Across Europe and throughout the world, McCann offices were now entrenched in their local markets. International billings, which had surpassed U.S. billings in 1969, were now a crucial driver of our profitability. We had already surpassed JWT as the leading agency in non-U.S. billings. And our London office was on fire. In two years alone (1971-72) billings leaped 85%.

Regional coordination. European clients were already aware of the benefits McCann could offer through our research-driven creative and our ability to drive efficiencies through our international network. In 1964, the agency had handled only six accounts in more than five European countries. By 1973, that number had tripled to 18.

An emphasis on testing—and results. At McCann, we had long emphasized standardized research and creative testing. Usually, campaigns that worked in one market also worked in others with few or no changes. This helped multinational clients reduce costs and helped overcome the "cultural" resistance of local clients.

Despite these strengths, we needed to prepare McCann's European offices for the coming reality of regional pitches and to ensure maximum cooperation between offices in accepting and adapting creative that would, by necessity, originate from elsewhere in the network.

This was crucial. Because already major clients were shifting their operational as well as their communications strategies. For American-owned companies, this meant more authority was being pushed to—or demanded by—their regional European HQs.

But the future wasn't being driven by the U.S. multinationals. In the "new Europe," the biggest opportunities were coming from clients such as L'Oreal in Paris, Henkel in Dusseldorf, Martini & Rossi in Turin, Unilever in London, Opel in Rüsselsheim, Germany, and Nestlé in Vevey, Switzerland.

Fortunately, McCann-Erickson was well positioned to serve these growing clients.

"Transferable power"

As European markets opened up, it became more important than ever for companies inside Europe to coordinate marketing and maintain brand consistency throughout the region. And for many of these companies, Europe was only the start. Global expansion was also on their minds.

To expand our European business, we knew that increased cooperation between McCann offices would be essential. Fortunately, the success of the London office gave us the leadership leverage to break down cultural barriers and improve coordination between all our European offices.

Between 1967 and 1973, Eugene Kummel, who headed McCann-Erickson International sent no less than 130 professionals overseas. This was a consistent strategy that he called "transferable power." Rather than focusing on local language skills, Kummel was more concerned with finding people who "spoke the language of soft drinks, or gasoline, or automotives, or beer." In sending so many executives overseas, Kummel turned McCann into the first agency that mirrored what its own clients were doing—building a culture of executives dedicated to global business careers.

This was a tremendous advantage to us in Europe. "Transferable power" meant that we could call upon a core team of executives who viewed themselves not as local, nor even regional, leaders. These executives were dedicated to the overall success of the McCann-Erickson global operation, understood the McCann culture, knew our clients' challenges and could work together across markets to win new business.

Of course, winning business always led to more opportunities. It's interesting to note that before the 1970s were over, many McCann executives in both creative and management roles had worked for the agency in six or more countries.

Within the worldwide agency, the phrase "transferable power" quickly came to be applied to European as well as American executives. Just a few of the stars of that time included Barry Day, the creative director we hired in London in 1969, who rose through the years to become the agency's worldwide vice chairman; Ann Burdus, the London agency's research director who went on to top posts in Europe, the U.S. and other markets; Nigel Grandfield, who became group chairman of the U.K. agencies; Jens Olesen, the great Dane who started at McCann in London and worked for us in 19 offices in 10 countries, ending up as president of our South American division based in Brazil; and Mike Ferrier who worked for us in nine countries—from Europe to the Americas to Regional Director for the Far East—before retiring to live in Monte Carlo.

The secrets of regional success
1. Compelling global case studies (e.g. Coke and Esso)
2. Established capabilities in clients' regional headquarters markets
3. Strong regional cooperation and reporting
4. Standardized research techniques and creative testing
5. "Transferable power" to enhance local expertise, reinforce agency culture
6. Measurable benefits for clients: cost effectiveness, brand awareness, product sales and market share

Remember: Your expertise makes you competitive. But it's your ability to execute that sets you apart.

"The Right One" for Europe

One of the first accounts to talk to us about expanding from a local to a regional campaign was Martini & Rossi.

We had won the U.K. account in 1970 and developed a very successful campaign for the Martini vermouth brand around the slogan "The Right One." In fact, our creative strategy drew heavily on the success of Coke's 1969 "The Real Thing" campaign, but in Martini's case, the imagery was transported to a new level of sophistication. Our Martini ads depicted a lavish lifestyle of yachts, luxury hotels and upscale locales such as Monte Carlo.

Count Victorio Rossi, a grandson of one of the company's founders, oversaw the company's brand marketing. He loved our new campaign and, with the support of the family's executive committee, was keen to expand it across Europe.

Of course, convincing his strong-willed local teams, especially in the home market of Italy, to embrace a campaign originating from the U.K., presented a challenge.

Rather than taking the traditional, country-by-country approach of presenting to each client in their home market, we took another idea from of the Coca-Cola playbook. Whenever Coke sold a new campaign, they always convened a regional meeting to review the worldwide campaign.

In what was to become a standard approach for McCann's regional pitches in Europe, we worked with Count Rossi to convene a regional meeting, in this case in London. The general managers from all the major European markets were invited along with their agency counterparts from McCann.

The meeting was held at McCann's Howland Street office. Even though we knew we had the Count's backing, he wanted to position the launch of a regional Martini campaign as a group decision – not something he was forcing down the throats of his people.

Our presentation hit all the right notes. We had the right creative, the right imagery, the right music and an aspirational "right one" strategy that connected the Martini brand with mass audiences in every market.

Still, as the meeting drew to a close and I studied the faces of the various national managers, I knew they hadn't yet fully accepted our regional idea.

Alarm bells started ringing.

As my assistant burst into the conference room, I realized they were real alarm bells.

"Sorry to interrupt," she said, "but we need to evacuate the building."

For a few seconds, nobody moved.

"Please hurry!" she said. "They think there's a bomb in the Post Office Tower."

Suddenly, everybody understood what was going on. The McCann office was just a block or so away from the GPO Tower (now the BT Tower). At the time, it was London's tallest building. Just months before, the Provisional IRA had exploded a bomb in the restroom of its "Top of the Tower" restaurant.

We all hurried outside, where police shepherded us through the streets, until we were a safe distance from the Tower.

The bomb-scare evacuation kept us out of the office for more than two hours. During that time, as the immediate drama of the moment dissipated, the local McCann people sought out their Martini counterparts, striking up conversations, starting to build relationships and helping close the loop on the local level.

Back in the conference room, I suggested we adjourn the meeting and allow the local agencies more time to discuss with their Martini counterparts the possibility of adapting the advertising to ensure it worked successfully in their local markets. I recommended that each agency present a localized version of the campaign for each client to consider without obligation.

There was complete agreement. Within four months, Martini was working with McCann-Erickson throughout Europe. Not long after, McCann was awarded the account on a worldwide basis.

Martinis all round: How to sell a unifying idea to a diverse group

1. Good strategy and creative makes a difference.
2. Know your client—what he wants to achieve and how he wants to be perceived.
3. Have an agency team that takes advantage of every opportunity for informal communication, bonding and consensus building ("transferable power" in action).
4. Dramatic presentations help (though the excitement of this was not by design).

I tell L'Oreal "I'm Worth It"

In the early '70s, every full-service advertising agency relied heavily on two financial drivers: creative production fees and the 15% commissions earned on media buys.

For an agency like McCann-Erickson, the emphasis on global and regional campaigns allowed us to offer savings to clients on the creative work.

Of course, "savings" on creative for clients meant lost revenue for us. But as we planned and bought media in more and more countries for the same client, the increase in media commissions more than offset the reduced creative production fees.

The system worked well for both sides. But it was only a matter of time before it started to be challenged.

In 1975, I received word from our Paris office that François Dalle, the CEO of L'Oreal, wanted to talk about our fees.

By this point, Dalle was legendary in the industry and one the most prominent figures in French business. Since becoming CEO in 1957, he had transformed L'Oreal into an international powerhouse in the health and beauty category. McCann had won L'Oreal's U.S. and Italian business in 1972 and, based on the success of our "Because I'm worth it" campaign, the relationship had since expanded to 13 countries, including a regional campaign in all the major European markets.

The success of McCann's work for L'Oreal had only reinforced Dalle's reputation as a forward-thinking global marketer. His business was going from strength to strength. Now, all of a sudden, he was worried about media commissions in France.

As I boarded my plane for Paris, I contemplated the problem. I knew that in France the advertising industry had established a different compensation system. Some local agencies, the ones that delivered the largest volume of advertising to French media companies, charged clients lower fees for media planning and buying than the 15% commission charged by international agencies. Because of their large volume, these local agencies also received year-end rebates from each media company, based on a formula agreed upon at the start of the year.

French clients who paid less upfront were happy with this way of doing business. From my point of view, the French system was flawed for three main reasons.

First, it made agencies more focused on maintaining relationships with media sellers and less focused on the qualitative and quantitative media research that would help increase advertising effectiveness.

Second, it had the potential to distort the agency's judgment in placing media for specific clients; once an agency had passed a spending threshold with a certain media company, they were incentivized to spend more with that company for their own good, even to the possible detriment of an individual client.

Third, the French system, if accepted by McCann for L'Oreal and extended to all our French clients, would cost my agency a great deal of money. McCann and the other international agencies simply didn't have enough local volume to drive the kind of rebates French agencies were seeing.

I arrived at L'Oreal headquarters with my French colleague Jean-Max Lenormand. Based in Paris, Lenormand was the worldwide coordinator for the L'Oreal account. His job was to make sure that everything we did on an international basis was understood and approved by the French client team, as well as to oversee our work within the French market itself.

I had met François Dalle before and knew he understood English well. Still, he wanted to conduct this meeting in French, with Lenormand translating.

After the usual pleasantries, Dalle shifted gears. He had a well-rehearsed and forceful speech prepared.

He pointed out that L'Oreal paid its agencies in France far less for its media buys than McCann was charging him. And that the work we were doing for him was generating tremendous volume for us, even as we were using the same basic campaign in every market with just minor adjustments. He was demanding I agree to reduce his agency fees.

I paused, waiting to see if Lenormand would translate into English the French for "or else."

Even if Dalle didn't say it, the threat of him pulling his entire international business hung in the air.

I couldn't agree to his terms. But I knew my response to his challenge would make or break our future relationship. By now, I was very familiar with the European style and knew that some bosses—particularly in France—used provocative gambits like this as a way of taking the measure of their business partners.

I also knew Dalle was reveling in his commercial success and thoroughly enjoying his reputation as a genius who, since working with McCann, had doubled his rate of worldwide growth. Looking at him across the table, I figured the last thing he was going to do was risk his business success and personal glory over an issue like this. While he certainly had the power to do it, switching agencies would be a big gamble for him. His own people would be in an uproar.

I responded with a well-rehearsed and forceful speech of my own. It went something like this:

"Monsieur Dalle, you say that McCann-Erickson is charging you too much. But let's take a look at what you're actually paying for. You're paying for the talents and experience of a worldwide agency with dedicated, on-the-ground personnel in every market, people who thoroughly understand L'Oreal and its products, its image and its positioning. You are paying for an agency that takes every nuance of your marketing message seriously. Remember how we worked with you in Italy to test the different ways of translating 'because I'm worth it' so it didn't sound too presumptuous to Italian women? In a different agency's hands, a great campaign could have been ruined. Our research and our sensitivity to all the issues related to your cosmetics brands ensured it was a huge success. Over the past three years, we've put in a place a well-oiled, seamless operation that is the envy of every other major personal care company in the world. And we're investing back a part of the media commissions you're paying us into the kind of brand research no other agency offers. Do you really want to tear that apart to shave some Francs from your global advertising budget? We're not going to change our agreement. Because to use a phrase you know very well, *we're worth it*."

As Lenormand translated my words, I saw the color draining from his cheeks. Then, as soon as I finished, I started to get up as if I were leaving.

It was a calculated risk. But sometimes you have to take risks for principles you believe in, particularly when you're pretty sure you've got the winning hand.

I was halfway to the door when François Dalle spoke in perfect English and said: "Come back here and sit down. We have not finished our discussion."

Needless to say, I sat back down. Our commission structure stayed in place. Less than two years later, Dalle extended McCann's L'Oreal assignment to all its worldwide markets.

Proving your worth: How to justify charging a "fair" price

1. Provide superior service – for L'Oreal, we combined the best coordinated regional network with unrivaled local expertise.

2. Quantify the results – testing demonstrates your commitment to results and a focus on continuous improvement.

3. Deliver what your client really wants – in this case, business success was highly intertwined with personal prestige.

Your clients can always find a cheaper option. Make sure you're delivering the best value.

"The Eagle" has landed

One of McCann-Erickson's most enduring client partnerships through the years has been with Henkel, the German-based marketer of household and personal care products, such as Persil laundry detergents, Fa deodorants, and Pritt glue sticks. (Among its more recent acquisitions, Henkel bought Dial Corporation in 2004.)

Like many German companies, Henkel took a scientific approach to all aspects of its business—from product development to consumer research. In the 1970s especially, the company was an avid student of American marketing practices as it sought to regionalize its brands and grow share against the likes of P&G and Unilever.

Right around the time I assumed responsibility for McCann's European business, Henkel went through its own management change. Dr. Helmut Seiler became Managing Director.

For our first meeting, we planned a general review and discussion of Henkel's European business and future plans. But when I saw a French language memo on his desk, I knew the issue of compensation in France was also on his agenda. (Even reading upside down in a foreign language, I knew right away what the subject was going to be.)

Sure enough, halfway through the meeting, he broached the topic: Henkel's French subsidiary felt that there should be an adjustment in the commission, the typical French disease.

I explained why there couldn't be one and how McCann was reinvesting back in our business in ways that would help his overall business grow through better coordination and research.

He pretended to be unimpressed, saying, "my people don't really need all that."

I pointed out that his competitors were in the process of building their own regional capabilities and would be coming at him more aggressively than ever.

He got up, walked over to his bookshelf, and pulled out a German dictionary. "Mr. Geier," he said, "did you know that your name means 'vulture' in German?"

I laughed. "I think that's a misprint," I said. "I thought Geier meant eagle, and eagles only prey on live animals, not dead."

He turned to me with a little chuckle. "Eagle, huh? I guess I'll let France pass."

Having bonded with some German humor, Seiler and I formed a lasting partnership. And McCann-Erickson began expanding its relationship with Henkel both in Europe and with worldwide brand assignments. Key to the relationship was the fact that every time I met Dr Seiler I endeavored to bring to him new research or competitive information he could not get elsewhere. Bringing additional knowledge to the table is always a good idea when visiting top management at a company. In Seiler's case it was especially appreciated.

In one of our early meetings, I presented an overview of best practices in relation to multinational brand coordination, highlighting the fact that the American companies had standardized systems and procedures covering all aspects of communications from the advertising brief to creative testing to brand research. I pointed out that Henkel was still using different briefing documents in each country and a multitude of different measurement techniques. There was no regional coordination and no clear way to evaluate advertising effectiveness from one market to the next.

"As a matter of fact," he said, "I'm talking to McKinsey about hiring them to help us develop a complete brand management coordination system."

"McKinsey?" I said. "They'll take months of your time, create a lot of work for your people and charge you about half a million Deutschmarks for the pleasure. I could have McCann put together a proposal to update all your branding coordination tools in a just a few weeks. Because of our knowledge of the business we can do it better and faster than any consulting firm."

He asked me to go ahead, even as he went ahead and hired McKinsey to do the same kind of work. Within six weeks, McCann provided him a complete new brand management protocol that combined the best methods of P&G and Gillette. Later, he was good enough to come back to me and say he had wasted his money hiring the consulting firm. He implemented the McCann recommendations virtually as written.

"I should have listened to you in the first place," he said. "It would have saved me a lot of time, money and aggravation."

Because we always went "above and beyond" in areas that helped clients like Henkel create lasting change, McCann's reputation in the beverage and packaged goods categories continued to grow. Even as we expanded our relationship with Henkel in Europe, we were winning assignments from major European clients such as Unilever, Nestlé and GM's Opel division who were developing regional and global growth strategies of their own.

Building a relationship: Always bring something extra to the table

1. **Competitive learnings**–Knowledge of how similar companies operate in different markets

2. **Best practices** – Example: standardized methodologies that make coordination easier

3. **Research** – New data—especially when accompanied by customized analysis

4. **Humor** – even in Germany

Number one in the new Europe

As early as 1972, McCann-Erickson had leapfrogged its competitors to move from #4 to become the #1 agency system in European billings. We were the first agency to truly drive the regional brand coordination concept and that provided a key advantage against the likes of J. Walter Thompson and Ogilvy & Mather. Our competitors were doing some great global work as well as great local work in many major markets. But it was McCann that anticipated and responded fastest to the changes happening in Europe at that time and developed systematic regional approaches that were eventually expanded to South America and the Far East as well.

In the same way that Coke's centralized decision-making gave it a global edge over Pepsi, so too did our centralized regional approach prove highly effective for clients as varied as Martini & Rossi, L'Oreal, Henkel, Rothmans, Unilever, Nestlé, Lufthansa, and Zanussi (home appliances).

For every client, we combined strategic thinking with powerful creative. We tested, tested and tested our work to ensure its ongoing effectiveness and local relevance. We developed and expanded our category expertise. And we nurtured and promoted the best people, using the concept of "transferable power" to put the right people where they were needed when they were needed.

Our relationships with European clients were hard-won, but long-lasting. I've mentioned earlier that European clients take longer to "warm up" to a business relationship, but compared to their U.S. counterparts, they are far less likely to abandon it at the first sign of trouble.

To keep our client relationships on track in this the new era of regionalization, we instituted a process designed to identify and remedy any harmful frictions that occurred on the national level. We put in place a simple agreement that ensured that local disputes could be brought to the regional decision makers to resolve. Usually, there was a coordinator assigned to each worldwide account out of the home office location that provided that support system.

Any problem with the agency relationship would be spelled out in writing, with a copy going to the local agency head and also to the coordination center of the client. If there was a problem the agency had with the client organization locally, a letter was sent to the headquarters of the agency to review. How did it work in practice? For example, if one of our local account people was not working well for a client, we would move quickly to switch him off the business. If necessary, we sent regional or global SWAT teams into the local agency to ensure that the problem was resolved satisfactorily. On many occasions, this approach not only saved business, it helped strengthen the overall agency-client relationship.

In fact, the system worked so well in Europe it expanded worldwide throughout Interpublic and is now used by many agencies that work with multinational clients.

Two keys to maintaining client relationships

1. Establish a process that allows you to communicate with—and resolve problems at—every level of the client organization.

2. Provide outside help to fix internal problems, particularly people problems at the local level.

The author gets shipped off to Europe by Paul Foley, the incoming CEO and Bob Healey, the retiring CEO of IPG.

The author at 8 a.m. in the London office—looking forward to seeing someone by 10 o'clock.

British Prime Minister Edward Heath joins me at McCann-Erickson's London office.

Ted Heath meets with CEOs of major U.K. clients in the McCann dining room.

Henkel Managing Director Dr. Helmut Seiler explains that "Geier" means vulture in German. I convince Dr. Seiler that in my case it means eagle.

International partners: Meeting with General Mills CEO Steve Sanger, his wife Karen, and Nestlé CEO Peter Brabeck in Salzburg, Austria.

Chairman of Milk Board with Mrs. Faith Geier at Cocktail Art Exhibit held by his wife at the Agency.

The author and Jack Nicholson take a break from working their clients at the Wimbledon Championships.

CHAPTER SIX

Be Creative—Strategically

*How to develop marketing platforms that allow you to
create centrally, improve locally – and succeed globally*

"If it doesn't sell, it isn't creative."
—*Advertising maxim coined by the Benton & Bowles agency*

"Did you see that ad?"

Whether you work in advertising or not, you can probably remember at least one time when a friend has told you excitedly about a great commercial he or she saw on TV. See if this sounds familiar:

> YOUR FRIEND: "Have you seen that great new ad?"
> YOU: "Which one?"
> YOUR FRIEND: "The one with the talking pandas."
> YOU: "I don't think so."
> YOUR FRIEND: "You gotta see it. These two pandas are sitting in the zoo. Everyone is watching them through the glass, hoping they're going to mate with each other to make some panda babies. All the time they're talking about how they want to decorate their cage with bamboo furniture so they can eat it if times get tough."
> YOU: "Sounds great. What's it for?"
> YOUR FRIEND: "Um... I don't know. Does it matter?"

Yes, it matters.

If your friend is excited about an ad but doesn't know who paid for it, that's not really advertising. It's merely entertainment.

Of course, creativity is a key ingredient in all successful advertising. More than ever, the "business of ideas" that Marion Harper described more than six decades ago thrives on creative solutions that cut through the clutter, capture the attention of DVR-savvy TV viewers and create new ways to engage online consumers.

"The first job of an advertisement is to get noticed," said the former Ogilvy & Mather creative director Norman Berry. And the ad that thrilled your friend may have met that standard.

But Berry's boss, David Ogilvy wouldn't have been satisfied. He said: "When I write an advertisement, I don't won't you to tell me you find it 'creative'. I want you to find it so interesting that you *buy the product*."

I can't tell how to be creative. There are other books for that. But I can tell you some of the right ways to use creativity to help build your business. I'll also give you a few examples of campaigns that successfully use strategic creativity to connect with consumers, communicate effectively and, yes, sell the product.

What is strategic creativity?

When I talk of "strategic creativity," I'm referring to the kind of creative work that is:

1) *Built around a strong, central idea* – a recognizable brand platform that can be integrated and communicated through every media channel
2) *True to the brand* – communicating fundamental product benefits in ways that are both believable and memorable
3) *Research-based* – inspired by market-based insights and a sound analysis of the competitive business environment
4) *Tested for negatives* – I've learned that it's far less important to test comparative ads to see which one is better than to understand the negatives as a way of exposing and embracing the positives.
5) *Approved by the ultimate decision-maker* – whatever the professionals think, the only person who decides if a campaign works or not is the consumer to whom it is directed.
6) *Adaptable to changing circumstances* – in a changing world, strategic creativity allows for campaigns to evolve without altering the essence of the brand.
7) *Successful over time* – strategic creativity leads to campaigns that resonate with consumers over extended time periods, growing sales and building enduring brands.

Strategic creativity is advertising first, entertainment second. It is designed to sell products, not win awards. But when it is done well, strategic creativity can be as award-winning and entertaining as the work produced by the hottest creative shops in the world.

"Create centrally, improve locally"

Strategic creativity isn't about creating one great ad or winning over consumers in a single market. It's the stuff of long-term, brand-building, multinational, market-share-driving *campaigns*.

Strategic creativity isn't about chasing creative trends or jumping on the latest pop-culture bandwagon. It's about developing sound insights into your brand, your customers and your competitors, and using those insights to solve well-defined business and communications challenges.

What's the difference between an insight and an idea? The late Phil Dusenberry of BBDO, who for many years led Pepsi's relentless assault on Coca-Cola, summed it up in his book *One Great Insight Is Worth a Thousand Good Ideas*. He wrote: "ideas, valuable though they may be, are a dime-a-dozen in business…Insight is much rarer—and therefore more precious. In the advertising business, a good idea can inspire a great commercial. But a good insight can fuel a thousand ideas, a thousand commercials."

For global advertisers, strategic creativity that's based on unique brand insights can lead to campaigns that run for years, feature a variety of executions and evolve in ways that keep the advertising fresh and the message consistent.

At McCann-Erickson, the mantra for such campaigns has long-been: "Create centrally, improve locally." This basic philosophy has led to many powerful and long-running campaigns, each based on a strong central campaign idea, adapted where appropriate to individual markets and researched in each market using the same methodologies to gauge its impact and effectiveness.

Many of the campaigns I talk about elsewhere in this book reflect McCann's—and Interpublic's—approach to strategic creativity. Here are the stories behind the creation of three of the world's most successful and best-loved strategic, creative campaigns.

"Priceless"

For more than a decade, MasterCard's "Priceless" campaign has been one of the world's most instantly recognizable campaigns. The campaign appears in more than 100 countries and four dozen languages. As proof of its success and cultural acceptance, it has inspired countless parodies, from "The Tonight Show" to "The Simpsons" to all manner of humorous international variations (many of which can be found on YouTube).

Since it launched in 1997, the "Priceless" campaign has featured more than 160 commercials in the U.S. alone and hundreds more targeted executions have been produced to reflect the local tastes and experiences of consumers around the world.

But what was MasterCard before "Priceless?"

As a brand, MasterCard was competing with two powerful and long-established competitors:

- American Express represented exclusivity and prestige—a positioning reinforced by its celebrity-based imagery and the promise that "Membership has its privileges."

- Visa represented convenience and ubiquity for the active consumer. It was the card that for years had told consumers it was "Everywhere you want to be."

MasterCard, though instantly recognizable as brand, lacked a clear point of differentiation with American Express or Visa. Most consumers, even if they carried a MasterCard credit card in their wallet, felt no strong emotional connection with the brand. In the ten years before 1997, MasterCard had shuffled quickly and unsuccessfully through five different brand campaigns.

The challenge of creating a new brand strategy fell to McCann-Erickson's New York office.

In studying the available consumer research, and by commissioning their own custom studies, McCann was able to pinpoint an important trend in consumer attitudes that MasterCard could address with tremendous credibility and impact.

The research showed that consumers felt comfortable in many ways: Times were good. Brand names and designer labels were popular. And consumers had long grown comfortable with using their credit cards for all forms of everyday and big-ticket purchases. At the same time, a certain uneasiness was creeping in. The end of the millennium was approaching. Technology, especially the Internet, was transforming life in new ways. Despite their prosperity, consumers were searching for more meaning in their lives.

McCann's central insight was this: In this time of prosperity, simply buying more stuff wasn't giving people the fulfillment they craved. It was quality of one's experiences that mattered people wanted more time with family and friends, new ways to enjoy life and create shared memories.

This insight led McCann-Erickson to a simple, resonant tagline: "There are some things that money can't buy. For everything else, there's MasterCard."

The "Priceless" campaign revolutionized the MasterCard image in the U.S. market and was embraced quickly by MasterCard around the world. It reintroduced the brand as one that understood that consumer purchases were merely the stepping stone to the experiences that mattered in people's lives.

It was a strategic positioning that associated MasterCard with the most emotional moments of people's lives, while reinforcing the everyday utility that MasterCard provided.

Equally important, this was a strategic positioning that MasterCard could not only own, but one that would also help differentiate the brand from the exclusivity of American Express and the conspicuous consumption associated with Visa.

The "Priceless" campaign has all the hallmarks of the best global campaigns: a consistent brand strategy, a powerful emotional connection with consumers, and unlimited ways to express its central concept locally. While many of the best "Priceless" ads appear multinationally, even globally, 60-70% of all the commercials that appear are created specifically for local markets. In India, for example, ads will feature cricket instead of baseball.

"Priceless" insights

1. **Start with the consumer**: Use research to get a clear picture of your customer's rational and emotional needs.

2. **Create a constant brand strategy**: Find language that uniquely articulates your brand—and resonates with consumers.

3. **Express yourself locally**: Establish the creative boundaries—then give local agencies the freedom to play within them.

The warmth of shared moments

Throughout my career, right from my first days at McCann-Erickson's New York office, I've been pleased to work with many of Nestlé's brands. In the U.K. and other international markets, one of Nestlé's major brands is Nescafé instant coffee, known in the U.S. as Taster's Choice.

McCann-Erickson's work for Nescafé has been built around a consistent brand image that reinforces the quality of the coffee, its drinkability and the warmth of the shared moments Nescafé helps create. These are the constant elements of Nescafé advertising and, while most executions are produced locally, they all build toward a consistent brand image.

Sometimes, though, the creative from one market is so good and becomes so popular that the creative goes from local to global.

In the 1980s, McCann-Erickson's U.K. agency created a popular campaign for Nescafé, in which each commercial played like the episode in a soap opera. Each installment dramatized the developing on-screen relationship between two neighbors who meet by borrowing and returning each other's coffee, before starting to share "warm moments" with each other over cups of Nescafé. As the campaign developed, new characters and complications kept the sparks flying and the suspense high.

The campaign was a huge success, with the on-screen drama prompting an equally dramatic rise in Nescafé Gold Blend sales. The commercials also inspired a best-selling romance novel and a music collection that hit #2 on the U.K. charts.

In the 1990s, the series was adapted for the Nestlé Taster's Choice brand in the U.S. market. The spots, featuring the same two actors, soon had U.S. consumers clamoring for the next "soap opera" episode.

Sales volume in the U.S. jumped 40%, propelling Taster's Choice ahead of its competitors. The U.S. campaign was then adapted for other English-speaking markets and ran with subtitles in continental European countries. A Spanish-language "telenovela-style" was created featuring new actors for the Latin American market.

The campaign was named the "Best Global Television Campaign" by the International Advertising Association and in every market in which it aired, it generated huge publicity and similar sales success.

The Nescafé "soap opera" campaign underscored the new possibilities created by consistent global brand strategies. With agencies around the world developing ads based on the same strategic platform, it was now possible to take a locally successful campaign and replicate that success on a global basis.

The "warmth of shared moments" was a brand insight that every local agency could build on to create effective local advertising. But it was also an insight that could be applied universally so when the right creative came along, it was easily expanded to reach a global audience stretching from New York to New Zealand.

How to "succeed locally, expand globally"

1. **Let ideas come from everywhere**: Make sure all local agencies are working from a similar global brief—built around the central strategic brand insight.

2. **Spread knowledge across all markets**: Through consistent research and shared information, a global agency sees how patterns emerge and which creative approaches work best.

3. **Export and adapt the winning creative**: With a product that offers the same benefits—and has the same brand position—in all countries, successful campaigns almost always travel well.

"The Real Thing"

As I mentioned in Chapter One, Coca-Cola ushered in the modern age of global advertising with its "one sight, one sound" strategy in 1963 and a successful campaign based on the theme "Things Go Better With a Coke."

By 1969, Coca-Cola was ready to carry its idea of integrated marketing to the next level of global coordination, with a new advertising campaign and a globalized approach to in-store displays, vehicles, delivery uniforms, and vending equipment—in fact, all aspects of the consumer experience.

The campaign McCann-Erickson created to accompany this new merchandising stance revived the slogan "It's the Real Thing," which Coke had first used in 1942.

In that slogan, Coke and McCann recognized an essential brand strength that set Coke apart from its competitors—not just refreshment, but a promise of enjoyment, quality and, equally important, authenticity.

"It's the Real Thing" allowed Coke to present itself as a brand that could serve as an anchor in a sea of change. The advertising was hip and contemporary but also heavily based in the powerful memories that the Coke brand, even the Coke bottle, stirred up in consumers, both young and old.

This was 1969, remember. The year of Woodstock and moon walks and John Lennon singing "Give Peace a Chance." In America and around the world, cultural changes and political differences were causing rifts in society. But somehow the Coke brand found a way to navigate itself through those swirling currents and allow consumers of all ages to agree on one thing: The Real Thing.

The Real Thing campaign is best known for the memorable "hilltop commercial" I mentioned in Chapter Four. But over most of the 1970s, this Coke campaign continued to find new ways to express its message of "authentic moments." In one popular 1973 commercial called "Country Sunshine," for example, a young girl travels by train and car across America to return to her family's rural home. She's lovingly greeted by her parents and siblings, and everyone celebrates the moment with a cold bottle of Coke.

Coke's "Real Thing" positioning was so successful, it has been revived or alluded to in campaigns that have appeared in every decade since the 1970s, with campaigns such as "America's Real Choice" in 1985, "Can't Beat the Real Thing" in 1990, and 2003's "Real" campaign.

The power of "The Real Thing"

1. **A recognition of heritage**: Coke's "Real Thing" campaign honored the brand's history—and its emotional relationship with consumers.

2. **A promise of authenticity**: Beyond a promise of product quality, the "Real Thing" resonated with consumers' own personal experiences and memories.

3. **A contemporary flavor**: Though many older consumers may have remembered the slogan, the campaign itself was fresh and youthful—with images and music that appealed to the younger generation.

CHAPTER SEVEN

Act Quickly in a Crisis

How to retain clients, restore confidence and replace lost business

"We won't make a drama out of a crisis."
—*1980s slogan used by U.K.'s Commercial Union insurance company*

Do the right thing

SOMETIMES EVENTS BEYOND your control will threaten to overwhelm, even sink you.

The Tylenol tampering scare of 1982 showed how leading brands could be attacked, damaged, restored and ultimately strengthened by a crisis. At the time, Tylenol's market share dropped form 35% to 8%. But Johnson & Johnson's handling of the incident—including a complete recall of the product and the introduction of new, tamper-proof packaging—has rightly become a casebook study in crisis management.

In recent months, we have seen many standard business practices challenged in the face of public outrage over the taxpayer bailouts of the financial and insurance industries.

AIG was one of the most obvious targets, especially in regard to executive bonuses. It reached the point that in March 2009 CEO Edward Liddy appealed to his own people to "do the right thing" and return at least 50% of any bonuses above $100,000. Many (but not all) of them did.

What would you do in similar circumstances?

In any business crisis, it's important to grasp quickly the broader ramifications of the situation—and what's at risk in terms of revenue, brand image and corporate reputation—then focus on removing the biggest thorns first.

In this chapter, I'll relive the seven crises that broadsided me in my early days as CEO of Interpublic and some of the lessons I learned that may help you address similar challenges today.

"When things are going well, it's time to worry"

The 1970s were a fantastic decade for the McCann-Erickson agency and the Interpublic Group (IPG).

I did pretty well, too.

I was named vice chairman of IPG in 1975, and moved my family back to New York in 1976. In 1977, I was named President of IPG and, in 1979, proposed to CEO Paul Foley the acquisition of SSC&B-Lintas, a U.S. agency with $1 billion in billings. It was a very big deal. At the time, the biggest the industry had ever seen.

The SSC&B-Lintas acquisition sent a powerful message through the industry. Interpublic was on the march. In addition to buying the U.S. agency, we also acquired 49% of SSC&B-Lintas International with a commitment to acquire the remaining 51% three years later. Historically, Lintas had been the in-house agency for global packaged goods giant Unilever. The acquisition would allow Interpublic to establish a second global agency network, one with deep international experience in major multinational categories such as foods, detergents, personal care, packaging, plastics and chemicals.

Meanwhile, the original global agency—McCann-Erickson—was on fire, both creatively and in terms of business success. The creative resurgence began early in the decade, with Bill Backer's "hilltop commercial" for Coke, which had become a worldwide sensation. Backer was the creative director who led McCann's work for Coke, Brown-Forman (wines and spirits), the New York Racing Association and the Miller Brewing Company, an account that had flourished through the decade, propelled by the hugely successful Miller Lite launch. ("It's Everything You Always Wanted in a Beer. And Less.")

By the end of the decade, McCann's International agency was #1 in the world. The U.S. agency was, once again, in the top 10. And on a worldwide basis, the agency's total billings of $1.4 billion put it just $70 million behind the still-strong J. Walter Thompson.

Elsewhere in the Interpublic family, the Campbell-Ewald agency, which we had acquired in 1972, was thriving under the leadership of CEO Tom Adams. Headquartered in Detroit, Campbell-Ewald had established itself as a fast-growing, independent creative agency doing great work for clients such as Chevrolet.

As president of Interpublic, I worked closely with Paul Foley and, as Foley approached retirement, I was a clear contender for the top spot. This was made official in May 1979, when the IPG board approved Foley's recommendation that I succeed him as chairman and CEO upon his retirement at the end of the year.

Naturally, I was delighted. The Interpublic Group had a superb client roster, a growing creative reputation, and, with the addition of SSC&B-Lintas, the strongest group of agency systems the advertising world had ever seen. Everything at the company was running well. The future had never looked brighter.

But Don Keough, Coca-Cola's Chief Operating Officer, who was at the time McCann Erickson's major client on the Coke account, has always told me: "When things are going well, that's the time to worry."

Boy, was that true in the spring and summer of 1979 and for the 18 months beyond.

As the news of Paul Foley's succession plan was made public, I faced a series of crises that sent Interpublic revenues into a steep decline and caused a crisis at McCann-Erickson so acute that, as *Business Week* later reported, "Madison Avenue was taking bets that the agency would never recover."

Crisis #1: Spielvogel quits. Backer follows.

Paul Foley had been a boss and a mentor to me. He had begun his career in advertising as a copywriter. And he always remained a writer at heart. One of his best remembered sayings was, "writing is to persuasion as breathing is to health."

In 1979, what none of us realized was that Foley's own health was failing.

For months, I had an intuitive sense that something was wrong. Paul seemed less and less sharp when it came to addressing the details of agency or client business. The only time his legendary Irish wit burst forth was when he told stories rooted in the distant past. During Paul's last year at the company, I volunteered to travel with him on many business trips inviting myself along even though my presence wasn't officially necessary and it meant I would be out of the office for big chunks of time.

Today, most people would recognize his symptoms for what they were: the early stages of Alzheimer's. But back then, neither I nor my colleagues could put a name to what was happening.

When I was named as Foley's successor, questions naturally arose about the roles other key executives would assume. Carl Spielvogel, formerly of *The New York Times* (and much later the U.S. Ambassador to Slovakia) had joined McCann-Erickson in 1960 and risen to be chairman of the executive committee there before moving to Interpublic as one of three vice chairmen. Through backdoor channels, Spielvogel promoted himself as the potential future chairman of the company. When Foley and the board made the decision that I should become chairman and CEO, Spielvogel came to me and said he wanted to be my president and COO. Knowing the board wasn't likely to buy into the idea immediately, I asked him to wait six months, after which I would recommend he be named president, overseeing administration and PR, but not operations directly. He agreed, but didn't want to wait.

Unbeknownst to me, Spielvogel prevailed upon Foley to release him from his contract. He quit the firm, announcing a plan to go and work on Wall Street.

Spielvogel's departure was a blow, but not a disaster. He was extremely close to George Weisman, who had recently been named Chairman and CEO of Philip Morris. And, of course, Philip Morris had purchased The Miller Brewing Company several years earlier. But we had nothing to fear. McCann, under Bill Backer's creative leadership, was doing great work for Miller and Spielvogel had told us he was exiting the agency business.

A month later, Bill Backer told me he was quitting too.

By 1979, Backer had risen to become vice chairman and chief creative officer of McCann-Erickson USA. As creative director, he was responsible for many of the world's most unforgettable campaigns. But he wasn't enjoying his executive responsibilities or the agency's internal politics: Backer was continuously butting heads with COO Dick Lessler, a man whose success was built on his strategic brilliance, as opposed to his people skills. Even though I had arbitrated what I thought was a workable "power-sharing" arrangement between the two of them, Lessler always found a way to get under Backer's skin. Even such a simple thing as switching the order of their names on a client presentation without telling Bill could set Backer off.

Now, Backer told me he had had enough. Having worked for years with many of the world's greatest songwriters and musicians on songs and advertising jingles, he wanted to move full-time into the music business.

I knew we couldn't afford to lose Backer. He was the creative leader beloved by the Coke and Miller clients and one of the key pinch-hitters whenever there was a crisis on other major accounts.

I should have known that when Bill Backer was talking of leaving, the thought of starting his own agency wouldn't be far from his mind. Over the years, he had come to me several times about starting an agency together. But the last time we spoke, about a year before, I told him my commitments to the company and its people were now so deep that I could never imagine myself leaving.

Rather than thinking about Bill's future plans, though, I focused instead on convincing him to stay.

If there was anyone who could persuade him, I knew it was Paul Foley. Paul was like a father to Bill. They had worked together for years with tremendous success and were both "horse people", a bond which was strengthened by their work on an account they truly loved: the New York Racing Association.

Foley was in Italy. I reached him there and explained the situation. I told him it was imperative that he curtail the rest of his trip and return to New York immediately to talk to Bill Backer.

Foley was as concerned as I was. He promised to fly back to New York the next morning.

Unfortunately, Paul Foley woke up in his Italian hotel room and, completely forgetting our conversation, looked instead at his travel itinerary. He was booked on a flight to Moscow. Without a second thought, he flew there.

Foley didn't return to New York for another three days. Neither Backer nor I knew enough about Foley's medical condition to comprehend the reason for this apparent snub. Backer let his emotions guide him and Foley's delayed return only solidified Bill's determination to quit. Foley, because of his close relationship to Backer, agreed, as he had done with Spielvogel, to release him from his contract.

Perhaps if Paul Foley had flown home sooner, he could have persuaded Bill Backer to stay. But we both could see at least one silver lining: Backer hadn't jumped to a competitive agency. Even as he left, I had faith in Bill. And to this day, I still believe the decision to launch Backer & Spielvogel three months later was not initiated by him. When the news broke that the two former colleagues were starting an agency together, it seemed an unlikely pairing to anyone who knew their background at Interpublic and McCann. Backer didn't much appreciate his dealings with Spielvogel when they both worked at McCann. In fact, he had been one of the key people most influential in persuading Paul Foley to shift Spielvogel out of McCann and into his Interpublic role.

What to do when key people want to leave

1. **Understand their emotions**: Large agencies are filled with larger-than-life personalities—and personalities always make things personal.

2. **Consider their intentions**: Find out what professional motivations are driving the decision—can you make a counter-offer to satisfy them?

3. **Act fast if you want to keep them**: Treat the situation urgently. Hesitation—even if it's inadvertent—can be costly.

Crisis #2: Calming the Coca-Cola client

Backer's departure upset a lot of McCann-Erickson clients, none more than Don Keough at Coca-Cola. He hinted it might be time to put the account in review.

I called Keough, who happened to be in England, and asked if I could meet with him as soon as possible. When he agreed to a breakfast meeting the next day, I hopped a plane to London and took a cab to the Berkeley Hotel, where he was staying.

I knew Keough didn't have much time to give me, so after waiting impatiently at a breakfast table about ten minutes, I called him in his room.

"Do you know what time it is?" he screamed in my ear.

"Ten past eight," I told him.

"Look at the damn clock," he said.

I was standing a few feet away from a grandfather clock in the hotel lobby. The time on the dial read ten past seven. I hadn't adjusted my watch properly.

"I'll be there when I get there," he barked.

I drank three cups of coffee to help with my jetlag, then told the waiter to set two bottles of Coke on the table.

I waited patiently for Don Keough. I knew he was the most powerful decision maker at Coca-Cola. He was deeply involved in all its operations and loved working closely with Bill Backer and the creative teams on Coke's advertising campaigns. On a global basis, the Coke account by now represented an astounding $750 million in billings.

Don was known for his cheerful, gregarious personality, But when he arrived for breakfast that morning, I saw a different side: he was one pissed-off Irishman.

Thankfully, Keough had tremendous respect not only for Bill Backer, but also Paul Foley. Because of that relationship he was willing to hear me out. He listened to me explain how I planned to handle the situation and my promise of a new creative leader to handle the account. I hoped to convince him that the rest of the team we had in place wasn't entirely dependent on Backer and that, after working on the account for more than 20 years, McCann-Erickson possessed the kind of deep brand knowledge he couldn't afford to give up lightly.

I asked Keough to give me 90 days before putting the account into any review.

"What makes you think you can get everything done right in 90 days?" he asked. "If you let me down, I'll have a real problem."

"Look," I told him. "I'm half Irish myself. My mother is Irish. She'll tell you when I make a promise I always deliver."

Keough sat back in his chair and chuckled. "Anyone who can come up with a bit of blarney like that deserves six months. Just get it fixed…and don't let me down."

Three months later, McCann-Erickson launched what *Adweek* readers called the year's best campaign: Coca-Cola's "Have a Coke and a Smile," featuring the famous "Mean Joe Greene" spot created by Penny Hawkey and Roger Mosconi.

Despite my early morning hiccup with the time-change, I had solved one potential crisis with what looked like refreshing ease. But another crisis, far more serious, was already brewing.

> **Lessons in saving Coke**
> 1. **Demonstrate your commitment**: Move fast—and get wherever you need to be to talk to your client.
> 2. **Present a plan—and a timetable**: Show that you understand the business problem—and have thought through how to solve it.
> 3. **Deliver on all your promises**: Having an Irish mother sometimes helps—beyond that you just have to roll up your sleeves.

Crisis #3: Backer & Spielvogel win the Miller account.

It didn't take long for Carl Spielvogel to sour on Wall Street and Bill Backer to grow disenchanted with the music business. Within just a few months, they announced the formation of Backer & Spielvogel Advertising. The partnership surprised many people, since the two executives had previously been known to have a poor working relationship.

But Spielvogel's relationship with George Weisman at Philip Morris, which dated back to their *New York Times* days, gave him the inside track to the Miller account. Now in partnership with Backer, the creative star who had built Miller High Life and launched Miller Lite, it was obvious Backer & Spielvogel would be talking to Philip Morris about doing some work for Miller.

While Backer & Spielvogel were making "secret" presentations to

John Murphy at Miller and George Weisman at Philip Morris, rumors were flying through the industry. Everyone was speculating that Miller would give the new agency an assignment, perhaps a product launch, or conceivably even one of the three Miller brands currently at McCann-Erickson.

Despite the rumors, McCann's overall relationship with Miller looked solid. Paul Foley rightly viewed McCann's various campaigns for Miller as possibly the best creative work ever done for a brewery. Plus, Foley himself had great relationships at Philip Morris. He had been deeply involved in the Miller family's original decision to sell to Philip Morris, convincing them the company would continue to operate independently and that the sale would allow the family to expand its philanthropic work with Catholic charities.

The shocking news came on August 8, 1979. Miller was moving all three of its brands—High Life, Lite and Lowenbrau—to Backer & Spielvogel's startup agency. With billings close to $90 million, primarily on TV, Miller generated 15% of the agency's total U.S. billings and 65% of the profits of the New York office.

Not only had Backer & Spielvogel won the biggest first account for a new agency in advertising history, they had also dealt a crushing blow to McCann-Erickson's seemingly mighty New York office.

Many years later, on a flight down to Jamaica, Joe Cullman, the founder and retired chairman of Philip Morris told me the personal reasons why the Miller account left.

Crisis #4: A massive liftout of McCann-Erickson's New York talent

Dick Lessler, Backer's old nemesis at McCann, told *Advertising Age*, the loss of the Miller account had left him "fighting mad."

And that was before his best people started quitting.

Among the people who followed the Miller account as it headed across town to Backer & Spielvogel were a large creative team, the manager of the New York office and head of the account, plus the agency's top media director.

Within a few short weeks, the New York agency had not just lost its major account, but also its entire top management team, along with many other talented people.

The industry was buzzing about the problems at McCann. And even though we had stabilized the Coca-Cola situation, other clients were not happy.

What McCann learned about protecting its "people business" from its (former) people

1. **Hold onto your stars**: The best way to keep your best clients is to keep your best people.

2. **Enforce your contracts**: If your key people have the protection of a contract—that protection needs to work both ways.

3. **Use "non-compete" agreements**: Before losing the Miller account, it was hard to imagine losing such a big account—or so many key people—to a startup agency. Now, non-competes apply to more than just the highest-levels.

Crisis #5: Fixing McCann-Erickson causes big problems at SSC&B: Lintas

As I surveyed the damage to the McCann agency, I knew I had to act fast to steady the ship. Complicating matters, the agency's chairman and CEO was out on medical leave. The agency's two units—U.S. and International—were reporting directly to Interpublic. Willard Mackey, the highly experienced McCann executive (and former Marschalk CEO) was running International. But within the decimated New York office, there was no clear candidate to take charge.

I made the decision to promote James Agnew, a rising star who had been running the Los Angeles office, to be McCann-Erickson's new U.S. president and CEO.

The only problem: During the SSC&B-Lintas acquisition, the Unilever client had already been informed that Agnew would be moving to London to run Lintas' international network.

Unilever, which still saw Lintas as something akin to its own in-house agency, was severely jolted by the news. The client expected everything, especially major executive transitions, to be well-planned out and seamlessly executed.

Even though I communicated why McCann's abruptly changed circumstances had forced my hand, the client was still upset. There was a real concern that losing Agnew might affect our agreement to close the International part of the acquisition.

Crisis #6: Instability leads to high-profile account reviews

While Unilever was still steaming mad, my quick fixes at McCann-Erickson weren't enough to reassure every client.

Two of our oldest clients, Exxon (dating from 1912) and Del Monte (which we'd worked on since 1917), both announced they were putting their accounts in review.

Given the success I'd enjoyed with the Esso brand in Europe, the Exxon review hit me on a personal as well as a business level. I made it my personal mission to save the account.

Clearly, McCann's highly visible problems had created an enormous amount of uncertainty in the market. Each day, it seemed like competitive agencies were circling like vultures over all our accounts.

Crisis #7: The board has second thoughts about the new CEO.

My first year as CEO of Interpublic was not a pleasant one. Still reeling from McCann-Erickson's loss of the Miller account, total income for the holding company declined 9% in 1980.

As far as the Interpublic board could tell, none of the biggest challenges facing the company had been solved.

McCann-Erickson USA was still a shadow of its former self. Even though we had won the $20 million Pabst Brewing account to partially replace the Miller loss, profits at the agency were still way down. And the Exxon and Del Monte reviews only added to the concerns.

The executive situation at SSC&B-Lintas had created such bad will with Unilever that some people inside Interpublic had started questioning whether I was the right man for the job.

With all the recent troubles we had faced, I knew there were some behind-the-scenes maneuverings taking place within IPG. So, ahead of my first board meeting in 1981, I turned to a few "well-placed sources" to find out exactly what was going on.

I discovered that some of my most senior colleagues, including Neil Gilliatt, the Interpublic vice chairman and Tom Adams at our Campbell-Ewald agency were pitching ideas for a "new look" top management team. Adams was "offering" to serve as chairman and CEO out of Detroit, and a CEO at one of our New York agencies had agreed to serve under him as Interpublic COO. Gilliatt, meanwhile, was willing to delay his upcoming retirement for the opportunity to play a larger role in running the company.

I knew what was going on. But I didn't plan on addressing it directly unless it came up.

Throughout my career, I had been known for getting things done, but not always for trumpeting whenever I had solved a problem. It was always my natural instinct to move directly on to the next most urgent challenge.

That's why, when that board meeting began, I was the only person in the room who knew all the details of the results we were finally starting to deliver.

First up, I told them that both Exxon and Del Monte were staying put. That alone caused some sighs of relief.

Next, I celebrated the fact that McCann-Erickson had just beaten out six other agencies to win the $20 million Texas Instruments account. The Texas Instrument client would be replacing its assortment of 26 foreign and domestic agencies with McCann Erickson, a powerful endorsement of the McCann-Erickson network and its coordinated global methods.

Coke was happier than ever at McCann. Our new creative director, John Bergin, whom I had brought over from the Lintas side, had previously worked on Pepsi at BBDO. He had already built a great team, connected well with Don Keough, and was relishing the opportunity to get back into the cola wars. Meanwhile, Bill Mackey, who had worked on Coke for many years, was providing the leadership and continuity to ensure that the global effort was coordinated and effective. Crucially, the Backer & Spielvogel "liftout" had not touched two of our most important, but less visible players: McCann's heads of research and strategic development. These two executives provided continuity with accounts like Coke and had reinforced our ability to win clients like Pabst and Texas Instruments.

I also told the board that, at that very moment, SSC&B-Lintas was working on a "top secret" project for The Coca-Cola Company that even the McCann-Erickson people knew nothing about. The project would lead to the most successful product launch of 1982: Diet Coke.

Then I gave them some testimonials from Unilever in London. It turned out that Bill Weithas, the man I had put in place to run SSC&B-Lintas International in place of Agnew, was getting rave reviews from the senior client people. He was doing such a great job, they'd almost forgotten how upset they were over the Agnew affair. (Putting Weithas in London was a decision that was already making me look good. To quote *The New York Times,* he ran the agency "with aplomb from London" for many years. Agnew, meanwhile, quit McCann in 1981.)

The board meeting was going well. Gilliatt and Adams were squirming just a little. Then my assistant rushed in.

"I'm sorry to interrupt," she said. "But I have the president on the phone."

I looked around at the agency presidents and CEOs on the Interpublic board. "Which president?" I asked

"President Reagan," she whispered loud enough for the whole room to hear.

I rushed out of the meeting to take the call. President Reagan had just been elected in a landslide. And now he wanted to talk to me.

As an actor, Ronald Reagan had appeared in commercials produced by McCann-Erickson back in the 1950s. As it turned out, it was his brother Neil, a man who had headed McCann's West Coast operations many years earlier, who had suggested the President call me. The matter itself was relatively minor, and we chatted just a few minutes. When I returned to the Interpublic boardroom, though, I had no problem acting as if we had discussed some weighty and confidential matters.

While I was gone, the discussions in the boardroom had continued and the mood had changed completely in a positive direction.

If anyone had been planning to raise an objection to my running of the company, now was clearly not the time to do it. Interpublic was back to business as usual.

I'm sure the details in my presentation would have been enough to convince everyone that things were back on track. But the phone call from Ronald Reagan hadn't hurt, I'm sure.

What my "baptism of fire" taught me as CEO

1. **Reputation matters**: Negative publicity causes everyone—employees, clients, competitors and, of course, the media—to question what you're doing.

2. **Problems attract more attention than solutions**: Quietly saving the Coke account was nothing compared to Exxon publicly announcing a review.

3. **It's great to have bench strength you can trust**: Knowing in-depth the abilities of key personnel throughout the company, I was able to fill open positions quickly with smart, reliable leaders who could hit the ground running.

4. **Communicate, communicate, communicate**: With so many fires to put out, you focus on clients first, second, and third. I still needed to do a better job communicating internally and with my board. I kept working on that for the next 19 years.

Emerging from a time of crisis

Having survived not just my first year as CEO, but also a potential boardroom problem, it was time to start planning for the future. Finally, it seemed as if Interpublic was ready to emerge from its crisis mode and start regaining control of its own future.

Many leaders would have chosen to rid themselves of the "rebels" in their ranks. But I was painfully aware that Interpublic and our major agencies had endured a traumatic two-year period marked by major business losses, tremendous internal tension and highly public executive turnover.

Rather than getting upset with the three individuals in question, and maybe doing something about it, I left well enough alone. They knew and I knew what had gone on. Now I needed to get everybody working together as a team.

I kept Gilliatt close as a vice chairman of Interpublic. He was approaching retirement age but had a long history at McCann-Erickson and knew our people and our systems.

I gave Tom Adams an even bigger challenge. A former footballer and sportsman, Tom had done wonders at Campbell-Ewald. Seeing an opportunity to build out a third network, I asked him to build out a global group of independent creative agencies under a new Marschalk Campbell-Ewald Worldwide banner.

The goal was simple: create a network of local creative agencies primarily focused on local accounts. But make sure that the agencies were networked and able to work together, so that, where necessary, Interpublic could provide another agency option for major international clients.

Tom decided he didn't want to be running the worldwide aspect of the business. He didn't like the travel and he knew he wasn't always the best with international clients. Richard O'Connor moved to New York to run the worldwide agency, with Les Delano heading the International operations. With his creative background, Delano was key to the international growth of this third network. He oversaw the expansion and could communicate well with the local agencies, which were mostly run by creative people.

It was just as well that Tom Adams stayed in Detroit, as he might not have had the sensitivity needed for this particular business. In a meeting with the Managing Director of a Japanese client in Japan, the client asked Tom what he had done in the war.

"Well," he said, "I flew over Guadalcanal and shot down quite a few Zeroes," referring to the Japanese fighter planes.

"I was there, too, but you must have missed me," said the client. "Or maybe it was I who missed you."

We were able to negotiate with Hakuhodo, McCann's partner in Japan to create Hakuhodo Campbell-Ewald. But the deal allowed us only to work on International, not Japanese, accounts. That was a mistake on our part, and was ultimately the reason the Hakuhodo partnerships were disbanded.

Back at McCann-Erickson, we recombined the U.S. and International agencies under chairman Eugene Kummel, later agreeing with Gene that the globetrotting Willard Mackey be named CEO of the new McCann-Erickson Worldwide. Mackey's nickname was "The Healer," and he proved to be just that. Under his leadership McCann very soon won the global $100 million

Camel cigarette account. Shortly after, both Black & Decker and Goodyear consolidated their overseas advertising with McCann-Erickson.

Meanwhile, Bob James, who had moved to Interpublic from his spot as Marschalk CEO (and stayed there long enough to cleanse himself of any account conflict concerns) was named head of McCann's U.S. agency. Mackey and James worked well together and the U.S. agency rebounded remarkably over the next few years. In the latter part of the decade, as the process of globalization sped up even more, McCann's U.S. and International billings accelerated sharply and, for once, simultaneously.

What about the advertising itself?

In 1982, John Bergin hit a home run with the new Coke campaign "Coke Is It!" John was an unusual creative man and always interesting to work with. I once went to his office after five o'clock to ask him to consider a change in some creative work. Just a suggestion. He pulled a gun out of his desk, pointed it me and said: "Quit being an account man." I hightailed it out the door and was halfway down the corridor before he called me back. "It's only plastic," he laughed.

The timing of Bergin's "Coke Is It!" campaign was much appreciated by the client, because Coca-Cola itself was in the process of launching its own new competitor to the Coca-Cola brand.

The SSC&B-Lintas "Just or the Taste of It" campaign not only launched Diet Coke in a hugely successful way. It also marked the Lintas agency's emergence as a legitimate and powerful creative agency beyond the packaged goods arena.

In 1982, Interpublic acquired the 51% of Lintas we didn't already own. As a holding company, we were still unique in the advertising business. And once again, we were firing on all cylinders.

Remembering Don Keough's advice, I never did stop worrying. But as new opportunities to grow and expand the business began to appear, it was time to start planning strategically for the future and to get back to having some fun.

CHAPTER EIGHT

Plan Ahead

*How to create a "blueprint" for future growth—and
adapt it during fast-changing times*

"If you want to be a big company tomorrow, start acting like one today."
—*Peter Drucker*

The growth imperative

WHATEVER THE PREVAILING economic conditions, you and your company
always need to be thinking ahead and planning for your future growth.

You need to fully understand your Strengths, Weaknesses, Opportunities
and Threats (SWOT analysis). But remember, too, that SWOT analysis will
always be just a snapshot and it always will be incomplete.

In business, today's strengths are often tomorrow's weaknesses; seemingly
brilliant opportunities fail to pay-off as expected; the biggest threats often
come from the most unexpected places.

Just look how the media world was impacted when three former PayPal
employees started YouTube in 2005. MySpace grew to become the worlds
#1 social networking site before being bought by NewsCorp in 2006—two
years later it was overtaken by Facebook, a still-independent company formed
by three Harvard students in 2004.

Your plan for growth must be based on your best, most honest analysis
and expectations. But it must be continually adapted and updated. Because

even if you predict the future better than most, something unpredictable is sure to happen along the way.

Case in point: The global advertising industry was transformed during the 1980s and 1990s in ways that no one could have foreseen. In this chapter, I'll tell you: How we created the blueprint for growth at Interpublic in the 1980s. How we approached acquisitions. How we responded to our changing clients' needs. And how we responded to the emergence of new, aggressive and deep-pocketed competitors such as WPP, Omnicom and Publicis.

If your industry is going through a similarly sweeping transition, the lessons in this chapter will be particularly relevant today.

Three networks, three personalities

In the early 1980s, Interpublic was the only holding company in the advertising world.

Our plan for growth was based on strengthening our two major global networks, McCann-Erickson and SSC&B:Lintas (which became known as Lintas Worldwide) and building out a third system under the Marschalk Campbell-Ewald Worldwide banner.

Our main global competitors were U.S.-based agencies such as BBDO, J. Walter Thompson and Ogilvy & Mather. But British-based agencies such as Saatchi & Saatchi were also looking to make their mark on the international scene.

At Interpublic, we viewed ourselves as a management company, uniquely positioned to serve an increasingly global client base.

Our two existing global agencies had distinct—and different—personalities.

- *McCann-Erickson Worldwide* was brash, hard-charging and, wherever you went, recognizably American. Its New York office had been the source of much of the "transferable power" that had carried McCann around the world. The agency's major clients—Coca-Cola, Esso, General Motors, Henkel, Nestlé, and Unilever—were blue-chip clients drawn from all of the major categories. McCann offices buzzed with energy. Its people were confident, impatient with a "get-it-done-then-ask-permission" attitude.

- *SSC&B-Lintas Worldwide* was a quieter, more process-driven agency. Walking the halls of Lintas, you sensed the agency took its work seriously, much like the packaged goods clients from which it drew much of its business. Even as it grew its creative reputation with work for brands such as Diet Coke and Maybelline, Lintas remained structured, orderly and efficient.

Putting together a global "Marschalk Campbell-Ewald" network was creating a different, less well-defined result. Our goal was to create the first worldwide network of independent creative agencies able to compete with local creative agencies while providing a system approach for multinational advertisers. Marschalk's traditional home was in New York, Campbell-Ewald's was in Detroit. As a U.K. agency, we had added the Park Lane office of Erwin Wasey (an American-owned agency acquired by Interpublic in 1963), renaming it Wasey Campbell-Ewald. Across much of continental Europe, we structured the network around the offices of the Troost agency (acquired in 1975).

While we had succeeded in assembling a 3rd international network, it lacked a personality that defined it separately from McCann and Lintas. And it lacked a creative leader.

We decided to adapt our approach.

Having spent most of the 1970s in London, I had seen first-hand how British advertising had come into its own and how British agencies had developed a truly global reputation for creativity.

In the five years since I had returned to New York, the competitive landscape had continued to evolve. Collett Dickenson Pearce—the creative agency where Charles Saatchi, John Hegarty, future movie director Alan Parker and producer David Puttnam all made names for themselves—had been hit by legal and tax problems. The financial director was indicted for making payments into off-shore accounts. And Frank Lowe (now Sir Frank), the agency's Managing Director who had to leave CDP, went on to start his own agency, Lowe Howard-Spink.

By 1983, with London firmly established as a creative counterweight to New York, it made sense to look to the U.K. to help define the personality of our 3rd network. We took a 35% stake in Frank Lowe's two-year-old agency, and eventually merged it with the Wasey London office.

We were looking for a strong personality. And Frank Lowe delivered.

Lowe was flamboyant, British and always independent. His creative principle was similar to the one Doyle Dane Bernbach had used in New York in the 1960s: he believed in presenting only one campaign idea to the client.

Lowe's successes were legendary. Advertising like Heineken's "Refreshes the parts other beers cannot reach" campaign was instantly recognizable in the U.K. market. And his belief that he knew best – combined with the passion of his presentations—would generally convince clients to go along with his recommendations.

When Lowe presented a campaign, he did it with a conviction that his agency had thoroughly vetted its options and was presenting the idea that would be the most successful. He stood on principle and was willing to lose clients if need be. At one time, Unilever fired him because he refused to create a back-up campaign.

Creatives, naturally, flocked to his agency.

The Lowe brand gave our 3rd network instant creative credibility and a British personality that was sophisticated, witty and contemporary.

As a holding company, Interpublic now had three distinctly different networks. We were global, multidimensional, and structured to give local, national and global clients even more options in how they worked with us.

We had adapted our plans to fit with the evolving global landscape and had recognized early the rising power and influence of U.K. advertising.

Best of all, we had given ourselves increased flexibility to attract and manage competing accounts and propel the next stage of our growth.

Where's the problem: Idea or execution?

1. **Ask yourself the right questions**: Don't abandon a sound strategy just because your execution is less than perfect. First, re-evaluate.

2. **Respond to external factors**: In the case of our 3rd network, we realized the time was right for a U.K.-led global agency.

3. **Make the necessary changes**: A mid-course adjustment is often better than abandoning a plan and starting over.

During the current "Great Recession" these questions need to be asked with brutal honesty. Don't use the downturn as the all-purpose excuse for poor execution—nor as the reason to abandon an otherwise sound strategy.

Lowe: From public to Interpublic

We merged Wasey Campbell-Ewald into Lowe for 35% of the new company. It was a big help in attracting creative talent to our expanding 3rd network. It also gave us some immediate business advantages. We brought General Motors's Vauxhall division into the Lowe fold and strengthened the U.K. volume base. We rebranded and merged our continental European offices as Lowe-Troost, which gave the Lowe network expanded options to add additional GM brands and ancillary services. (Saab, for example, became a Lowe client following the acquisition of a Swedish creative agency.)

Meanwhile, McCann-Erickson continued as GM's lead agency on Opel business, while Campbell-Ewald, which we separated out from the Lowe network, continued handling Chevrolet, with the benefit of now coordinating the account through McCann's international offices.

The Lowe-Troost network also gave us expanded capabilities to work with Henkel. By the mid 1980s, Henkel had consolidated all their household and personal care business at Interpublic agencies: McCann-Erickson and Lowe-Troost. Meanwhile Lintas continued to enjoy great success with Unilever.

Around this time, U.K. agencies were trading at high multiples on the London Stock Exchange. We decided to list the Lowe Group on the London exchange to give the agency more flexibility to pursue acquisitions beyond the European market.

The idea was sound. But the reality of running a publicly traded company didn't always jive with Frank Lowe's idiosyncratic style. Lowe had to come to grips with his new responsibilities to shareholders. And he had to get used to working for bigger, multinational clients and their highly structured approval systems.

Of course, Frank had a big personal stake in making it work, and that helped. But it wasn't always easy.

One time, General Motors insisted, based on their internal policy, that they be given different campaigns to choose from.

Frank insisted on not doing it, sticking to his creative principles.

I intervened with an approach that would appeal to both his pocket-book as well as his ego.

"Look, Frank," I said. "This client isn't as sophisticated as the British executives you're used to. But what are you worried about? You're the best presenter in the business. You know which idea is the best. All you have to do is sell it. Everybody wins."

Lowe grudgingly gave General Motors the alternatives they wanted.

The Lowe Group thrived through the 1980s, but its ability to grow as a stand-alone company was limited by its need to meet the quarterly targets investors and analysts demanded. When the market dipped in 1990, we made the move to acquire 100% of the Lowe Group and bring it inside Interpublic.

Our offer was designed to give Lowe more leeway to focus on a long-term plan for the agency and, crucially, assume more leadership of the U.S. part of the network, which was being run through Marschalk's New York office, which became Lowe-Marschalk.

I thought Frank might resist the offer, but his personal interest prevailed once again. The investment paid out in less than four years.

During the eighties and nineties, Interpublic and Lowe had a very successful business partnership. But the relationship was rocky and ultimately broke apart, with some of the problems being exposed to the outside world, sometimes through third parties.

Now when people ask me why I invested so much in Frank Lowe, I tell them: First, I'm a great believer in risk taking. And if Lowe was a risk it certainly paid off for many years. Second, I believed I could control his management style since Frank always reported directly to me. Many of the problems that developed over time were caused by expanding into areas that were neither Frank's nor Interpublic's expertise (more on that in a later chapter).

But egos, when they get too big, are not always controllable. Ultimately, IPG couldn't dial back his competitive nature as he continually sought to outdo McCann-Erickson. The results of several of his off-strategy acquisitions ended up creating strategic and operational problems in the parent-agency relationship.

Managing larger-than-life personalities
1. **Assess the upside**: In a creative industry, big personalities will attract attention—and win business.

2. **Consider the management challenge**: Not every culture—nor every manager—can handle every type of personality.

3. **Understand what it will take to make it work**: Knowing what motivates a person is crucial in how you manage them.

London vs. New York

One of the most interesting aspects of how the advertising business changed in the 1980s was the way U.K. agencies emerged onto the global stage.

In the 1960s and for much of the 1970s, the Madison Avenue approach—and the deep pockets of U.S. agencies and clients—had given the international advertising scene a distinctly American tone.

By the 1980s, though, British creativity was being globally recognized and one financially strong British agency was beginning to acquire agencies in the U.S. market.

It's also interesting to note that many of the new independent agencies that emerged in the U.S., such as Fallon McElligott Rice in Minneapolis, found inspiration in the work of British agencies. Many award-winning campaigns from the hot new U.S. agencies of the 1980s had striking similarities to work found in the previous year's U.K. award-show annuals.

As a global holding company, we had recognized early the need to add some British flair to our mix. And the decision had paid off exceptionally well.

The success of the McCann, Lintas and Lowe networks was helping Interpublic grow its stock at a 15-20% compounded growth rate. Clearly, the three-tiered network was working for investors as well as clients.

It was only a matter of time before our competitors started taking notice.

New York's "Big Bang" merger

Interpublic's first real competitor from a holding company perspective appeared dramatically on the scene in 1986.

Omnicom was born in April 1986 when three of the top 20 agencies agreed to a "merger of equals." New York's BBDO and Doyle Dane Bernbach agencies, joined forces with Chicago-based Needham Harper Worldwide. With

10,000 employees and annual billings of $5 billion, Omnicom immediately became a huge competitor to Interpublic.

The new company was headed by Allen Rosenshine, the former CEO of BBDO. Norman Campbell took over at BBDO and Keith Reinhard, the head of Needham Harper, ran the now-combined DDB-Needham agency.

Interestingly, the Doyle Dane Bernbach board approved the merger despite a higher last-minute bid from London's Saatchi brothers. Later that year, the Saatchis swooped in to buy the Ted Bates agency for the surprisingly high price of $507 million, to become, temporarily, the new global leader, with $7.5 billion in billings. Interpublic had been involved in the negotiations for Ted Bates. We were offering stock, so knew we would have to offer a premium to the Saatchis' cash offer. When our first two bids were topped by the London agency, we knew they were highly determined. We realized that the key to the deal would be the price paid for the controlling shares owned by Bob Jacoby. He was a short little guy but much taller when he stood on his money. Knowing that our offer would be subject to final due diligence—and that the head of Bates International was biased toward the Saatchis and sure to communicate the details of any renewed offer—I put in a much higher bid than I would have actually wanted to pay. Even at this higher level, the Saatchis agreed to pay more.

Meanwhile, Omnicom's "big bang" merger wasn't proving an immediate success. The agencies had distinctly different cultures and were not instantly adept at managing client conflicts. Accounts such as Honda, IBM, Procter & Gamble and RJR Nabisco all left. Altogether, client defections directly attributable to the merger reduced Omnicom's billings by $184 million. Word on the street was that Omnicom actually stood for "Operations May Not Improve Considering Our Merger."

In addition, the new holding company didn't have the same global history as agencies such as McCann-Erickson and J. Walter Thompson. BBDO had built a system of coordinated local agencies to serve clients such as Pepsi and Gillette. DDB Needham was a combination of two of America's best creative agencies, but it didn't start life with a strong overseas reputation.

But Omnicom and its agencies were run by smart people. Allen Rosenshine not only replaced the business lost in the merger, he actually grew total billings nearly 30% by 1989 to $6.3 billion.

At that point, he surprised everyone by announcing he wanted to be running an agency, not a publicly listed company. When BBDO Chairman Norman Campbell retired, Rosenshine stepped down from his Omnicom role and went back to a job he found more fun: being Chairman and Chief Creative officer of BBDO. To replace himself, he persuaded Bruce Crawford, his predecessor at BBDO, who had been running the Metropolitan Opera to great reviews, to return to Omnicom as Chairman as CEO.

The New York Times reported that Crawford's return to the advertising business "surprised the operatic community," while Rosenshine told the Times, "With Bruce's availability and Norm's desire to retire, this became an irresistible solution."

In 1997, Bruce Crawford named John Wren as his successor as CEO, while Bruce stayed on as Chairman.

I always thought that John was very smart in keeping Bruce Crawford on as Chairman. John had made his name running Omnicom's Diversified Agency Services (DAS) division. He had a strong business and financial background, but Bruce's presence gave him credibility in regard to the advertising side of the business. To this day, Bruce has stayed visible and involved, right on the same floor, not parked away in a corner office downstairs. John also brought in a CFO with a great background in the public and private equity markets, Randall J. Weisenburger, who joined from Wasserstein Perella & Co.

With Bruce Crawford as an invaluable sounding board, Wren and Weisenburger have kept Omnicom on a steady course in the years since 2002 surpassing Interpublic as the #1 advertising holding company by revenue, as ranked by *Advertising Age*. In 2002, Bruce Crawford was lured back to the world of music as Chairman of Lincoln Center, while continuing as the non-executive Chairman of Omnicom.

Interpublic and Omnicom have always been fierce but friendly competitors. At Interpublic, my CFO Gene Beard and I respected the fact that the Omnicom team were straight shooters. Omnicom adopted many of the best approaches Interpublic had in place, in everything from worldwide account coordination to personnel training to incentive programs. Their use of stock options and restricted stock programs was similar to ours. At that time, we had a pension plan; they did not, but they provided a special program for their key executives.

It's worth mentioning that Omnicom's successful model is built around three major global agency networks: BBDO, DDB Worldwide and TBWA Worldwide.

Three global networks. What a concept!

The benefits of competition

1. **It helps to be part of a "competitive set"**: Omnicom's creation validated Interpublic's holding company model—setting the stage for even greater client acceptance.

2. **A good competitor improves your game**: Competing with another New York-based holding company created rivalries throughout our two organizations.

3. **It changes the dynamics of the industry**: Competition at the holding company level gave everyone—from Wall Street to creative professionals—a new way to evaluate the advertising business.

A healthy industry generates strong competition—and ensures innovation.

"Sir Martin" conquers the world

The Saatchi brothers shook up the advertising world in the 1980s. But the Saatchi & Saatchi that exists today is just one of four international agencies within Publicis, the fourth largest advertising holding company. It was the man once known as "the third brother," Martin Sorrell who ultimately had more staying power.

Martin Sorrell (now Sir Martin) was the CFO who helped engineer some of the Saatchis' early acquisitions. But he quit the agency in 1985 and reappeared in 1986 as the CEO of the publicly listed WPP Group, a shell company formerly known for the manufacture of shopping carts and wire baskets.

Sorrell began quietly. Using the leveraging power of his company stock, he successfully acquired several "below the line" agencies. Then he stunned the advertising world by making a hostile play for the JWT Group. When the JWT board approved the deal, the world was surprised to discover that a tiny, virtually unknown U.K. company had gobbled up one of Madison

Avenue's most venerable institutions.

The purchase price of $566 million was stunning. But then so was the audacity of Sorrell's move.

William Muirhead, one of Saatchi & Saatchi's joint chairman, called Sorrell "a brilliant deal maker… who combines amazing ruthlessness with great charm."

Sorrell himself told *The New York Times* he had been tagged by the British press as "a boring, diminutive, well-fed health nut." He also admitted he knew little about advertising. But his financial acumen allowed him to pull off the hostile deal.

It's important to note that favorable U.K. accounting rules made it easier for British companies such as WPP to pursue acquisitions in the U.S. Under U.K. rules, companies are allowed to write off goodwill (the premium paid for a company above its book value against net worth) rather than depreciate it gradually against profits. The British system enhances earnings per share; the U.S. approach depresses them. For Martin Sorrell and WPP, the rules made it easy to swoop in with an all-cash offer that American companies found difficult to match. The WPP approach was particularly effective when Sorrell targeted privately held companies. At a private company, shareholders—especially those in top management and close to retirement—normally have to sell back to the company at book value when they leave. When a cash offer is made at three or four times a company's book value, it is usually impossible to refuse.

Having digested his huge JWT acquisition, Sorrell came back two years later and repeated the feat. WPP acquired The Ogilvy Group, including the legendary Ogilvy and Mather agency, this time for $825 million.

At first, the Ogilvy management resisted Sorrell's hostile bid. Ken Roman had only recently taken over as Chairman and CEO from the now-retired Bill Phillips. Ken was steeped in the Ogilvy culture and the agency's sense of independence was so strong that the board was not keen to approve any deal. Ogilvy was one of the best known names in advertising; the agency was famous for work on great worldwide accounts such as American Express and IBM.

Ken Roman cast around for a white knight and Interpublic stepped forward. Ogilvy proposed that Interpublic take a minority stake, leaving existing management in control of the historic agency.

From the outset, there were concerns about possible account conflicts, but we at Interpublic were confident, based on our proven holding company model, that any account losses would be minimal.

Ogilvy was earning $800 million in revenue and a net profit of $33 million. The stock had traded at $32 before WPP bid $50 a share. Knowing that WPP would have trouble leveraging the Ogilvy acquisition, we offered an all-stock transaction at a premium to WPP's all-cash offer. But Ogilvy's advisers were concerned. Supposedly, if account losses did occur after the deal was announced and Interpublic's share price declined as a result, shareholders could have sued Ogilvy management for not accepting WPP's all-cash deal. In addition to possible shareholder lawsuits, Martin Sorrell was already well-known for using litigation to his advantage. These concerns, combined with pressure from Ogilvy's international board members, led the Ogilvy board to accept WPP's sweetened bid of $54 per share.

Knowing both Ken Roman and former Chairman Bill Phillips as well as I did, I knew that Ogilvy was a first-class, professional organization. I was sorry we were not able to work out a satisfactory arrangement, partly because of their financial advisers' belief that account losses would take place. I did feel that concerns about account losses were overblown. And in the end, there were very few account losses between Ogilvy and JWT.

Within two years, two agencies with great reputations had been taken over by the British invader. As *The New York Times* noted at the time: "in four years (Sorrell) has turned a $518,000 investment in a company that manufactured supermarket baskets into the world's second-largest marketing-communications company."

When the accounting rules are working in your favor, it's amazing to think what you can do with a little cash and a lot of financial leverage.

The WPP way to take a small company into the big time.

1. **A "reverse IPO"**: With relatively little cash, Sorrell took control of a small, publicly listed company, then redefined its business model.

2. **Favorable accounting rules**: From his U.K. base, Sorrell had a competitive advantage in bidding for American companies.

3. **Offers that couldn't be refused**: Especially for privately held companies, it's impossible to ignore all-cash offers made substantially above book value.

WPP on the brink of collapse

For all of Martin Sorrell's legendary financial acumen, his highly leveraged deals made WPP particularly vulnerable to any business downturn. The recession of the early 1990s, coinciding with the first Gulf War, hit the ad industry hard and WPP hardest.

By the end of 1990, WPP was in trouble. By July 1992, the group was forced to announce: "WPP will be dependent on the continuing support of its bankers...Without this support, WPP will be unable to continue to trade."

The future of WPP was hanging by a thread. And major clients, particularly brand managers at Unilever, were concerned. Virtually of all Unilever's worldwide advertising business was assigned to four agencies—Interpublic's Lintas and McCann-Erickson, and WPP's J. Walter Thompson and Ogilvy & Mather. Unilever called these four agencies "the Club."

Around this time, at least two of Ogilvy's Unilever clients indicated to McCann-Erickson they were interested in switching agencies. These accounts could have been easy wins for Interpublic. But I chose not to attack. If WPP had collapsed, the disruption to the industry would have been enormous.

Unbeknownst to Sorrell, I informed top management at Unilever that no Interpublic agency would target any of WPP's Unilever accounts for a period of 12 months. The Unilever client appreciated that gesture, knowing that there could have been a major disruption to their global marketing efforts if WPP had gone bankrupt at that time.

We gained credibility with Unilever, but I'm sure that, even to this day, Martin Sorrell wonders why he didn't lose any Unilever business during his time of crisis. (If he did find out, he was not the kind to send thank-you notes.)

Sorrell was able to renegotiate with his major investors and managed to steer WPP through its financial storm. Then he went right back to his aggressive, acquisitive ways.

Martin has always been outstanding in how he runs his company. While he was not always loved by clients, he was persistent and deeply involved in many aspects of the business. Clients knew Sorrell worried about his business first and their business second.

Sorrell exerted control not through his people skills, but through contracts that he enforced to the letter. If someone left, there would be no early release. He would sue at the drop of the hat, no matter how unimportant or small the issue.

But he got results and continued to build the company. He acquired two more of America's largest agencies—Young & Rubicam and Grey Advertising—along the way. He also did particularly well in acquiring research companies and moving early to set up independent media buying companies.

Throughout the past 20 years, the "ruthlessness" noted back in the '80s has always been a part of his approach and it seemed to work. He mellowed a bit by the time we entered the 21st century and we now enjoy exchanging war stories.

What Interpublic achieved during WPP's crisis

1. Credibility: By not attacking a weakened competitor, we gained credibility with a major client—and saved that client from the upheaval of moving accounts in the midst of bankruptcy.

2. Stability: Allowing a competitor to breathe allowed the whole industry to better weather the recession—and prevented any new competitors from filling the vacuum.

3. Trust: In the longer term, a strengthened client relationship allowed us to compete for and win more Unilever business.

In a recession such as today's, you may achieve short-term benefits if a competitor folds. But the perceived vitality of your industry may also suffer. Case in point: the once-mighty newspaper industry.

Publicis makes four

The ad industry's fourth major holding company grew out of the French agency Publicis, founded in 1926 by the 20-year-old Marcel Bleustein. Publicis grew from its origins above a Parisian drugstore to become a dominant agency in France, known for its work for clients such as L'Oreal, Nestlé and Renault. It also built a strong European network.

When Maurice Levy became President, and eventually Chairman, the agency embarked on a more ambitious international expansion. Many times, I tried to convince Maurice to join forces with Interpublic, and at times he may have been willing to do so. But the Bleustein family didn't want to relinquish control.

Levy spent a good deal of time in the U.S., finding ways to strengthen his business here. He made a big move into the U.S. market in 2000 with the purchase of Fallon McElligott. The same year he also purchased the Saatchi & Saatchi agency. Two years later, he made an even bigger move with his $3 billion acquisition of bcom3, which included the historic Chicago-based Leo Burnett agency and the old DMB&B agency.

This 2002 transaction established Publicis as the world's 4th largest advertising holding company.

Before bcom3 was formed, Interpublic had attempted to move on DMB&B, which was run by Roy Bostock. DMB&B had the Cadillac, Pontiac, and General Motors accounts, along with a lot of Procter & Gamble business. An Interpublic acquisition would have created some problems between Unilever and P&G, but probably more so for P&G. We thought we could solve it, but Bostock went ahead with the merger with Leo Burnett that created bcom3. Later, Interpublic tried to purchase bcom3 and Bostock was a great ally in this. We got as far as figuring out a way to adjust some Unilever business so there would be no category conflicts within the group. The bcom3 management agreed in principle to our deal.

Then a problem emerged from Japan. Dentsu, Japan's largest agency, owned 20% of bcom3 and had been trying to expand their own U.S. operations with small agencies in Los Angeles, London and Germany. McCann-Erickson, meanwhile, owned 51% of Hakuhodo-McCann-Erickson, a partnership with Japan's second largest agency. If we had closed a deal, it would have ended up with Dentsu continuing to control 20% of bcom3 and Interpublic owning 80%. Face was important in Japan. And Dentsu, which saw itself as a holding company in its own right, didn't want to be seen owning 20% of an agency that was part of the holding company associated with their closest competitor. No matter how I tried to work out the problem, it just was not acceptable to the older management.

Shortly after, Maurice Levy came in with an offer that allowed Publicis to acquire bcom3, establishing a strong foothold in the U.S..

Interestingly, following Publicis' acquisitions, the strict alignment policies of major global marketers loosened up considerably.

Changes in ownership had wrought so many current and potential conflicts that things really needed to change.

General Motors changed its policies so that Publicis ended up being able to handle Toyota through Saatchi & Saatchi, while GM continued with Leo Burnett.

What was unthinkable a few years ago—that clients such as Colgate Palmolive, P&G, and Unilever could all work with the same holding company—is now a reality at WPP.

The fact that Interpublic proved the holding company model could work over several decades opened all sorts of doors for competitors. Today, the big four holding companies account for 80% of the global advertising business.

Why the holding company "blueprint" transformed the business

1. **It worked for clients**: The holding company provided strong worldwide coordination systems, creative options and less disruption when it became necessary to move business.

2. **It worked for the holding companies**: Interpublic's established systems allowed competitors to adopt proven ideas in terms of structure and coordination.

3. **It delivered long-term growth**: Organically and through acquisition, the holding company model allowed companies to adapt to marketplace changes, respond to client needs—and develop new competitive advantages,

How did Interpublic hold up?

While the new holding companies made a lot of bold moves, created a lot of noise, and gave the advertising business a whole new shape, Interpublic went about its business a little more quietly, and in many ways more effectively. Our primary objectives in the 1980s and '90s were threefold:

1) To strengthen our agency systems in the world's major advertising markets through organic growth and acquisitions
2) To build out our worldwide systems into developing markets
3) To continue to provide integrated communications services within our global agency systems

In later chapters, I will talk about how we pursued acquisitions and why some worked while others failed. But perhaps the best way to explain how Interpublic viewed itself and executed its strategy through the '80s and '90s is to reprint here some excerpts from an interview I gave to an Italian media publication in June 1988. It gives insight into how we looked at our clients, our business, our people, and our competitors at a key moment in the history of globalization. It also helps explain why Interpublic was able to grow its earnings faster than any competitor, allowing Interpublic stock to deliver a 22% compound growth rate over a period of 20 years.

The View from 1988

By the late 1980s, Interpublic faced intense competition from several new and aggressive global competitors. In June 1988, I gave an interview to Media Key, a European advertising publication, in which I was asked about how Interpublic was navigating the changes in the industry and my personal approach to the business. Here are some excerpts from that interview.

On "mega-mergers" and globalization:
The much-publicized mergers in advertising and the new groups that have been formed are caused by a phenomenon created by the clients. These clients have consolidated and they're looking for worldwide efficiencies of operation, which is driving the agencies in the same direction. There aren't many big agencies that can service worldwide clients well. Our agency systems have been at it for many years. They've made all the mistakes.

On what made Interpublic different:
We learned a long time ago that Interpublic must have a separate office from the agencies and to have a name different from the agencies. We're dedicated to a philosophy of maintaining each agency system with their own, very particular business philosophy, which differ one from the other. As you look at the Thompsons, the Ogilvys, the Saatchis all have that problem. When Paul Foley, a great creative man, was chairman of Interpublic, it was very difficult for him to stay out of the creative problems of the agencies. Because Interpublic has a businessman running the company, it circumvents any possible conflict problems, real or imagined. We save 10-12% of the agency's management time to put against growing its clients' business by freeing them of responsibility in areas such as cash management, legal, real estate, tax benefit plans, human resources, stockholder relationships, and acquisition work.

On the Interpublic approach to acquisitions:
Our three key considerations are: First, the merger must bring a benefit to the client either in resource terms or people terms or better overall efficiencies and supply better, effective advertising. Second, the chemistry among the people has to be right. It won't work otherwise. And third, the seller as well as the buyer must have a mutually satisfactory deal. We won't force synergies to the detriment of servicing clients and marinating key people that are needed against the business.

On building brands for clients:
We still have to convince clients of the importance of the emotional bonding of the product with the consumer that it's a major asset and an investment that has to be nurtured. When it is done right and enough money put behind it and a total communications package developed around it (not just advertising) you can grow a business with better margins over a longer period of time. Brand equity builds and provides the buffer against the continued price off, discount approach that some businesses are taking.

On advertising research:
One thing I have learned is not to test ads to tell which one was better than another, but to help find the negatives and to know whey they were negative and to help find the positive elements and expose them. In the end good analysis helps, but the talent of judgment after the analysis is the solution.

On why I succeeded within Interpublic:
I believe it was a combination of elements. First of all, I wasn't as smart as a lot of people and therefore I had to work harder and longer. I always tried to work and develop a team attitude and bring people along with me and let everybody else share in the success. I really enjoyed growing and building a business and particularly the success of a new business win or a client's breakthrough success.

On my own "low profile" approach to the business:
The agency people who develop advertising strategy and creative should be the most visible in the marketplace. The chairman of Interpublic should

never be the chairman of the 4A's (the American Association of Advertising Agencies). That responsibility should be given to an agency head who is an advertising professional.

On recruiting talent:
I have a point of view that is different than most on hiring young talent. I'd rather take an innovative, aggressive experimenter who does not have an MBA title because that type of person seems to have a less know-it-all attitude, a more learning attitude and they seem to be people who find ways and means to be successful by working the business, and working it long and hard. *(Note: This was despite having an MBA from Columbia myself.)*

On risk-takers:
I look favorably on employees who come up with ideas soundly developed, who are willing to take risks, but risks that are based on careful analysis and study—these are the ones that I want in our company.

On taking the pulse of the business:
I learn by keeping my finger on what's happening in the marketplace. I want to know what my competitors are doing. I have an open door policy and see various people, particularly creative people from our agencies. I want to find out their problems and where they think they can do better. Yes, it may be one or two layers down, but that's where you learn what's in the wind and what's coming next.

On victory and defeat:
You get the best learning from experiences on the job. If you lose, know why you lost and learn from it. If you win, enjoy it – there's nothing like it.

CHAPTER NINE

Put Clients First

*How to be your client's best business partner—and communicate
a client-centric philosophy throughout your organization*

"Every business is built on friendship."

—*J. C. Penney*

Make it your business

GOOD RELATIONSHIPS ARE essential, especially in a client-driven business
like marketing communications. At Interpublic, our mission has always
been to build the businesses and brands of our clients. We develop long-term
partnership with clients by understanding their business needs, by bringing
forward new ideas to help meet their sales goals, and by fostering productive
relationships at every level where our organizations intersect.

It's not always easy.

These days, agency-client divorce rates are soaring. According to a recent
article in *Advertising Age*, the average relationship between client and agency
now lasts just two years.

The reasons for these short-lived marriages are plenty. As the pace of business
accelerates, CMOs and Marketing Directors are being given less time than
ever to demonstrate results. The ever-shifting competitive environment means
brands are constantly facing new and unexpected challenges. Consumers are
elusive. Media choices are evolving. Once agencies are hired, there's less time
for strategic thinking and more emphasis on short-term tactical solutions.

What's an agency to do?

Great work is a prerequisite. Beyond that, it's important to find ways to help your client in ways he doesn't expect to be helped and in ways that differentiate you from your agency competitors.

The first step is to recognize that advertising is a people business. Every client relationship is personal and you need to know and understand the personalities involved on the client side. The agency-client relationship is often defined as much by the day-to-day interactions on the account as it is by the work that gets produced.

Second, never forget that your agency-client relationship is not just about advertising. The things that keep your client up at night touch upon all aspects of her business or industry. You need to be aware of those concerns, the information needs connected to them, and the potential blind spots that you and your agency, with a valued outside perspective, can help reveal.

Third, demonstrate continually your commitment to your client's overall business success. It's not enough to be an "agency partner." You need to see yourself as a "junior partner" in your client's business, even if that means investing time and resources on business issues that are not strictly within your agency's purview.

From a client's perspective an agency that helps solve problems is far more valuable than one that concentrates on selling its services. Most large advertisers use more than one agency. If you and your agency can stand out from the pack as true business partners, you'll gain a real advantage when the client starts considering to whom he should award any new business assignments.

Never forget that your client's overall business success is the best route to a lasting relationship and the true secret of an agency's success.

The secrets of a successful agency-client marriage

1. **Business is personal – so know the personalities**: Day-to-day interactions are crucial to a successful relationship.

2. **Make your client's business your own**: Add value by supplying relevant information—and an impartial perspective.

3. **Stop selling and start solving**: The more you act as a "junior partner" committed to your client's success, the more the relationship will flourish.

The honest broker

Working in London in the early '70s, I got to know Dr. Anton Rupert, the head of Rothmans International, pretty well. With just ten British pounds to his name, he had started manufacturing cigarettes in his garage back in 1941. Three decades later, his ambition and entrepreneurship had helped him build a multinational tobacco empire, one that was particularly strong in Europe, Asia-Pacific, and his native South Africa.

One day, I got a phone call from Dr. Rupert, asking if I could meet him on short notice in London. I rearranged my schedule and headed to the meeting.

Rupert knew that I had good connections with Philip Morris and its chairman Joe Cullman.

He got right to the point.

"I've been talking to Joe Cullman. What do you think of our two companies working together?"

"What do you have in mind?" I asked.

Dr. Rupert laid out the novel plan. With Philip Morris dominant in North and South America and Rothmans strong in the rest of the world, he and Cullman envisioned a merger-of-equals, dividing the world between them and running the combined company as co-CEOs.

It was an interesting idea, one that would have created a global powerhouse to dominate the tobacco industry. But it had a couple of immediate drawbacks.

First, and easiest to point out, was the fact that Philip Morris and Rothmans were managed in distinctly different ways. Rupert preferred a decentralized approach giving the managers in every major Rothmans market a great deal of autonomy in how they ran their businesses. The one thing Rupert managed centrally was advertising, where he decided on the approach and had to approve any local changes recommended from the markets. Cullman, meanwhile, believed in a strong centralized approach, with head office controlling all of the major business decisions.

The second problem was the obvious personality clash. Both Cullman and Rupert were strong leaders and though they had different styles they shared one trait: The need to control.

Rupert, being a pragmatist, thought a power-sharing arrangement could not only work, it would also benefit both sides. In their analysis, the consolidation and additional leverage created by the merger would boost profitability at least 30% on a global basis.

In fashioning his discussion with Philip Morris, Dr. Rupert used me as a sounding board. Because I knew the cultures of both companies and the personalities of the CEOs involved, he wanted my honest opinion on the pros and cons of a possible merger.

From my perspective, a merger at that time would have been a huge benefit to McCann-Erickson as we would have likely picked up substantial new business. But at the same time, I knew that unless both partners fully embraced the idea of working together, the potential benefits would evaporate.

Discussions reached an advanced stage, but the control issues were never adequately resolved.

In the end, the two wise men realized their partnership wasn't to be. Rather than a merger that transformed an industry, this was a merger that didn't happen. But playing the role of honest broker enhanced my relationship with Dr. Rupert and served me and my company very well for the future.

As a footnote, several years later word leaked out that R.J. Reynolds was negotiating to buy a stake in Rothmans. Without hesitation, Philip Morris swooped in and quickly acquired 30% of Dr. Rupert's company.

Playing the role of honest broker

1. **Be impartial:** Give your best advice to both sides where appropriate.
2. **Respect every confidence:** Nothing is more valuable than a client's trust. Don't abuse it.
3. **Don't get invested in the outcome:** Don't impose your own interests into a negotiation of which you are not a full participant. Let the two parties come to their own conclusions.

How to be a conversation starter

One of the challenges for my German client Henkel was to increase its business in the U.S. market. Henkel had great sales and distribution in Europe and much of Latin America, but its U.S. business was based mainly on industrial adhesive products.

I knew Dr. Helmut Seiler, Henkel's Managing Director, would appreciate being exposed to any opportunities to gain a foothold in the U.S., so I analyzed the competitive set and suggested that he might consider a global strategic partnership with SC Johnson & Company.

SC Johnson was a family owned company very successful with its household products in the U.S. but, at the time, not particularly strong in international markets.

The idea had appeal to me, too. Interpublic didn't do any business with SC Johnson at the time, and I thought this would be a great way to get to know the company outside of a new business pitch.

On paper, the Henkel-SC Johnson partnership made perfect sense. In addition to being family owned companies, both of them could be of enormous help to each other by handling marketing and distribution in the geographies in which they were strongest.

I made contact with SC Johnson and verified that there would be interest in engaging in discussions with Henkel.

Several meetings took place, but in the end, both parties felt the fit would not be right.

Still, Dr. Seiler at Henkel appreciated the effort, which only enhanced our expanding business relationship. And I had made useful contacts within SC Johnson.

In fact, Sam Johnson tried to hire me, so I know I did the right thing in trying.

Being a conversation starter like this is one of the valuable, often unseen roles the ad agency can play in furthering its client's business interests.

An enduring partnership

One of the most remarkable and enduring agency-client marriages of the 20th century was that between Interpublic, particularly McCann-Erickson, and The Coca-Cola Company.

In my many years working closely on the account, we built a good relationship with Don Keough, who rose to become President and Chief Operating Officer of Coca-Cola Americas in 1981 and stayed in that position until his retirement in 1993.

Keough was the living embodiment of the Coca-Cola Company—a powerful personality, a rousing public speaker, and the executive most trusted by Coke's bottlers and retailers. He knew the facts and figures inside out, but more than anything, Keough understood the emotional side of the Coke brand.

Keough and the Coke team appreciated how Interpublic and its agencies worked. Our account planning system and drill-down approach to the business ensured that Coke's global coordinator knew what was happening on their business anywhere in the world, while local managers were continually updated about strategies and creative executions.

Don himself was the drill-down master, always on top of what was happening around the world in both the filtered and unfiltered versions. A terrific and demanding client, he always challenged Interpublic and its agencies, from top management on down, to take risks and push for new ways to expand his business. It was a true partnership. Things didn't always work out perfectly, but when Don signed off on something, he always shared the blame. And when things worked well, as they often did, he made sure the agency got the credit it deserved.

Here are some examples of our partnership in action.

Secrecy and sensitivity

The late 1970s were not a great time for Coca-Cola. The blind taste tests of the infamous Pepsi Challenge had begun in 1975 and had helped propel Pepsi's market share even as Coke stagnated. Coke was still number one, but its supremacy was being challenged. Meanwhile, at a time when counting calories was all the rage, Diet Pepsi and Pepsi Light, with a combined 4.4 share were outselling Coke's Tab brand, which was stuck at 4.2.

Despite its small band of loyal fans, Tab was an acquired taste for most soda drinkers. I liked it well enough. It had a slightly medicinal flavor, but I always thought it was perhaps doing me some good. It was marketed primarily to women as a diet drink that would help create the body shape they wanted. Given the dual challenges coming from Pepsi, everyone at Coke was feeling the pressure.

In 1980, Don Keough was looking to improve the Tab situation and considering the launch of a new, improved product.

We convinced him to assign this top secret project to Interpublic's new agency, SSC&B-Lintas. Bill Weithas and his Lintas team worked closely with Coca-Cola in researching the product. Everything was done under a cloak of secrecy. We didn't want to tip our hand to anyone at Pepsi, nor to our own McCann colleagues who were focused 100% on the Coca-Cola brand.

Coca-Cola's goal was to create a new diet soda with a sweeter taste – one much closer to Pepsi. Consumer taste tests and in-home trials could help refine the product, but the intense secrecy meant that only a very limited amount of creative research could be done.

Weithas and his team laid out three main options:

1. Relaunch Tab with a new formula
2. Keep Tab—and launch a new, stand-alone diet cola brand.
3. Keep Tab—and launch a new diet product using the Coca-Cola name

Coke's CMO Ike Herbert was very concerned that using the Coca-Cola name would cannibalize sales of the original Coke brand—a big risk at a time when Coke's leadership position was already under heavy attack.

The idea of relaunching Tab with a new formula was the first to be eliminated. A new, much sweeter Tab would likely alienate its current buyers and the relaunch of an already-weak Tab brand was not likely to generate much excitement with consumers.

Still, using the Coke name continued to be seen as a high-risk option.

The matter was only resolved when Don Keough saw Lintas' creative concepts. His gut told him that the "Just for the taste of it!" campaign would connect with consumers and that the new product would hurt the "taste-testing" Pepsi much more than it did Coca-Cola.

As always, Don invited feedback from his whole team, making sure everyone felt included in the decision-making process. But his own opinion was clear and his enthusiasm was contagious. Soon, everyone inside Coke and the whole team at Lintas was hyped up for the launch.

The final test would be when the new brand and the new creative were unveiled to the Coca-Cola bottlers.

For a launch of this magnitude, Keough and his team decided to put on a real show.

It happened at Radio City Music Hall in New York City in July 1982—a no-holds barred gala event that featured a performance by the Radio City Rockettes. The launch commercial, which Lintas had already shot in a Los Angeles auditorium, featured a host of celebrities attending what looked like the very same Radio City event. Stars such as Telly Savalas and Joe Namath were seen rising from their seats to sing "Just for the taste of it!"

Overnight, a new product sensation was born. By 1983, Diet Coke was the #1 sparkling diet beverage in America. It was launched as Coca-Cola Light in international markets. Within another three years, it was #1 in its category all around the world.

What happened to Tab? After the launch of Diet Coke, the Coca-Cola Company pulled back on marketing the brand and it went into a long decline. It's still available in many markets and its fans are still loyal, many of them travel hundreds of miles just to get the product.

Coca-Cola takes on French café culture

Throughout the years and throughout the world, Coca-Cola has pushed its bottlers to expand their distribution options.

In most markets, vending machines have been a huge success. But in France, Coke's ambitious plans backfired.

In the early 1980s, one of Coke's hotshot financial guys was running the European operations and trying his hand at marketing for the first time.

He developed a plan to install vending machines in major metropolitan areas and invested in about 10,000 ultra-modern, all-purpose beverage units. The only problem: French café and bistro owners, who at that time were big sellers of Coca-Cola, rebelled. Even when Coke offered a profit-sharing deal, giving the bar owners a cut of the revenue from the machines nearest their establishments, the plan proved unworkable. In crowded neighborhoods, no one could agree which machines should be designated to which establishments.

The plan hadn't been thought through properly. This was France, remember, where emotions often run high, especially when a big American company wades in trying to change the way you run your business.

Before long, the vending machines were shipped to other, less contentious parts of the world.

The man who installed the machines made a huge mistake by not really testing the proposition ahead of time.

But Don Keough was usually quick to forgive risk-takers for the mistakes they made. In this instance, the executive involved was the man who eventually succeeded Don as President of Coca-Cola.

Changing the formula

By 1984, the "Pepsi Challenge" had become more than an ad campaign. It had turned the #2 brand into a direct threat to Coke's status as the world's number one carbonated beverage.

Since taking over the reins at Coke in 1981, Chairman and CEO Roberto Goizueta had challenged the entire company to do things differently—declaring there would be no sacred cows, including the Coke formula.

The Marketing Director of Coca-Cola USA had recently arrived from Mexico, where he had worked for Pepsi before joining Coke. Together with Brian Dyson, Coke's Argentine-born U.S. President, he began working on a plan to reinvigorate the company's lead product. Interestingly, both men shared a Spanish-language connection with the Cuban-born Goizueta.

Coke hired a well-known consulting firm to assist in the process. I had already been exposed to the work of previous consultants engaged by Coke, so I had some idea what to expect. One of those earlier consultants had even suggested that Coca-Cola was a dying brand in which the company should no longer invest heavily. Apparently, the money being "wasted" on Coke would be better spent on a range of new products across the beverage spectrum. (The latter was actually a good idea, just not at the expense of the core brand.)

As the top-secret project—known internally as "Project Kansas"—progressed, we on the agency side were brought into the process and exposed to Coke's research and the thinking of the consultants. It was clear that a radical new idea was gaining strength: the launch of a new Coke formula, sweeter and less carbonated—a direct challenge to Pepsi on the basis of taste. In packaging this idea, the consultants and some at Coke glossed over key elements of the research, in particular the finding that a large body of consumers, especially adults 25+ in the South, had an almost religious attachment to the Coke brand and its existing formula—and didn't like the taste of the new, sweeter product. Despite this finding, the consultants pushed the idea of the new formula, arguing that even die-hard lovers of the original Coke would eventually be won over.

Clearly, one option would have been to launch a new brand and sell it alongside Coca-Cola. This new brand, with its new sweeter formula, could be marketed as "the taste that Pepsi drinkers prefer," an answer to the challenge by Pepsi.

But Coke decided that bold action was needed and the decision was made to go "all-in" with the launch of New Coke, completely replacing the world's best-loved carbonated beverage with a new product designed to restore Coke's dominance in market share.

Once the decision was made, we all got behind it. The launch of New Coke was a major event—with ads featuring superstar spokesperson Bill Cosby applauding the improved taste.

It was one of the biggest disasters in marketing history.

Looked at in isolation, the sales figures themselves weren't terrible. But something far more damaging had happened. Virtually overnight, all of the history, the passion, the memories—every part of the emotional experience that consumers associated with the Coca-Cola brand was destroyed.

Many consumers simply refused to buy the product. Hundreds of thousands of people wrote letters to the company or called to personally complain.

But as the backlash grew more vocal, especially in the South, Don Keough stepped in. Just as Jim Burke of Johnson & Johnson had acted boldly when faced with the Tylenol tampering scandal three years earlier, Keough knew this situation demanded an equally unequivocal response.

On July 10, 1985, less than three months after the launch of New Coke, viewers of the ABC soap opera *General Hospital* were interrupted with important breaking news from network anchor Peter Jennings: Coke was coming back.

As Don Keough said at a press conference: "The simple fact is that all the time and money and skill poured into consumer research on the new Coca-Cola could not measure or reveal the deep and abiding emotional attachment to original Coca-Cola felt by so many people."

Interpublic and McCann worked with Don Keough and the Coca-Cola Company to rush through the "America's Real Choice" campaign. Created by

"Big John" Bergin, the campaign announced the return of what was now called "Coke Classic." By the end of the year, the original formula was outselling both the New Coke and Pepsi. A huge disaster had been transformed into an unprecedented success.

And, as always with Don, the agency and client took shared responsibility for the failure and success that came out of the whole experience. The partnership held strong—win, lose, or draw.

The end result of the New Coke debacle was that Coca-Cola saw the kind of share growth it hadn't seen for decades and reestablished an unquestioned leadership position it maintains to this day.

How to avoid or correct your biggest mistakes

1. **Don't go into a major launch blind**: Test your strategic communications options, even if means risking some secrecy.

2. **Don't argue with consumers**: When they're mad at you, act fast to appease them.

3. **Don't assume consultants are always right**: They're not.

Global brands, local tastes

No company embraced globalization in the food industry faster or more efficiently than Nestlé. The company, which dates back to 1867, expanded from its base in Vevey, Switzerland, to open its first U.S., British, German, and Spanish factories in the early 1900s. Today, the company is a global packaged food giant: a leader in baby food, breakfast cereals, bottled waters, coffee, confectionery, dairy products, pet foods, prepared meals, and more—with over $120 billion in revenues and more than a quarter of a million employees around the world.

I got my first taste of Nestlé business on the Morsels account at McCann New York in 1960. In Europe during the 1970s, I got to know reasonably well Max Glore, the company's European director, and also an up-and-coming executive Helmut Maucher, who ran Nestlé's West German operations before moving to the Swiss headquarters.

Glore and Maucher were highly aware of the success Nestlé's competitors, especially archrival Unilever, were having as they worked with worldwide agencies on global strategies and brand campaigns. They were keen to push for a global approach to marketing their own brands. But the Nestlé culture pushed back. The company, whose CEO had a financial background, had always profited based on its commodity purchasing expertise, global distribution efficiencies, and long-term financial planning. In addition, because Nestlé's brands and products were often reformulated to suit local consumer tastes, it was comfortable handing off control of marketing to its local managers.

Things changed in 1981 when Maucher took over as Nestlé CEO, a year after I had assumed the same position at Interpublic.

Maucher was plain-spoken, action-oriented and determined to stir things up at the company. One of his first decisions was to order managers to stop creating lengthy 10-year business plans and start focusing on driving their short-term business. "Forecasts of the future are almost always wrong," he said. He told national managers he only wanted a one-page summary of their business each month. "Let's have more pepper and less paper!" was his motto.

As CEO, Maucher also recognized how important it would be to expand Nestlé's U.S. presence, energize its marketing efforts, and increase its corporate influence. During his 15 years as CEO, Maucher consulted me and my Interpublic colleagues on a wide range of issues, affecting everything from global communications and agency assignments to public policy issues and long-term strategic initiatives. It was work that continued when Maucher became Nestlé Chairman in 1996 and Peter Brabeck succeeded him as CEO.

Here are a few examples of how Interpublic's client-centric approach benefited Nestlé through the '80s, '90s and beyond.

Refining the global approach

One of Helmut Maucher's first challenges as CEO was to find a way to consolidate Nestlé's global advertising relationships. Maucher was intensely competitive with Unilever—so much so that he had actually quit Nestlé in 1970 when the frozen-food operation he was running in West Germany was put into a joint venture with Unilever.

Now, as Nestlé CEO, he had the chance to compete head-on with his Anglo-Dutch corporate rival.

Maucher immediately began to push for the global consolidation of advertising assignments. He delegated the challenge to his new marketing head Camille Pagano and asked if I would work with Pagano to develop a new blueprint that could be rolled out globally.

Pagano and I worked on a plan that rationalized the way Nestlé worked with advertising agencies around the world. Nestlé already worked with the four main global agency networks of the time—McCann-Erickson, Ogilvy, J. Walter Thompson and Publicis. Our plan consolidated the category assignments so that each of Nestlé's major categories was assigned to a lead global agency.

Maucher and Pagano knew that McCann-Erickson was already the lead agency for most of Nestlé's big-spending coffee brands, so that assignment was a straightforward one. But they also respected the fact that I didn't treat the assignment as a chance for a major "land-grab" on behalf of Interpublic.

There was an inherent fairness to the proposal and that was an essential component as the plan was sold internally at Nestlé.

Remember, this was a culture where local markets had run their own marketing for many years, so the shift was a potentially jarring one.

With Swiss efficiency, Maucher and Pagano presented, sold, and rolled out a plan that moved Nestlé, step-by-step to a truly global marketing structure. They:

- Encouraged every relevant brand assignment to be moved to the lead global agency every time the opportunity arose, particularly if there was a concern in how the account was being serviced in the local market.
- Set up accountability reviews with each lead agency every six months to highlight if any problems existed and where.
- Put in place a system that required the local office of the lead agency to be informed in writing if there was a problem, and that Nestlé headquarters be informed at the same time. This system alerted both the agency and the client to the problem, locally and globally. The local agency was given the chance to solve the problem or, in some cases, McCann-Erickson used its new concept, the global "SWAT team" assigned to the category.
- Even set up a final "court of appeal" back in Vevey, Switzerland, where the worldwide brand team could get involved to give a local agency a final hearing and a last chance to avoid losing a piece of business.

For Nestlé, the complexity of moving from a patchwork of local agency and brand assignments to a coherent global system was made easier by the systematic approach that was taken.

The company's problem resolution system ensured that every agency was treated fairly. And the fact that problems were put in writing meant they could be understood and addressed by the relevant parties in a timely manner.

It's a system that came to be used successfully by many global clients.

Integrating Nestlé into the U.S. market

As CEO, Maucher was away from his Swiss office at least 50-60% of the time, criss-crossing time zones, and drilling down to understand the challenges of each brand, each category and each market.

Maucher knew the U.S. market would be a crucial component of Nestlé's continued global success—so, in addition to his CEO duties, he personally assumed responsibility for the company's North America Zone.

Nestlé had a huge and dispersed U.S. presence, including chocolate products (and later Carnation) in Los Angeles; the beverage division in San Francisco; Stouffer's frozen meals in Cleveland, Ohio; and the Alcon vision care division in Fort Worth, Texas.

In the 1980s, understanding the U.S. market was crucial to Maucher for several reasons. It was:

- The largest market for Nestlé's consumer products
- One of the fastest, most reliable regions in terms of economic growth
- At the forefront of product development in all areas of the food business, from convenience to health consciousness to weight-loss
- A tremendous source for potential acquisitions in the packaged food category
- The center of global advertising expertise

Despite the importance of the U.S. to Nestlé's success, Maucher inherited a company that had no deep corporate roots in the market. Before the 1980s, Nestlé's brands were well known and heavily promoted, but the company did very little public relations work at the corporate level. And it had only limited contact with government agencies, including the crucially important Food & Drug Administration.

Maucher asked me to help put together an Advisory Board that would brief him and his corporate managers on the key issues, trends, processes, and players in the U.S. market and deliver points of view on issues that cut across all the various divisions of Nestlé's business. Specifically, he wanted to know how Nestlé could serve itself more effectively in the areas of:

- Government relations
- Consumer public relations
- Media relations
- Diversity and multiculturalism
- Working with the FDA

The board we put together included Dick Monroe, CEO of Time, Inc.; Mel Jacobs, Chairman of Saks Fifth Avenue; former Congresswoman Yvonne Braithwaite Burke, who was then Los Angeles County Supervisor; Faith Whittlesey, retired ambassador to Switzerland; Tom Wyman, CBS chairman and board director of S.G. Warburg Group; and Dr. Sandy Miller, former head of the FDA's Center for Food Safety and Applied Nutrition.

Maucher asked me to join the Nestlé Advisory Board, too. I pointed out that my involvement might cause a problem with then Unilever Chairman Morris Tabaksblat. But when Maucher insisted—pointing out that we would be focusing on macro and relationship issues—I broached the matter with Tabaksblat.

I was pleased to discover that Morris was comfortable with me playing a formal part in this Nestlé initiative. It was a clear sign that he trusted me with his confidential issues as much as Maucher did. As I said in a previous chapter, business relationships with European clients take longer to develop, but once established they tend to be more resilient than those with Americans. Both of these men knew that whatever they discussed with me stayed in their own backyard.

The Nestlé Advisory Board met twice a year for many years, long after Nestlé established its U.S. corporate headquarters in LA. This board gave Helmut Maucher a reliable way to stay on top of the overall market, to validate what he was hearing from his own managers and, most important, to build closer personal relationships with key decision makers in government, finance, and the media.

Food shopping with Nestlé

Nestlé's $3 billion takeover of Carnation in 1984 was at the time the world's largest ever non-oil acquisition. Overnight, it doubled the size of Nestlé's U.S. operations.

The friendly takeover was a coup for Helmut Maucher and created a huge windfall for the heirs of Carnation Founder Elbridge Amos Stuart, who still owned 35% of the shares. It was also a deal that further strengthened Nestlé's relationship with Interpublic because we had helped set the table for the purchase.

By 1984, I had already been involved with several major acquisitions on behalf of Interpublic. I had negotiated directly with owners and managers. And because of that experience, I knew how advantageous it could be to line up all the pieces and get all the key decision makers on board before anyone else approached the company with a competing offer.

In the case of Carnation, Interpublic had a long-standing advertising relationship with the company through our agency Erwin, Wasey & Co, which we had acquired in 1964. Elliot Plough who managed the Carnation account out of the Wasey's West Coast office was an executive straight from central casting (Jon Hamm playing the character Don Draper on *Mad Men* always reminds me of him). He was very close to Carnation President Dwight Stuart and had helped his client through two or three divorces as well as several proposals in Las Vegas.

By 1984, Stuart, who personally owned about 20% of the company, had fallen out with Carnation's 77-year-old Chairman H. Everett Olson and told us he might be interested in selling the company. Olson was himself a unique personality. I'll never forget walking into his office the first time, where he had his desk raised up on a foot-high platform. Being short in stature, this was the way Olson arranged things so he could always look down on his guests or at least be at eye level with them!

I alerted Maucher that this might be a good time to initiate a discussion with Carnation, and he asked us to arrange a meeting. The companies had a distribution arrangement in Mexico, so the business relationship at a low level was already very good. It was suggested that Maucher prepare a pre-emptive proposal for the meeting. I briefed him on the personalities involved: how Stuart had clearly reached a point in his life when, at 59, he felt ready to move on from the family business and pursue other interests; and how Olson, closing in on 80, had managed the company successfully from a financial and sales perspective, but had not kept pace in the marketing and advertising area.

Maucher made his offer and the deal was closed in an amicable manner before Nestlé's competitors had a chance to respond.

After the deal was done, Al Gordon, a neighbor in my New York apartment building who worked for the Kidder Peabody investment bank, which Carnation appointed to advise them, asked me, "How did you possibly manage to get them to agree on a price before we had a chance to shop it?"

"I didn't get them to agree on anything," I smiled. "I merely suggested."

Carnation, its chairman and its family owners wanted to know that the company would be in good hands. And Nestlé was able to get its proposal right first time with all the necessary assurances of Carnation's continued autonomy within the much larger corporation.

Mars exploration

Over the years, with Helmut Maucher and later Peter Brabeck, we explored opportunities with Quaker, Hershey, and even Mars.

Mars is one of America's largest family-owned corporations. And as in any family, frictions sometimes arise. That was the case in 1991 when, following the retirement of Forrest Mars, Sr., the two sons running the company seemed to have fallen out.

I suggested to Helmut Maucher that he might approach Mr. Mars Sr., who was now retired and living in Las Vegas running a small candy company. They hit it off together and agreed in principle to move forward with a possible acquisition. The only problem was that the final vote came down to the family itself. The only way for the brothers to block the deal was to bury their differences and vote together to block it. That's exactly what they did.

On September 20, 1991, *The New York Times* reported:

> The Swiss food giant Nestlé S.A. said it was not in merger talks with Mars Inc., the American family-owned candy company, but it declined to deny reports that contacts had taken place. "There are no negotiations going on with Mars," a Nestlé spokesman said. But asked whether there had been other, less formal contacts, he said, "That is as far as I'm prepared to go."

Not all deals are consummated. But, especially as globalization accelerated in the '80s and '90s, clients like Nestlé always appreciated the chance to get the first bite at a possible acquisition target.

Redefining Nestlé's product and branding strategy

In 1992, Helmut Maucher put one of Nestlé's most ambitious and persistent executives in charge of global marketing.

Peter Brabeck had built his reputation as a trouble-shooter in Latin American markets such as Chile, Ecuador, and Venezuela. His willingness to take on the toughest assignments in times of political turmoil and labor unrest proved his mettle.

The marketing challenge Brabeck was given by Helmut Maucher was a daunting one. Nestlé had several thousand different brands, many developed specifically for local markets, and a lab-driven approach to developing new products.

Brabeck managed the Strategic Business Unit (SBU) structure that allowed the company to group all its products under the company's six global brands, including Nescafé, Nestea, and Nestlé. We worked with Brabeck to help Nestlé formalize a new set of global brand hierarchies and strategies that could be executed at the global, regional and local level. Meanwhile, we also worked with Nestlé to push the idea that new product concepts should be consumer-driven.

It sounds like a simple change. But for a big, successful company, truly listening to customers isn't always as easy as it sounds. For Nestlé, the scientific approach—and the idea that the company could develop new ways to improve consumers' lives—had been central to its corporate philosophy since the 1860s. Founder Henri Nestlé was a trained pharmacist who launched the company with a baby formula specifically created to address the problem of infant mortality.

In the 1990s, we, subtly but effectively, helped to adjust Nestlé's philosophy. The company became more responsive to customers around the world, while still maintaining its reputation for scientific leadership and product innovation.

Beyond product development, the notion that Nestlé's future efforts should be driven by the realities of consumer research, not just the possibilities created by science, opened up a new era in how the company viewed itself, its role in the global community, and its own global strategic initiatives.

Listening to consumers. It's a simple, but important lesson for every global company. Because no matter how big you get, no matter how much brainpower you employ, getting feedback from your customers never goes out of style.

Better nutrition leads to healthier growth

Peter Brabeck succeeded Helmut Maucher as Nestlé CEO in 1997. Born in Austria, Brabeck has always been an adventure-seeker—an avid pilot, helicopter skier, loyal Harley-Davidson enthusiast, and lifelong mountain climber.

He ran Nestlé with a sense of urgency—always looking to increase sales and market share—but also with respect for the company's traditions and a managed approach to risk.

Brabeck co-authored a company brochure about "The Nestlé spirit," communicating to employees such dictums as: "Nestlé is skeptical of short-term fads and self-appointed gurus," and the simple advice: "Nestlé people do not show off."

While he had a true sense of adventure, it was combined with the pragmatism and patience that made him an effective long-term business leader.

In 2000, he attempted to climb Switzerland's most famous and daunting mountain, the Matterhorn. Heavy snow turned him back. And even though he didn't feel his life was in danger, he said, "the risk was too high for the responsibility I have." Needless to say, the Nestlé board agreed with his decision.

Once again, Brabeck demonstrated his persistence. Two years later, at the age of 58, he went back and climbed all the way to the 14,492-foot summit.

Later, as CEO, he developed a corporate initiative for Nestlé built around a theme of—and commitment to—Nutrition.

The concept was simple. All of Nestlé's product lines were in some way connected to fueling or sustaining the body. Many products that Nestlé had developed and marketed over the years had distinct nutrition and health benefits. And Nestlé's products catered to all life stages—from formula for newborn babies to dietary supplements for elderly consumers.

As Brabeck looked for ways to accelerate growth, a focus on healthier products and additional health-oriented services offered a clear opportunity.

The strategy has proved so successful that Nestlé has established a separate division within the company and the Nutrition philosophy—summed up by the line "Good Food. Good Life"—flows through every product category, and to every corner of the world. It took time to implement but is the key corporate priority today.

In developing countries, providing access to fresh water has been a major part of the strategy. In a world where more than one billion people do not have access to fresh water, and more than 2.4 billion do not have access to sanitation, Nestlé has taken the lead in water management and distribution.

One example is the way Nestlé distributes the purified water that is created as a by-product in its instant coffee manufacturing towers. In markets where no clean water is readily available, this product has gone a long way to help reduce disease and provide a reliable supply of drinking water.

In the developed world, Nestlé promotes a full-range of nutrition-oriented products for people and their pets. The company also promotes consumer awareness of nutrition issues to help enhance the quality of people's lives all over the world.

By emphasizing Nutrition in these and other ways, Brabeck created a platform for Nestlé that enhanced its reputation for social responsibility and its ability to work more effectively with governments, communities, and consumer groups around the world.

How successful is Nestlé's Nutrition approach? Through 2007, Brabeck's last year as CEO, the company reported 12 straight years of organic growth exceeding 5-6%, in an industry used to 1-2% growth rates. Despite the global economic slowdown in 2008, Nestlé, under Chairman Peter Brabeck and new CEO Paul Bulcke, delivered profits of $16.6 billion and 8.3% organic growth on top of the previous year's milestone results.

Nestlé and Interpublic: How nourishing the relationship increased its longevity

1. **Aligning global agencies**: We put the clients' needs first—and didn't attempt a "land-grab."

2. **Enhancing U.S. operations**: We helped our Swiss-based client think and act like a major U.S. corporation.

3. **Consulting on acquisitions**: By presenting meaningful opportunities and facilitating conversations we demonstrated a commitment to Nestlé's broader business mission.

4. **Redefining brand strategies**: Our research and branding expertise helped simplify a complex branding challenge—and reinvent the new product development process.

5. **Developing global platforms**: Helping Nestlé respond to long-term opportunities.

Pulling the right levers for Unilever

Unilever is a global giant in foods, beverages, cleaning agents, and personal care products. For advertising, it works with two main holding companies: Interpublic and WPP. Within Interpublic, Unilever has been most connected over the years with the Lintas network, which began its life as "Lever International Advertising Services"—Lever Brothers' in-house agency.

Historically, and especially from the Unilever perspective, Lintas had a reputation for effective creative, not award-winning creative.

Frequently, Unilever's U.S. and U.K. offices appealed to the head office for the chance to work with local creative agencies. One year, we gave them the chance. We collaborated with Michael Dowdall, Worldwide Director and Coordinator of Household Products, to produce a special presentation for Unilever's worldwide category meeting in Florida. The presentation showed advertising from three "hot" creative agencies—one in the U.K., one in the U.S., and the third from a new agency no one had ever heard of.

Many of the Unilever managers expressed an interest in working with the third agency which, as you may have guessed, was revealed to be a reel of Lintas's non-Unilever work. The agency, it seemed, was capable of producing award-winning creative—but only when its clients allowed it to.

"Perhaps we're the problem," Dowdall told his Unilever colleagues. "Why don't we go back and give Lintas the opportunity to do this kind of work for us?"

We suggested to Dowdall that a lot of the best work Lintas had produced for Unilever was being "no'd to death" by cautious staffers lower down in the chain of command. If the national managers wanted to see better creative, they should be encouraged to get involved in the creative process a lot earlier.

This experience led us to work more closely with Unilever managers around the world ensuring they became more involved with—and invested in—their creative output.

We suggested an annual meeting at which the Chairman would sponsor creative awards in Unilever's four key categories. Within each category, both the agency and client were recognized in the areas of:

- Best New Product Launch
- Best Overall Creative Campaign
- Best Integrated Communications Program

In addition, an overall prize was given to the best campaign across the categories. The awards show was held each year in conjunction with a meeting between Unilever clients and top management at its agencies. Invariably, agency compensation became one of the big issues under discussion. Invariably, it was Interpublic—not WPP—that led the way in combating cuts.

How Maybelline became attractive to L'Oreal

In the early 1990s, SSC&B-Lintas, Maybelline's U.S. agency, was venturing more and more into the global cosmetics arena with its work for Unilever. It was an account conflict that could have caused the end of a beautiful relationship.

At the time, Maybelline was owned by the New York investment firm of Wasserstein Perella, which had acquired the brand from the Schering-Plough Corporation. I persuaded Bruce Wasserstein and his colleagues to keep Maybelline within the Interpublic family and move it to our new agency, Gotham.

As always, Wasserstein tried to drive a hard bargain. He wanted to invest ("at a reasonable price") in an equity stake in Gotham in exchange for keeping the business with us.

I pointed out that ownership of the agency by a client organization would make it more difficult to attract new clients, who might assume that Maybelline would always come first. It would be far better, I told him, to start investing in Interpublic, where the margins were just as good and the growth more predictable. He didn't take my advice, but we kept the account.

I knew that, eventually, Wasserstein would want to sell Maybelline, so I watched the situation closely. Soon after, I was able to let Lindsay Owen-Jones, the chairman of L'Oreal, know that the time might be right to make an approach.

Maybelline was an attractive target for L'Oreal. It was especially strong in the U.S. market, with an expertise in mascara and eye shadow, major product areas in which L'Oreal was not particularly strong. Plus, the addition of Maybelline would give L'Oreal more shelf space at retail and more clout in its negotiations with retailers.

Owen-Jones recognized the opportunity and could see clearly the benefits of expanding Maybelline products through his worldwide system. L'Oreal and Lancôme were brands that conveyed a French aura; adding Maybelline New York to the mix was a smart move at a time when American fashions and brands were becoming increasingly popular in the global marketplace.

As with all acquisitions due diligence, properly done, made a difference. It was obvious that the two management teams got on very well, which would ensure a smooth transition.

L'Oreal made an attractive offer to Wasserstein that he agreed to. Bruce, great negotiator that he was, engineered some last-minute interest from a German company that helped motivate L'Oreal to sweeten the bid slightly and close the deal.

Knowing both companies as I did, I was pretty sure that Maybelline management would click with the L'Oreal system. And that proved to be the case. Owen-Jones and the L'Oreal team proved so successful at expanding the Maybelline brand throughout the world that they recouped their investment within five years.

> **Bringing buyers and sellers together**
> 1. Understand both sides of the deal: Know what the seller wants to achieve—and how the buyer might unlock value through the acquisition.
> 2. **Make the necessary introductions**: Set up the meetings and suggest the reasons why both sides should work together on a proposal.
> 3. **Then get out of the way**: Let both players handle their own negotiations.

Make it your priority

How do you instill a client-centric philosophy throughout a global organization?

Clearly, one way is to create and share examples of how well the client-centric approach pays off in terms of:

- Account longevity
- Organic growth from existing clients
- Additional product assignments

The best way, however, is to make client-centric behavior a component of your forward-planning process.

At Interpublic, we made focusing on the needs of clients a formal part of our annual forecasting meetings.

Agency leaders were required to put in writing specific new client initiatives they would undertake in the year-ahead. And the success in executing these goals—in areas not just related to advertising—became an element in executive compensation.

The goal was to encourage Interpublic people to go "above and beyond" for their clients at every level of the organization.

How did that play out?

On the one-to-one level, agency people got involved with helping local clients as they wrote and designed their own internal presentations and speeches.

On the agency business-planning level, we set measurable targets for specific "out-of-the-box" initiatives, like developing four new sales promotion ideas for existing local clients.

And on the senior executive level—both at the holding company and at the agencies—we created personal objectives to encourage and reward meaningful consultative work on behalf of Interpublic clients.

—————————

CHAPTER TEN

Expand Wisely

How to grow a global business organically and through acquisitions

"Never invest in a business you cannot understand."

—Warren Buffett

Growth opportunities

WHATEVER THE MARKET conditions, there are always opportunities to grow your business.

No one has taught me that more than Warren Buffett.

Consider this scenario from the recent past: The stock market was down 40%. The economy was slumping. The president's reputation was at an all-time low. And Warren Buffett went bargain hunting.

While it may sound a lot like 2008 (when Buffett took big stakes in GE and Goldman Sachs), the year I'm talking about is 1974.

That was when Warren Buffett started buying Interpublic stock, quickly establishing himself as the company's largest outside investor, with a stake of more than 15%. He also took a big position in the independently held Ogilvy & Mather, increasing his investments in both over time.

In buying advertising stocks, Buffett seized on an opportunity to invest in companies whose prices were temporarily depressed, but which offered reliable cash flow, sound growth prospects, and excellent potential for long-term return on investment.

At the time, Buffett was tracking at least seven major agencies. But he chose Interpublic and Ogilvy because he liked not only the valuations, but also the people—namely, Paul Foley and Bill Phillips—running the companies.

With Buffett, trust was and is a major factor in his investment philosophy. I saw that first-hand when in 1982 we were closing our deal to take 100% ownership of SSC&B:Lintas Worldwide.

We ran into a problem in West Germany, which had some of the strictest anti-trust laws in Europe. Interpublic already owned McCann-Erickson and Troost, which were both strong in the market. With Buffett's investment in Ogilvy, the West German Monopolies Commission objected to the deal, arguing that the Lintas acquisition would give the combination of Interpublic plus Ogilvy too high a concentration of the international ad business in West Germany. Their position was that Interpublic and Ogilvy would together control 40% of the international advertising market. And Warren Buffett, who now owned more than 20% of Ogilvy and Interpublic combined, would have what they saw as a controlling interest, creating a problem with their anti-trust law.

I was traveled out to Omaha to discuss the problem with Buffett.

In all my business travels, the offices we entered were the furthest thing from Madison Avenue I had ever seen. Throw rugs only partially covered the linoleum floors. The mismatched furniture looked like it had seen better days. (Buffett later acquired an office furniture company and a rug company, leading to a significant upgrade of his facilities.)

I noticed there weren't many people working in Buffett's head office, either. That's something I tried to emulate at Interpublic. At both companies, this emphasis on keeping corporate overhead low was maintained during my tenure.

We outlined the antitrust problem to Buffett and he surprised me with his response.

"I'll put my stock in escrow and have you vote it," he said.

I was stunned, but we took his suggestion back with us.

In the end, we were able to overcome the Commission's objections with a different argument. We convinced them that when the entire German advertising market was measured (including retail and other local accounts), Interpublic and Ogilvy would only control 10-12% of the market, which would be under the allowable 20% ownership threshold. That argument was good enough to win approval of our Lintas acquisition.

Still, giving up voting control of his stock was an unusual demonstration of trust, and it said a lot with respect to Warren Buffett. For the "Oracle of Omaha," investing in companies also means investing in people. It's not just about money. It's about trusting in the relationship and believing in the way management runs its business.

Time and again, in all of the acquisition work we did at Interpublic, I found that the one key element in negotiations is building trust with the potential acquisition partner. The man that taught me this through example was Warren Buffett.

The Oracle in action

Two years later, Buffett informed me he was going to take his profits on Interpublic, which had grown 900%. He had just bought a Buffalo newspaper and a stake in *The Washington Post*.

In selling his shares, Buffett told me he would do it over a six-month period, selling into our highs, so as not to cause problems for our stock. He also indicated that if we had shareholders who wanted to purchase his shares directly and quietly he would be happy to oblige.

Buffett was also, as it turned out, about to make a major investment in Cap Cities, run by one of the best managers, not only in the media business but in any business, Tom Murphy, with his partner, Dan Burke. The following year, with Buffett's backing, Cap Cities acquired ABC to become Cap Cities/ABC, a company sold to Disney for $19 billion in 1995. (Despite the success of his Cap Cities investment, Buffett told me at a wedding in Atlanta in the 1990s that he would have made more money if he had kept his money in IPG.)

Another interesting conversation I had with Warren Buffett concerned the issue of goodwill in the package foods business. For the purposes of our discussion, we used General Foods as our "hypothetical example." He said that if you looked at the diversity of General Foods' business it was hard to put a value on the goodwill of the company.

I explained to him that the company's coffee business (Maxwell House), because it was driven primarily by highly variable commodity pricing, could not command the same value as other General Foods brands. But in its other categories, General Foods brands like Cool Whip, Jello and Kool-Aid had better margins and more price stability.

I should have been paying more attention to Buffett's "hypothetical" situation. Shortly after our conversation, he began acquiring shares of General Foods, much to the disdain of many Wall Street hotshots. He eventually acquired 4 million shares at an average price of $37 per share, which netted him a tidy profit when Philip Morris swooped in to buy the company in 1985 for $120 per share.

Looking back on those conversations with Buffett, I realize he was probing me for more than just a financial assessment. We knew the food business, its various categories and all the major players. In evaluating General Foods, Buffett also probed for clues as to the quality and style of company management.

When he makes up his mind about a company, Buffett is usually right. At the time of his Interpublic investment, he let it be known he was not a fan of employee stock options, which Interpublic used. But beyond that he was a patient and supportive investor. The trust he puts into a company's management, combined with his long-term focus, makes him a great person to have as a large minority shareholder.

What Warren Buffett taught me about investing

1. **Establish trust**: It's the single most important factor. If you're not comfortable with the people running the company, be willing to say no to the investment.

2. **Find value**: Look for quality companies that are currently undervalued but offer reliable cash flow and solid long-term prospects.

3. **Understand the business**: Don't invest in companies whose business and prospects you can't explain in plain English.

4. **Think long-term**: When it comes to value investing, patience is a virtue that's often rewarded.

   Attack business and revenue problems with urgency. But when you've planted seeds, give them time to grow.

How to deliver consistent growth

Throughout the '80s and '90s, Interpublic delivered continued growth through a combination of organic growth and acquisitions. By the time of my retirement in 2000, the company had 650 offices in 127 countries and revenues of $5.6 billion. Over the course of two successful decades, Interpublic stock delivered a 22% compound growth rate, a performance that had even Warren Buffett admitting he sold too soon.

The ability to win new business was crucial to our overall success. But as we looked to deliver consistency, our strategies for growth focused on seven basic areas:

Three Keys to Organic Growth

1. **Winning new business from existing clients**: The most profitable internal growth comes from developing existing clients. At Interpublic, our client-centric focus helped us win additional assignments by demonstrating a commitment to the client's business that went above-and-beyond the day-to-day assignment.
2. **Delivering "local-to-global" growth**: Interpublic's global networks made it easy to expand local successes into other international markets. While successful U.S. campaigns were often exported overseas, we also championed successful campaigns from smaller markets and looked to grow those successes efficiently and effectively for our clients.
3. **Expanding through integrated services**: As global clients began demanding total marketing solutions for their brands, our agencies' abilities to offer coordinated direct marketing, sales promotions, public relations and digital solutions became a source of productive and profitable growth.

Four Factors that Drive Acquisitions

1. **Building on strength**: In any business, when your share of market is strong in a particular category, you can grow faster and with less cost through acquisitions that build on that strength. For example, a global agency with a strong knowledge base in package goods is well-positioned to acquire local agencies with a similar profile in their home markets.

2. **Remedying a weakness**: Within a global network, it's always possible for a local office to suffer setbacks through account losses or personnel defections. At such times, the scale of the holding company makes it possible to buy the right local agency and merge it with your current operation to re-establish a strong presence in the market.
3. **Expanding the footprint**: As the advertising industry globalized and clients expanded their operations into developing nations, acquisitions that filled out gaps in our geographic coverage offered a key area of growth.
4. **Investing in innovation**: In a creative industry, it's important to anticipate and respond to changes in consumer behavior. At Interpublic, we invested in companies at the cutting edge of media and technological innovation, offering clients new ways to maintain their own competitive advantage.

How to approach acquisitions

By the mid '80s, Interpublic owned three worldwide agencies—McCann-Erickson, Lintas and Lowe—each with a different set of growth priorities.

The challenge for each of our agencies was to expand both geographically and in the breadth of marketing services offered.

Global marketing was no longer just about advertising. Direct marketing, sales promotion and public relations were all part of the mix and these "below-the-line" disciplines were growing faster than paid media advertising.

On the client side, the buzzword was "global communications strategy"—as brands from all over the world began competing head to head for awareness, shelf space and market share.

Global clients were looking to work with agencies that could seamlessly integrate their branding efforts on a worldwide basis.

Interpublic had, of course, pioneered the concept of "total marketing communications" back in the 1960s. In those days, it had centralized many of these non-advertising services at the holding-company level and failed. Twenty years later, as the pace of globalization accelerated, it was clear that each of our agencies needed to offer clients its own version of the complete "global communications" package.

- *McCann-Erickson* was in the process of becoming the number one global agency. McCann worked for leading global clients in every major category and was looking to build its local client base in every market. The challenges for McCann were to: 1) Continue expanding into the developing world; 2) Expand the range of integrated services the agency offered.

- *Lintas*, with its package goods focus, had already expanded alongside its major client Unilever into most of the world's developing markets. The challenge here was to broaden its client base and develop parallel worldwide systems within the agency to offer the full range of integrated services.

- *Lowe*, our newest network, needed to expand geographically beyond the top 10 international markets. As our most creatively positioned network, Lowe also needed to find ways to add integrated marketing services through acquisitions, but without eroding its creative reputation.

Strategically, the challenge for each agency network was to develop worldwide systems for each major marketing discipline, creating fully integrated marketing services offering under the agency's own brand.

By owning and operating its own subsidiary agencies, each of our networks would be able to compete for a client's "global communications" budget.

Meanwhile, each subsidiary agency, such as McCann Direct (now MRM), would also be able to pitch for local and global budgets allocated to their particular discipline.

In executing this strategy, Interpublic's main role was to provide the criteria for acquisitions, plus the administrative and financial services that would take a load off the managers at the agencies.

The goals for Interpublic's agency networks

1. **Go global**: Expand through careful acquisitions into new and developing markets.

2. **Expand integrated offerings**: Develop worldwide capabilities in direct marketing, public relations and sales promotion (digital and healthcare agencies would be added later).

3. **Remain client-centric**: Focus on the services clients need now—don't get too far "out of the box" (for those examples, see Chapter Twelve).

Managing the acquisition process

In the late '80s and early '90s, Interpublic's acquisition efforts were focused mainly on expanding our three global, multidimensional agency networks.

As we went about acquiring local agencies and expanding our service offerings, we faced new and fierce competition from holding company rivals such as WPP and Omnicom.

Finding the right acquisition targets was only the first step. Speed was also important. We devised a simple two-stage system to communicate the criteria and manage the acquisition process. At each stage, relevant information was gathered for review and quick approval.

Stage One: Following initial discussions with the management of the company being considered, our agency managers would present Interpublic with a document that included:

i) The strategic rationale for the acquisition

ii) An analysis of the acquired company's position in its market relevant to its competitive set

iii) Background on the career histories of company management (especially important in cases where start-up agencies were being acquired)

iv) Financial data, including revenues and profits for the past three years, five-year forward projections, and the full balance sheet for the prior year.

This documentation would allow Interpublic management to make a quick go/no-go decision in regard to further negotiations—as well as to set the parameters for those discussions.

Stage Two: After final negotiations and the completion of due diligence by the agency's CEO and management team, the final acquisition document was sent to the Interpublic finance committee for approval. This included all documentation from Stage One, plus:

i) Complete financial terms of the deal

ii) Details of management incentive plans and deferred bonuses

iii) A comprehensive management capability and succession plan

On the financial side, our rule was to use Interpublic stock wherever possible to finance each deal. Our stock had a good track record (a history of growing at least 15-20% per year), plus it offered a tax-free exchange for the seller. For Interpublic, stock transactions meant that we did not have to carry goodwill that would need to be amortized on our balance sheet, negatively affecting our earnings. If anything was important to Interpublic, it was the need to maintain a strong balance sheet. By demonstrating consistent investment returns, we were able to provide the leverage of IPG stock as our global agencies sought to expand their operations. As Interpublic CEO, I was frequently asked by the agencies to open doors for them and to sell the benefits of stock transactions to the management of companies we wished to acquire.

In an acquisition, the devil is always in the details, especially when you are making agreements with the owners of a business. Some owners want to stay on. Others want to cash out and retire early. The details of cash vs. stock incentives have to be negotiated with owners and key individuals. Frequently, cash and/or stock incentives have to be pushed down to lower levels in the acquired company.

In addition to these details, our plans also took into account what might happen after the acquisition. Incentives were built into our agreements to ensure that succession plans were put in place. Sometimes we deferred certain payments for 12 months to ensure that a satisfactory succession plan was in place.

Management successions and business continuity are always a major area of concern, particularly when private companies are being purchased. This is all part of the due diligence process and must be monitored closely. (Unfortunately, this is one of the areas in which Interpublic became lax on its follow-through after 2000.)

The holding company role in agency acquisitions

1. **Establish criteria**: Define the requirements for an agency's acquisition targets to ensure they offer the right scale and strategic fit.

2. **Review and approve deals**: Create standardized documentation requirements to allow for a clear, quick approval process.

3. **Ensure continuity**: Make sure necessary follow-up takes place after the acquisition, especially in terms of audits and management succession plans.

4. **Integrate systems**: Assure that acquired companies migrate in a timely manner to corporate systems for IT, accounting, employee benefits, etc.

How did it work in practice?

Just like at Warren Buffett's Berkshire Hathaway headquarters, Interpublic was run by a small, close-knit team. Our number one rule was that the holding company should focus on efficiency and effectiveness. We did not take on any tasks that belonged at—or could be performed better by—our agencies.

We kept lines of communication short. Agency heads reported directly to me as Chairman and CEO of the company. Agency financial directors had a strong dotted line into my CFO Gene Beard.

During acquisition work, all Stage One and Stage Two documents came directly to a financial coordinator inside Interpublic who made sure that the numbers were checked internally by our Accounting and Treasury departments.

After that, the documents came directly to me and Gene for quick approval or review prior to submission to the board.

In many cases, acquisition work comes down to the wire. Competing bids create situations that call for quick decisions. At Interpublic, where acquisitions above $10 million required board approval, we had a special agreement in place to accommodate the realities of fast-moving negotiations.

As CEO of Interpublic, I was authorized to review any negotiated revisions to board-approved deals with the Chairman of the Finance Committee, who was an outside board member. In situations that required a response in 24 hours or less, this option ensured that we were not shut out of any deals because of time issues and the inability to convene a full board meeting or conference call.

Our system allowed for quicker review and decision-making than most of our competitors and there were times when that made a real difference. At the same time, we made sure that checks and balances were in place in the key areas of due diligence and internal auditing. As part of our due diligence, the CEO of the Interpublic agency involved met with the principals of the acquired company, and his management team was responsible for conducting and signing off on the documents related to the acquisition. Our internal audit department automatically reviewed the financial details of the stage documents and visited the agencies where appropriate. This included direct talks with the auditors of the acquired company if necessary. For larger acquisitions,

Price Waterhouse, Interpublic's auditor, also reviewed the financial details.

It's important to note that while we encouraged our agency heads to bring forward the best strategic acquisitions in their markets, the deals themselves had no impact on managers' compensation in the year in which they were made. Agency managers were not allowed to use acquisitions to "buy earnings" or make up shortfalls in their own business estimates for the current year.

Simply put, our policy was: "No deals to make the numbers." Acquisitions were intended to improve our overall business in the local market. From a compensation and bonus perspective, the acquisition was not factored into performance targets until the next fiscal year.

> **Keys to completing successful acquisitions**
> 1. **Enable speed**: Create systems and decision-making processes that allow you to respond quickly to opportunities.
> 2. **Ensure due diligence**: Make sure that all financial statements and business plans are fully reviewed and approved by the relevant departments.
> 3. **Be ready to negotiate**: When things come down to the wire, you need the ability to act fast to close the deal.

Some deals took us from strength to strength...others helped fix a problem

One of the key factors we emphasized with local agency management was that success breeds success.

It's far easier to make good acquisitions and be instantly acceptable to a target company when you are perceived as being a powerful and growing player in the market.

Many of our best "below-the-line" acquisitions were made easier because of the established presence and consistent organic growth demonstrated by the local offices of our global advertising agencies.

At other times, though, an agency might stumble in a particular market. Maybe it loses several accounts over a period of time. Perhaps key personnel have been lured away. Or maybe the agency is simply lagging behind its local competitors in terms of new business wins.

In these situations, the global strength of a holding company can help remedy the situation.

In the case of Lintas, a joint venture partnership with Hakuhodo, the number two Japanese agency, helped solve problems for the agency in Japan, while benefiting Hakuhodo in New York. Hakuhodo already had a partnership with McCann-Erickson in Japan. The 1987 Hakuhodo-Lintas deal helped improve our ability to service Unilever's extensive business in Japan. At the same time, though we controlled the joint venture, its restrictive terms meant we could not aggressively pursue local business, limiting our future growth. Still, the partnership served its purpose for many years.

Another example was Dailey International, which we acquired in 1983. Dailey had a strong presence in Los Angeles as well as offices in Hong Kong, Singapore and Australia. Dailey kept its own identity, but the acquisition allowed us to establish Dailey as the Asia-Pacific affiliate of the expanding Lowe system.

A third example was the London office of Lintas, which by 1989 was suffering from a loss of key people. We merged that office with the four-year-old agency Still, Price, Court, Twivy and D'Souza, which immediately re-established Lintas as the 10th largest agency in the highly competitive British market. Interestingly, our deal with agency chairman Chris Still thwarted Allen Rosenshine's efforts to acquire the agency for BBDO Worldwide.

Merging package goods with creative purists

One of our least successful attempts to revive a major agency happened in New York in 1994.

Lintas was again suffering—having recently lost the Diet Coke and IBM PC accounts—and was widely seen as being in a slump and lacking in the creativity needed to grow its business.

We acquired Ammirati & Puris, one of New York's most outstanding and principled creative agencies. The owners, art director Ralph Ammirati and copywriter Martin Puris, had already balked at one set of corporate owners, buying their agency back from Omnicom in 1990.

By 1994, though, they were ready to sell again, and the combination looked attractive for both creative and business reasons. In addition to the creative strengths Ammirati & Puris offered, their client roster complemented Lintas' own lineup: A&P handled MasterCard in the U.S., while Lintas handled the account in Europe. Both agencies handled business for Aetna.

Ammirati himself was very meticulous – known for checking to make sure that the cleaning person in his office hadn't moved his desk even a quarter of an inch.

Meanwhile, Puris, who became chairman of the new agency, was suddenly thrust into a new and challenging role as head of a worldwide agency.

In the past, Ammirati & Puris would rather lose accounts like BMW— which it handled from 1975 to 1991 and promoted as "The Ultimate Driving Machine"—than compromise its creative integrity.

We thought that transplanting this prestigious New York shop onto the global package goods agency of Lintas would create a powerful new system, combining creative leadership with international expertise.

But as Ralph Ammirati later said, the creation of Ammirati Puris Lintas was more like a "collision" than a merger.

Most of the leadership at the new Ammirati Puris Lintas agency came from the Ammirati & Puris side. Their attitude sometimes didn't sit well with Lintas clients such as Johnson & Johnson.

At my urging, Ralph Larsen, the Chairman of Johnson & Johnson, had become involved in annual reviews of advertising agencies. He pointed out to me that Martin Puris was pushing aggressively for creative overhauls of J&J's work. While he agreed that improvements were needed, Larsen wanted me to know that, in his company at least, radical changes couldn't happen overnight.

I let Martin Puris know that he needed to show a little more patience and a better understanding of how his more traditional accounts operated. He adjusted his approach, but he was not always comfortable with the need to compromise.

In addition, as CEO of Ammirati Puris Lintas, Martin was expected to travel extensively and be very involved in the agency's global operations. This was not how he enjoyed spending his time. His real strength—and his passion—was in talking to top clients about great creative advertising.

I knew the agency needed to be managed better operationally. I recommended to Martin that he put in place a COO, preferably someone from the international side of the agency, who could handle the necessary travel and help him run the global network.

Martin disagreed. His CFO pushed for the COO job and Martin wanted to give him the position. This caused an impasse between Martin and myself and the position went unfilled. Despite this, the agency did well for three or four years, but then problems began to arise again.

In retrospect, for Martin's sake, I should have forced the issue. By 1999, the situation had deteriorated to that point that we were forced to take bolder action.

When Martin Puris decided he wanted to retire, we moved forward with a major internal merger that reshaped the company and had a big impact on the advertising business. We combined two of our global networks: Ammirati Puris Lintas and Lowe & Partners Worldwide to create Lowe Lintas & Partners Worldwide. Frank Lowe became chairman and CEO of the new network.

At its creation, Lowe Lintas & Partners Worldwide had offices in 80 countries and billings of more than $11 billion. It immediately became the world's fourth largest agency network.

By 1997, this kind of scale was important. To win major global clients, an agency had to rank among the top 10 to be part of the consideration set. Being in the top 5 signaled to clients that an agency had the resources to be truly effective and responsive on a worldwide basis. Prior to the merger, Ammirati Puris Lintas was drifting toward the bottom of the top 10; Lowe & Partners ranked in the low teens.

But beyond the sheer scale of this merger, we thought it would work because the agencies were opposites, complementing each other on a worldwide basis. Lintas and its people needed better creative support. Lowe needed better international coverage and package goods disciplines. The combination was well received by employees, the business press, and clients, particularly Unilever.

But once again, personalities intervened. Frank Lowe had a problem working with an agency system he felt was beneath him. Which would have been fine, if he hadn't let everyone in the agency know it.

How to prevent a merger from becoming a "collision"

1. **Recognize the difficulties of combining different cultures**: When two cultures combine, understand which culture you want to predominate—and why.

2. **Evaluate leadership strengths and weaknesses**: Create a structure that allows leaders to play to their strengths—and ensure that the right management team is in place to deliver appropriate support.

3. **Make the right adjustments**: When problems arise, address them. Don't let the Peter Principle come into play.

The first change in acquisition strategy

By the early 1990s, the "new breed" of independent creative agencies had become firmly established in the U.S. market. Some of these independent agencies, such as the Nike "Just do it" agency Wieden and Kennedy (now known as W+K) are still independent. Others have been acquired by Interpublic competitors, including the Publicis-owned Fallon Worldwide, and Omnicom's Goodby Silverstein & Partners.

But several of the best independents of the 1980s and 1990s are now part of Interpublic, including such successful agencies as Carmichael Lynch, Deutsch, Hill Holliday, The Martin Agency, and Mullen.

Many people see Interpublic's pursuit of these independent creative agencies as just another way for us to leverage our growth and profits—what some call a roll-up.

The facts are a little different. In reality, we made a key strategic decision in the early 1990s to respond to the changing marketplace. It was a decision driven in part by Lintas' work with the Unilever client I mentioned in the last chapter, Michael Dowdall.

What we learned from Michael Dowdall at Unilever and subsequent conversations with other clients was that there was a growing desire inside global corporations to work with the hottest creative shops, even if it meant taking assignments—particularly new product launches—away from a major global agency.

The situation was similar to what I had observed with local clients in the U.K. in the 1970s. But within U.S.-based multinationals, it was a new and growing phenomenon.

At Interpublic, we realized that even though we had three global systems available to clients and great ways to offer alternative creative options within the holding company. We needed to position ourselves to succeed in this changed environment.

Looking at the situation, we made two important strategic assessments:

First, while we saw that big clients wanted to work with the most dynamic and attention-getting creative agencies in the business, we also knew they would be most comfortable if those agencies were financially stable and could grow with them, especially internationally.

Second, for the agencies themselves, we saw that creating great work for a client in the U.S. would not necessarily protect them when the client expanded that product internationally. If the client did assign an international network overseas, the U.S. business would always be at risk.

We realized we could position Interpublic most successfully by owning both the creative agencies that were being asked to handle new product launches and the global agencies that could take those products around the world.

We had a chance to test this new acquisition strategy when we acquired the great New York agency Scali McCabe Sloves in 1993, along with its subsidiary, The Martin Agency of Richmond, Virginia.

We merged the Scali agency with the New York office of Lowe to create an even stronger operation, Lowe/SMS.

Meanwhile, we left The Martin Agency alone. It didn't merge with any of our global networks. Instead, it reported directly to Interpublic, while gaining access as needed to the international support system of Lowe.

The continued success of The Martin Agency encouraged us to expand our new "creative independent" strategy. Interestingly, many of these agencies operated on a media-agnostic, fee-based approach, which allowed them to plan creative campaigns without regard to losing revenue based on how the work was executed. This concept, which was similar to what I had put in place in London 25 years previously, became very popular in the late 1990s and beyond.

We bought Minneapolis-based Campbell Mithun and connected it with McCann-Erickson Worldwide. Campbell Mithun worked with General Mills in the U.S., while McCann worked internationally on Nestlé's and

General Mills' joint venture brands. Now, they were able to coordinate and build that important relationship on a worldwide basis.

When we acquired Avrett, Free and Ginsberg, the renowned New York agency was handling Ralston-Purina pet foods. Those brands competed with the Nestlé pet foods handled by Dailey and McCann-Erickson in Los Angeles. But the holding company model allowed the three agencies to compete. Dailey was aligned with the Lowe network and, when Nestlé bought Ralston-Purina, Avrett was able to coordinate internationally with McCann, who handled the pet foods business overseas.

With one acquisition we deviated from our "creative independent" strategy to purchase a local agency for a straightforward business objective. Fahlgren & Swink was not known for its creativity, but it did have a major portion of McDonald's retail business across numerous Midwestern markets. We had an agency in Boston that had another piece of the McDonald's account, and we combined the agencies under the Fahlgren name. The idea was that we could move forward from that base to go after the whole McDonald's account. Smoot Fahlgren, the agency head, was a unique character, and he had a great relationship with McDonald's management. Smoot was making real progress with the client, who was having some creative problems with his agency. We thought we had a shot at winning a big piece of the business.

Then, lo and behold, Ammirati Puris Lintas won the Burger King account. No matter how much we tried to convince McDonald's management that the agencies were separate, it just didn't work. Reluctantly, we worked out an arrangement to sell the Fahlgren agency back to its management.

We were more successful with the acquisition of Minneapolis-based Carmichael Lynch and Boston's Hill Holliday.

Carmichael Lynch was one of the Midwest's hottest agencies, doing great work for Northwest Airlines and Harley-Davidson, a creative person's dream account. Carmichael Lynch plugged into Lowe's international system and enjoyed continued success.

In buying Hill, Holliday, Connors, Cosmopulos (now simply Hill Holliday), we got to work with that smart Irish lad, Jack Connors. The agency had reached a size where it was at risk of becoming a victim of its own success. It was doing great work for major clients, such as Price Waterhouse, which Ammirati Puris Lintas handled overseas. At the time, Price Waterhouse was building its consulting business and was a major global spender. Hill Holliday needed a better way to serve its clients on a global basis. The ability to plug into the global systems of Interpublic was a key selling point, and Ammirati Puris Lintas became the agency's international network.

Twice we offered Jack Connors the chance to run Ammirati Puris Lintas U.S. out of New York and twice he turned us down. He always was a great businessman and a smart negotiator. We bought his company for $150 million and it paid out in four years. One of the interesting parts of the Hill Holiday reason for purchase was its expertise in pharmaceutical event services. This was an unusual area of specialization, which none of our competitors was in at the time. It was a small operation, but it grew nicely over a couple of years. Jack then informed us that the company's managers wanted to buy fifty-one percent of the company back from Interpublic and resume control or leave. The mistake was they were specialists and were not under contract. Jack convinced Gene Beard, our CFO, to allow the buyback. It was valued at $5.5 million but we sold for $9.5 million.

Now Gene Beard and I were sharp, but not quite as sharp as Jack Connors. Jack next convinced us, by reminding us that Interpublic's policy was not to hold a minority, particularly in such a small operation; he offered to take the remaining forty-nine percent off our hands at a reasonable multiple by helping to place it.

We agreed to that deal, too. By that time, the business was worth about $30 million. The profit seemed very worthwhile, especially since others were coming into the field. Five years later, Jack sold the whole company for over $200 million to Bain Capital. In hindsight, we were too early and not smart enough. I've never known any manager at an acquired agency to be as grateful as Jack. He's the only one who ever called me to say "thank you" at Christmas.

One of the last acquisitions I was involved in was Interpublic's November 2000 purchase of America's largest independent agency, Deutsch.

I met Donny Deutsch at a 4A's convention. His agency had quadrupled in size over a three-year period. Now, like many independent agency chiefs before him, he realized the risks associated with being a large U.S. agency without an international outlet for the future.

Donny was unbelievably charming and a great presenter. He later became even more well-known as the host of "The Big Idea" on CNBC. (Though when he mentioned he was interested in dating my daughter Jody, thinking he was kidding, I told him *that* wasn't such a good idea. I suggested he stay focused on building the business.)

In acquiring his agency, I pushed hard to ensure that he give a certain percentage of his business to his people.

After due diligence was completed on both sides, the deal was finally completed in November 2000, one month before I handed over the Interpublic reins to John Dooner.

Like many deals, Donny's was heavily tied to Interpublic stock. I saw him after my retirement, and he expressed some disappointment that we hadn't met our full-year forecasts and the stock was down, along with many others in 2001.

I explained all the moving pieces that went into the budget estimates we made and how currency changes and client December spending delays, of which he was well aware, could affect the final numbers.

"We didn't miss by much," I reminded him.

Later, I was surprised to learn that Donny went to Dooner and convinced him he should have an adjustment. The board allowed it, though why they did I'll never understand. Donny would never have gotten it out of me.

Still, the Deutsch deal has done very well for Interpublic, paying back the investment in less than the five years that we projected. And Donny has moved on to a lucrative showbiz career.

The benefits of bringing creative agencies into the fold

1. **Creative options for clients**: When global clients began putting a greater emphasis on cutting-edge creative work, we adjusted our acquisition strategy accordingly.

2. **International connections for agencies**: The agencies we acquired retained their independence—but plugged into our successful global networks.

3. **Independent positioning and financial security**: These agencies benefited from the agency systems of the holding company—and reported directly to Interpublic, which protected their creative independence.

Investing in innovation

By the late 1980s, we realized the growing importance of TV programming to our clients' global communications strategies. An association with an appropriate show not only reinforces a brand's connection with its target audience, it also gives clients a comfort level about the quality level and suitability of the programming that surrounds their message.

The emphasis on programming has accelerated dramatically in the new millennium, where product placements are common in network shows such as "Heroes," and major brands are routinely integrated into popular reality shows.

Interpublic saw the trend early. We negotiated the international rights to "Wheel of Fortune" and "Jeopardy," two of King World's most successful U.S. game shows.

Our Initiative Media subsidiary developed production and distribution deals with broadcasters around the world. By themselves, these were good deals. The production costs on the shows were low. We earned an immediate and substantial markup.

But that was only half of it.

Initiative also worked with Lintas Worldwide to package the shows on behalf of our Unilever client. Because Unilever was able to make a long-term commitment to the shows, they enjoyed a discount of 25-35% on their advertising buys. Unilever's agreement gave them an "ownership" position in terms of product placement and advertising, with a portion of the advertising inventory sold to local, non-competitive clients.

The shows were wildly popular, becoming night-time ratings leaders in many markets. Unilever was delighted. They were enjoying tremendous exposure and advertising efficiencies in consistently formatted (no-risk) programming. And Interpublic's first foray into TV programming was an immediate success.

Building on this success, we then acquired Fremantle International in 1989 for $16 million. Fremantle had the international rights to the proven game show formats created by Mark Goodson Productions, such as "Family Feud," "Let's Make a Deal," "The Price is Right" and "The Newlywed Game."

Again, the shows proved to be big hits in Europe and other markets, which needed content at a time when European governments were privatizing the national networks. Again, Initiative and Lintas were able to package the shows for Unilever to create a powerful advertising showcase for the client's brands.

The game show phenomenon truly went global in the late '80s and early '90s. And many of these shows are still popular today. But all shows have a life cycle, whether they are drama, sitcoms, reality or game shows.

By 1994, we saw that our programs, which had begun to plateau in the U.S. market were also leveling off internationally. We decided to sell Fremantle International to All American Communications for $63 million in cash and stock, while taking a 20% stake in All American.

Later, they took the company public and we sold our remaining stock, earning a total profit of around $100 million on our initial investment. We had been on the leading edge of this new phase of advertiser-sponsored programming innovation and we used the proceeds to continue investing in new and innovative areas. Hollywood didn't always deliver the desired results. I'll discuss some of our less successful experiences, including our dealings with Mike Ovitz, in Chapter Twelve.

Investing in innovation doesn't always guarantee success. But when it works, you can really strike it rich.

Why investing in game shows worked—for Unilever and Interpublic

1. **We knew how to make a deal**: Having taken U.S. brands around the world, we knew the international TV world—and what consumers would respond to on a programming basis.

2. **The price was right**: Interpublic was able to make a profit on production and distribution costs even before we made the show; Unilever enjoyed extraordinary media exposure and advertising efficiencies.

3. **It was time to strike it rich**: As European governments were privatizing television networks, there was a quantum increase in the demand for proven programming content.

4. **You can't win unless you spin the wheel**: You never know exactly what will happen with an investment—even in an adjacent business you understand well. But this one paid off big.

With President George H. W. Bush at a White House dinner.

As chairman of the Ad Council, the author introduces President Clinton at a press conference endorsing the goals of the program.

Rupert Murdoch, Chairman of NewsCorp, Helmut Maucher, Chairman of Nestlé, the author, and Edward Horrigan, Vice Chairman of R.J. Reynolds at a n industry discussion.

First Lady Hillary Clinton, Faith Geier, and John Stafford, Chairman of Wyeth at a United Cerebral Palsy event.

On her visit to the U.S., Princess Diana spotted two former Sloane Rangers from London.

Albert Bellas, chairman of the American School of Ballet, honors the dancer of the year and the "business dancer of the year," who are joined by Christopher Plummer and Larry Bossidy, who chaired the event.

Talking with former Defense Secretary Casper Weinberger at the Interpublic Management Meeting "Toward 2000" in March 1989.

Treaury Secretary Larry Summers and Phil Geier (joined by Faith Geier) being honored for their work in government and business at Columbia Business School.

Faith and I celebrate with John Glenn on the anniversary of his historic, earth-orbiting Friendship 7 flight.

Kissinger and author discussing agency expansion in the Middle East.

Live from Sun Valley on CNBC.

Gene Beard, Retired C.F.O. and partner with author.

CHAPTER ELEVEN

Encourage Cooperation and Reward Success

*How to motivate managers, benefit clients
and propel overall performance*

"In motivating people, you've got to engage their minds and their hearts."
—*Rupert Murdoch*

Employing talent

TIMES ARE TOUGH. Unemployment is rising. We're living in an era of diminished expectations.

And people are still your most important asset.

Even if the global economic crisis has forced your employees to reappraise their short- and long-term career prospects, that doesn't mean you, as corporate leader, can take them for granted.

In fact, a recession makes it even more important for you to find the right ways to manage and motivate your people.

By engaging the minds and the hearts of your people you will help ensure the right ideas are executed most effectively. By offering the right incentive and training programs you will keep employees focused on the individual performance goals that contribute to overall results. By encouraging innovation and rewarding cooperation you will promote exceptional performance for clients and shareholders.

In this chapter, I'll outline six principles for motivating people and improving performance—principles that can be applied equally well in a recession as a recovery.

1. Set measurable goals—and track them

You may not be handing out big raises right now, but remember this: Most employees care as much about job satisfaction, the environment they work in, and the people they get to work with as they do about money. They also like to be told how well they are doing and what doors may be opening to them in the future.

Maintaining a corporate commitment to individual career development is especially important during a downturn. An annual performance review process gives each employee the opportunity to sit down with his manager and discuss in a constructive manner the successes of the past year and the areas that need to be worked on in the year ahead.

The performance management process should be designed to:

- Review performance
- Set new goals
- Identify strengths and weaknesses
- Discuss future career development

For the employee, the review provides the opportunity to get valuable feedback on current performance, guidance for the months ahead, and insights into the kind of future opportunities your company may offer.

For the company, the process is an invaluable management tool, helping to monitor overall performance issues while also spotlighting individual high performers who might be considered for new opportunities, executive training programs or future leadership positions.

A disciplined review system, based on actionable goals and constructive feedback, is well liked by employees and a highly effective management and HR tool.

2. Reward success

Money may not be the primary motivator for everyone, but offering competitive compensation is essential in terms of attracting and retaining good people.

Plans work best when they offer upside for most or all of these measurable objectives:

- Personal performance
- Retaining and growing existing business
- Winning new business
- Saving troubled business
- Delivering on corporate goals
- Succession planning (where appropriate)

My approach always favored incentivizing performance over paying big salaries. When recruiting staff to Interpublic and its agencies, we offered competitive salaries, but at the low end of the competitive range. The upside: our incentive programs were at the top end of the range; in most cases, they were at the highest.

3. Encourage cooperation

Especially within a global organization, today's employees need to work effectively with other offices and divisions. Sometimes that means a local office must make a business sacrifice for the greater corporate good.
The Interpublic approach—which likely will work for you—not only recognized this reality, it rewarded it. In designing our incentive programs, we sought to deliver significant performance-based rewards to employees based on their contributions not only to the office in which they worked, but also the their global agency system, and the holding company itself.
Annual bonuses were broken down into three components:

1) Local (office) incentive
2) Agency (network) incentive
3) Interpublic (corporate) incentive

Because our bonus pools overlapped at the local, regional and global level, every employee had a stake in the overall success of the company. These incentive principles took into account the need for local and global agencies to thrive and prosper, plus the interdependencies inherent in the holding company business model. Our competitors copied many of these programs with success, even after Interpublic gave a great deal of them up after 2001.

The bottom line: Making your employees invested in the success of their colleagues as well as themselves will give you a head start in achieving your corporate goals.

4. Drive short-term behavior

In this difficult financial period, revenue generation is a top priority within most corporations. Where appropriate, use temporary, short-term incentive programs to keep employees focused on immediate priorities, such as new business initiatives or revenue targets. These temporary incentives can add energy to your new business efforts and potentially help employees make up lost ground if annual goals are not being met.

Whatever metrics you are using for annual incentive programs—such as margin improvement, revenue growth and net new business—it's likely you are paying these in cash and/or with a lower number of options and cut-back allocation of stock.

In the short term, cash is king. But as you evaluate your remuneration practices and new programs take shape, the underlying imperatives of retention and reward remain constant. So make sure you are offering managers and key executives an appropriate blend of short-and long-term incentives.

5. Build long-term commitment

With stock prices down forty to fifty percent or more, stock options no longer deliver the kind of upside employees want or the retention value companies need. But it's still important to offer an incentive strategy and system that rewards key managers and executives over the long term for successful performance, while encouraging them to work together effectively for the overall benefit of the organization.

Make sure you signal to your key employees that their long-term commitment to the company will pay off in terms of both career advancement and wealth creation. In addition to cash and stock compensation, use leadership training programs to send a clear signal to "fast track" employees that the company values their current contributions and has confidence in their future potential. Bringing your corporate stars together to participate in executive training programs also creates an environment in which executives can meet and build relationships that will benefit the whole organization.

In tough times, it's important to show your people that your organization continues to offer the path to a more rewarding future. The right mix of short- and long-term financial incentives, including executive development programs and incentives based on multi-year stock performance, will help you do just that.

6. Pay for performance

In today's world, companies face new challenges in creating and delivering effective incentive programs. Many companies have come under a harsh spotlight for the executive remuneration practices especially when "performance" bonuses have lacked transparency and seem out of touch with real-world corporate or stock performance. In this new era, any "pay for performance" incentives need to be clearly justified using clear metrics such as revenue, margin, profit growth or comparisons to peer group performance. If not, even if you are operating in a turnaround situation, then paying bonuses at peer level or above is questionable unless explained in detail.

At the senior management level, it is important to reevaluate any outdated remuneration practices. I have always had a problem with paying any CEO a salary above $1 million. From a corporate standpoint, there is no tax deduction above this number. And with a "pay for performance" mindset, there are certainly better ways to motivate executives and demonstrate the performance-based character of a company.

A high-performance pay program—built on bonus payments, long-term restricted stock, and options, all of which release based on performance—is a much more effective and defensible way to go.

Six principles of effective incentive programs

1. **Set measurable goals—and track them**: A disciplined program, if properly managed, will be highly valued by key employees and is an effective management tool.

2. **Reward success**: Give employees a stake in meeting personal and business targets—with a high upside for exceptional performance.

3. **Encourage cooperation**: Everyone benefits when programs are designed to give employees reasons to work together—and a stake in each other's success.

4. **Drive short-term behavior**: Use an annual review process to focus individuals on immediate personal development priorities—and the year's business targets.

5. **Build long-term commitment**: Long-term incentive programs, restricted stock and options increase an individual's stake in the company's future—and are great retention tools.

6. **Pay for performance**: At least eighty percent of an individual's incentive compensation should be quantitative-based, and the rest tied to qualitative performance.

In today's business climate, transparency and pay for performance is the best practice.

CHAPTER TWELVE

Be Careful Whom You Trust

*How to avoid working with the wrong people
and executing the wrong ideas*

"Magnificent promises are always to be suspected."

—*Theodore Parker*

Tragedy and comedy

I RECENTLY WENT up to Stratford-on-Avon in Canada to see a play called *Caesar and Cleopatra* by George Bernard Shaw.

The marvelous Christopher Plummer played the title role of Julius Caesar. Plummer is, of course, a serious, seasoned performer—one of the great Shakespearean actors of our time. In Shaw's more comical play, he gave a humorous dimension to a traditionally tragic role.

What struck me most about the play was the way the people closest to Caesar, those in whom he placed the most trust, invariably conspired against him. Even Cleopatra, whom Caesar had schooled and guided in her progress to becoming Queen of Egypt, was willing to betray him (right up to the end at least).

Watching the cycle of trust-betrayal-forgiveness playing out on stage reminded me of a few of my own experiences in business. Times when I trusted too much and forgave too easily.

Many business leaders are less forgiving than I have sometimes been. They say that when trust is broken a person doesn't deserve a second chance.

I have always believed it is better to err on the side of giving people the opportunity to redeem themselves. Sometimes it pays off. In others, you get bitten a second time. So while I may not have the eloquence or stage presence of Christopher Plummer, I could relate to what his character was going through.

Et tu, Ovitz?

I first met Michael Ovitz in the early 1990s, when Interpublic was blazing new trails in the advertiser-sponsored TV programming business.

We were enjoying great success creating international versions of popular U.S. game shows and our client Unilever was reaping the benefits of the sponsorship and product integration packages we had developed.

We thought we could take this a step further and get involved in a broader advertiser-sponsored programming business. The idea was that clients would get involved in program development, gain the ability to integrate products in a seamless way and also take a financial stake in the show, participating in the back-end residuals.

We took the idea to Michael Ovitz and his powerful Creative Artists Agency. Ovitz was known as one of Hollywood's key power brokers and his relationships went well beyond talent management into the world of major acquisitions. He had been involved in Coca-Cola's purchase of Columbia Pictures and later worked with Coca-Cola and Allen & Company to help in the sale of that studio to Sony.

I was very impressed with Ovitz and, as our talks progressed, we reached the point where Interpublic began negotiating a possible acquisition of CAA, which was growing 15-18% annually. His basic business was movies, but the TV operation, run by Bill Haber, was the real growth area.

When it came to TV, CAA developed the complete package, bringing together writers, directors, and stars and selling the concept to networks as a "take it or leave it" deal. Our idea was to add advertisers into the mix upfront, making it easier to negotiate time slots as well as product integration.

We discussed terms with CAA, but the Screen Actors Guild proved too big a hurdle. Under California law, they did not let agents participate in ownership of companies that produce creative work like commercials.

A few years later, Ovitz used his Coca-Cola connections to make inroads into the advertising business. Coca-Cola was going through a management transition as Don Keough was retiring and Doug Ivester was assuming the presidency.

Also, since his work with the Columbia transactions, Ovitz had a direct line into Roberto Goizueta, the Chairman and CEO of Coca-Cola. Goizueta was sold on the idea that Hollywood could help add star power—and big-name directing talent—to his commercials.

The management of Coca-Cola asked Interpublic and Coke's lead agency McCann-Erickson to partner with CAA in the development of a far-reaching new campaign.

It was a major undertaking. Getting the project up and running required a huge information transfer from Interpublic to CAA. We had worked with Coca-Cola for almost 40 years. We had a vast archive of research into Coke's global consumers and detailed insights into what worked best in different regions and individual markets. Plus, Coca-Cola had been one of the first accounts for whom we had developed expertise in global account coordination.

Working with Ovitz and the CAA people he brought in, the McCann-Erickson team shared the information necessary to bring our new partners up to speed. The Interpublic account coordinator also spelled out a new approach to target marketing through mass media. Different commercials would be developed for different audience segments. And the commercials, targeted to different age and income groups would play on relevant programming—action, comedy, dramas—that delivered the desired audience.

No one knew Coke better than McCann-Erickson. But pretty soon, Mike Ovitz and CAA knew almost as much as they did.

Still, we worked closely with CAA in a spirit of partnership. After we had shared our knowledge and our strategic thinking with them, CAA developed some work for which they took full credit. At the same time, it was agreed with Bill Haber at CAA that we would share the creative work including production on the McCann-Erickson campaign "Always Coca-Cola." Haber was overruled by Ovitz three months later.

Then, lo and behold, Ovitz goes to Coca-Cola management and announces he can't work with McCann-Erickson. He will quit unless he is allowed to take full control of the account.

Suddenly, rather than having a creative partner on the account, we were thrown into a competitive pitch against the very company that had just picked our brains and raided our archives.

The first trust was broken.

Needless to say, when the presentations were made, Ovitz and CAA waltzed off with the U.S. account.

Like Christopher Plummer's comical Caesar, I didn't learn enough from that first betrayal.

A year or two later, Interpublic took another dive into the Hollywood pool. We bought a company called Addis-Wechsler. We were able to navigate the Screen Actors Guild regulations because, although Addis-Wechsler represented stars such as Leonardo DiCaprio and Cameron Diaz, it was primarily a production company.

In the meantime, Michael Ovitz had left CAA, spent a tumultuous fourteen months as President of Disney, and was now running his own start-up management company.

The managers at Ovitz' new shop began quietly circling Addis-Wechsler's top clients. Michael Ovitz, the biggest shark in the pool, called me up to let me know that Addis-Wechsler's employees were unhappy. I thought he was making amends for the past.

One time I called him to discuss the situation and reached him in August on a boat in the Mediterranean.

"Don't worry," he told me. "I'll be back in September. We'll work it all out."

By September, DiCaprio and Diaz had left Addis-Wechsler to join Ovitz' new company. Later, through a third party, I found out the Addis-Wechsler employees who worked with the talent were with Ovitz on his boat when I called.

I had trusted Ovitz a second time. But he didn't take his shot at redemption.

What Michael Ovitz taught me about Hollywood

1. **Contracts trump character**: Talk is cheap. Lawyers are not. Don't share valuable ideas or information until you have everything in writing.

2. **There's always a twist in the plot**: Don't believe in a character just because he says "trust me."

3. **When something succeeds, expect a sequel**: Judge people on their past behavior. If they cheat you once, expect them to do it again.

Sports marketing puts Lowe on the fast track

One of the hottest growth areas in the 1990s was event marketing. For marketers, the ability to connect with consumers through memorable live and televised events became an important part of the overall mix. This was particularly apparent in sports such as NASCAR and NFL, and globally through spectacles such as the soccer World Cup and the Olympics. In the business-to-business space, high-end sports such as golf and tennis offered targeted TV audiences as well as high-value corporate entertainment opportunities.

For Interpublic and its agencies, the event marketing area in general and sports marketing in particular offered a powerful way to enhance our clients' integrated marketing programs. When handled right, event marketing was a business that delivered high margins and continued growth.

The Martin Agency had great success with a special unit that connected advertisers to the consumer-driven passion for NASCAR racing.

McCann-Erickson built out Momentum, a promotion group that worked globally with professional associations and federations to develop opportunities for clients in major national and international sports, such as baseball, soccer, and rugby.

In the U.K., Lowe became increasingly involved in high-profile event marketing, starting with a major pre-Wimbledon tennis tournament sponsored by Stella-Artois, which they managed.

Before long, Lowe saw the opportunity to expand out of just providing marketing services guidance to become involved in actually marketing the events themselves. We set up a new company—Octagon—for three primary reasons: to create and promote sporting events, to represent athletes and to work with other Interpublic agencies to connect clients with relevant sports marketing opportunities.

This area proved very lucrative. Soon, Octagon was representing major athletes, producing successful golf, tennis, track & field and soccer events, including selling TV rights and becoming a real competitor to IMG. One area that nobody really marketed was motor racing, except for Bernie Ecclestone, Chairman of Formula One (F1).

F1 racing was hugely popular around the world, drawing large crowds and TV audiences. In the U.K., the famed Brands Hatch racetrack had recently announced it had regained the rights to Formula One in the U.K. and would resume hosting the British Grand Prix, starting in 2002. The Brands Hatch Leisure Company (BHL) owned five popular racetracks, hosting a wide range of motor sports. In addition, throughout the year, BHL produced sponsored events for clients such as Jaguar and Ford during which people got to race cars around the tracks. BHL generated eighty percent of its profits through ancillary events, marketing services, and advertising. It was a solid year-round business. And the return of prestigious F1 racing to Brands Hatch would be a significant driver of future growth. Ecclestone's contracts with the race tracks required the tracks to promote the races.

Frank Lowe had previously pitched Interpublic on the idea of buying soccer club Manchester United. After we turned him down, that franchise had sold for £400 million—a huge premium. But "Man United" had delivered. It was proving its global strength and, through successful marketing, it had turned into a global cash machine.

With Manchester United fresh in our minds, Lowe brought to the table the idea of Octagon acquiring Brands Hatch and its popular racetracks, along with the future potential of owning the F1 rights in the U.K..

The concept was good. The execution was disastrous.

Lowe's proposal made sense. If we could make the BHL business work we would have a solid, already functioning U.K. business, with 80% of the profits driven by corporate events and advertising at the tracks. The F1 connection would further enhance the value of our year-round events at which the public drove high-end cars on the track. If it worked in the U.K., this was a marketing concept we could take to other Formula 1 track venues.

At the same time, some of us had reservations. Acquiring BHL would require a huge upfront investment and take us into the realm of physical property management, an area outside any of our companies' core competencies. In addition, Brands Hatch, which had last hosted an F1 race in 1986, now required significant upgrades to its track and facilities—plus the necessary planning permissions and government approvals—before F1 racing would be allowed to resume there.

The due diligence process was supposed to help us overcome these reservations. Instead, it only served to obscure them. And because the acquisition was being handled through the agency, not at the holding company level, the most serious red flags were not communicated to senior management or the corporate law department. By the time it all ended, Lowe's deal to buy BHL had been transformed from a smart investment into the dumbest acquisition I've ever been involved with.

Red Flag #1: Due negligence

Because BHL was a public company, the London Stock Exchange required us to hire an outside investment banker to evaluate the deal. Price Waterhouse was the auditor on the transaction in England and had an investment banking consulting arm that Mr. Lowe hired to do the required due diligence.

Price Waterhouse's consulting group reviewed BHL's last six months' financials and forecast for the year. They recommended we go ahead. As it turned out, the past revenue, profits, and forecasts they signed off on turned out to be inaccurate. Making matters worse, the BHL contract for the rights to British Grand Prix contained a "hand-grenade" provision if the terms were ever disclosed. Because of this, access to and review of the contract was restricted to U.K. lawyers only, assisted by the very BHL management who were selling their company. A change of control clause in this contract was evidently satisfied by moving the annual increase in the sanction fees paid to F1 from 5% to 10% on revenue. A costly mistake.

Furthermore, Interpublic did not know that the head of BHL didn't sign an employment contract despite her being the marketing expert and key client contact. After stating she would stay on, she left within a couple of months. The CFO also left shortly after.

To sum up: BHL provided bad numbers. These numbers weren't sufficiently scrubbed by the Price Waterhouse auditors. They weren't challenged by the Price Waterhouse arm that was charged with conducting due diligence. After that, BHL's two key people left. Interpublic would never have approved the deal and bought out the shares of these executives, if we knew these contracts had not been signed.

It was a mess that could have been avoided by a more responsive due diligence process.

Red Flag #2: The wrong lobbyist

In order to gain the necessary government clearances and planning permissions, Frank Lowe hired a personal friend, Mr. Stevens, to be his consultant to the government. Stevens, who was close to the Royal Family, assured us that the government planning permissions would not be a problem and that he would concentrate on making sure the British government accepted the change of ownership and the moving of the race from Silverstone to Brands Hatch.

Even after the local permissions came through, the government refused to authorize our plans to switch the British Grand Prix—a globally televised F1 event—from Silverstone to Brands Hatch, despite a commitment to upgrade the track. It turned out that Silverstone's lobbying efforts were helped greatly by the head of their board, the legendary British F1 champion Jackie Stewart. Mr. Stevens' efforts on our behalf were no match for the popular, well-connected Stewart.

So even though we had bought five racetracks and the rights to the F1 British Grand Prix, when the time came to actually stage the race, we didn't have a track on which to run it. This development forced Octagon to make a deal with the British Racing Drivers Club to conduct the event at Silverstone. The deal required Octagon to not only lease and upgrade the Silverstone track, but also absorb the venue P&L and any losses. The analysis of the Silverstone P&L was done by essentially the same management of BHL, by now owned by Interpublic. In time, it became apparent that the Silverstone accounts were as deficient as those of BHL had been.

Red Flag #3: The wrong lawyers

The worst part of the deal was the way Mr. Lowe negotiated the Silverstone lease and future F1 rights with Bernie Ecclestone. We were told that both parties had put in an option to get out of the F1 contract after three years. When the final deal was signed, the option only existed on the other side. But Interpublic's lawyers didn't find that out until well after the fact.

The reason? A violation of corporate policy that stated all contracts had to be read, reviewed and approved by Interpublic in New York. Frank Lowe had a tendency, particularly during the Interpublic management changeover, to keep everything close to his vest. In negotiating the F1 deal, he and Ecclestone agreed that only their own U.K. lawyers would have access to all the details until signing. So while we approved the plan as presented by Lowe in London, the final contract differed in key details. In fact, the executed contracts didn't even reach New York until well after they were signed.

How did Interpublic let this happen? The discussions about Silverstone and F1 took place as I was leaving the company. Gene Beard, my partner and our CFO had left before this took place. John Dooner was due to become chairman in a month and Lowe/Octagon had been reporting to him as Chief Operating Officer for the previous eight months. When a board meeting was called to review the subsequent contract involving financing the additional commitments on the track at Silverstone, Dooner had already appointed a temporary COO at Octagon.

Interpublic approved the deal as it was presented. But that didn't stop Lowe, an operating company, deviating from the policy of the corporation. The rule that all legal documents had to be reviewed and approved by Interpublic was not adhered to.

Verbal assurances mean nothing once contracts are signed.

Bad as it was, the deal gave us control of Formula One racing in England and we had an agreement with Silverstone to lease their track and upgrade their facilities. In 2000, the return on investment was fine based on a U.K. Price Waterhouse-approved depreciation schedule, which stretched out our investment in Silverstone. (As a final insult, this depreciation method was later rejected by Price Waterhouse in New York.)

In 2001, due to the economic downturn, the dot-com bust, bad local weather, and an outbreak of foot-and-mouth disease that restricted outdoor events in England, Lowe's BHL investment started to stall. The private events and corporate sponsorships that provide the foundation of the year-round business were cut back drastically. Interpublic was stuck owning and controlling physical plants—racetracks—that no longer delivered a reasonable return on investment.

By now, it was clear that the BHL acquisition had been a strategic mistake. We had gone outside of our core competencies and the situation had been aggravated by a weak due diligence process and a fundamental betrayal of trust in the F1 negotiations.

In this kind of situation, my advice is simple: Always cut your losses early. Move on and don't look back.

However, it was no longer my decision. The new management at Interpublic was now in place. They wanted to get their arms around the situation. The chairman of the Audit Committee asked for a total review and asked me to take part as a background informer only. After one meeting, I was disinvited by Interpublic's incoming CFO, Christopher Coughlin, who arrived in the middle of the review process. Meanwhile, an outside consultant with no real knowledge of sports marketing was hired to investigate and recommend how to get out of the agreement, to no avail. The consultant believed if he could prove fraud, it would be enough to get Interpublic out of the agreement. But though the majority of his time was spent trying to prove fraud, any allegations that a person received money for pushing the transaction were shown to be false.

As part of this process, Octagon's COO now began reporting directly to the new Interpublic Sports & Entertainment executive, Mark Dowley, who spent most of his time overseeing West Coast programming and development. Octagon was doing fine except for the BHL part of the business. IPG had invested heavily upfront and poured money into the necessary track renovations. But executive departures had hampered the sales operation from the outset. Corporate sponsorship sales were down. Depreciation changes were hurting the P&L. Now, the economic downturn combined with bad local conditions had pushed the whole operation into the red.

Interpublic's head of Sports & Entertainment had seen enough. He renegotiated a hefty portion of the capital improvement plan from a contractually required $30 million to less than $14 million. He also negotiated a plan with Ecclestone to exit the F1 business with a one-time cash payment of $50 million.

The new agreement was set to be announced at the British Grand Prix taking place that July. It finally looked like Interpublic was going to cut its losses and put the BHL deal behind it.

Not so fast.

The new Interpublic management, led by the CFO, put the brakes on the deal and asked for a totally new review to be conducted by a group of former Morgan Stanley investment bankers who would work under Coughlin's direction. When Ecclestone found out that this new process would delay any deal at least three months, he pulled the plug on the negotiated agreement.

Notable at this time was a leak to *The Wall Street Journal* indicating that Interpublic's future losses on the BHL deal could reach an astonishing $500 million. Interpublic then moved to cancel the British Grand Prix contract, a move that cost the company $160 million instead of the $50 million negotiated just weeks earlier.

Six months later, Interpublic had to take another big financial hit, selling BHL at a substantial discount to the Motorsport Vision group. The head of Sports and Entertainment was shown the door. Interestingly, Dowley came a back a few years later when Interpublic (under new management) invested in the joint venture, which he had formed with Endeavor, a rising talent agency.

Meanwhile, the enormously popular British Grand Prix has been completely sold out each year, and the BHL real estate, now under new management, held a potential value well into nine figures before 2008.

How Formula One Racing took Interpublic off track

1. **An unnecessary detour:** Buying Brands Hatch involved Interpublic in physical plants and upkeep—an area outside of the company's core business competency.

2. **Bad directions:** Before now, due diligence had been handled internally by Interpublic. In this deal, due diligence work was handled entirely by outside investment bankers and accountants. Making matters worse, one firm was checking the work of a subsidiary of their own company. Mistakes were not apparent until too late.

3. **Loss of control:** With legal oversight assumed by the Lowe subsidiary, Interpublic's corporate lawyers had no advance opportunity to review details hidden in the final contract. Having started out with a faulty premise, this breach of trust all but guaranteed Interpublic's future problems with the venture.

4. **Slippery conditions:** While the projections associated with the BHL deal looked great conceptually, no one planned for the risks of economic downturn. Unlike service businesses, where cost adjustments can be made on manpower, Interpublic was stuck with the fixed costs related to owning physical plants.

5. **Running out of gas:** Even when it became clear that the BHL business model wouldn't get Interpublic to the finish line, the company didn't cut its losses quickly enough—and burned through more cash than necessary.

CHAPTER THIRTEEN

Learn from Disaster

*How to move beyond a perfect storm of business troubles—and
ensure the mistakes of the past are not repeated*

> "You could be a meteorologist all your life... and never see something like
> this. It would be a disaster of epic proportions.
> It would be... the perfect storm."
>
> *—Todd Gross, TV Meteorologist
> (played by Christopher McDonald in The Perfect Storm)*

Hurricane season

As THE NEW millennium began, Interpublic sailed into a sea of business
troubles. Many of the challenges the company faced were external and
unavoidable. But others were self-created, some might even say unnecessary.
Taken together, they created a perfect storm that left the company and its
employees battered and bruised—and Interpublic stock beaten down from a
high of $44.25 in December 2000, to a low of $2.61 in 2008.

Starting in 2001, and continuing for several years after, the "weather
systems" swirling around Interpublic included:

- The first CEO and CFO transition in 20 years
- The burst of the tech bubble
- Acquisition problems at McCann-Erickson
- Management challenges at Lowe
- Proceeding with a huge acquisition—True North—in a falling market

- The 9/11 attacks and the continued economic slowdown
- Implementation of new Sarbanes-Oxley regulations
- Management changes, including three new CEOs and three new CFOs in five years

If that wasn't enough, this list doesn't include the biggest challenge Interpublic faced to its business and its reputation.

Because if Interpublic faced a perfect storm, the eye of that storm was an ongoing Securities and Exchange Commission investigation into the firm's accounting practices that was launched in 2002 and was not concluded for almost six years.

Even as Interpublic's board and management battled significant issues in every operational aspect of its business, the SEC investigation created huge costs and distractions. By the time the matter was finally resolved in 2008, the company had no chance to catch its breath. A new global financial crisis had already begun.

The SEC investigation: The eye of a six-year storm

In May 2008, Interpublic agreed to pay a $12 million fine to settle an SEC investigation into accounting imbalances, an investigation that had begun in 2002. While Interpublic neither admitted nor denied the allegations brought by the SEC, the $12 million fine closed the books on a dark chapter in the holding company's and the McCann-Erickson agency's history.

If the size of the settlement seems insignificant, the fact that there was one wasn't. And the cumulative costs of the nearly six-year investigation went far beyond the fine itself.

It's impossible to measure the full impact that years of negative publicity and lost management time had on Interpublic. But in simple out-of-pocket costs, it's interesting to note that the company's annual expenses for corporate accounting and legal services ballooned from $8-10 million per year prior to 2002 to $40-50 million per year throughout the investigation. These costs included additional legal work conducted for the Board of Directors by Deloitte & Touche and an internal audit conducted by Ernst & Young, along with the fees for two sets of lawyers, one for the directors and one for the company. But the biggest beneficiary of this explosion in fees was Interpublic's long-time accounting firm of Price Waterhouse. After such a small fine, one wonders how an accounting firm could have spent so much.

Of course, this all took place in the post-Enron era when the onerous new Sarbanes-Oxley accounting regulations had just come into effect. It was a period of time when most accounting firms were running for the hills and blaming the corporations for some of the problems that they had overlooked in the normal auditing process.

But it's ironic that Price Waterhouse was the firm responsible for auditing Interpublic's accounts both before and after the investigation began. Having failed to alert Interpublic's management to unresolved accounting issues in 1998 and 1999, Price Waterhouse profited handsomely over several ensuing years as the firm "solved" the problems they themselves helped create.

What happened? Could it have been avoided?

The main focus of the SEC investigation was the overbooking of revenue by McCann-Erickson in Europe for the years between 1997 and 2002. By the fall of 2002, this overbooking, which stemmed from a failure to reconcile intercompany cross charges in a timely manner, had ballooned to close to $101 million and was the largest component of the $181 million restatement of IPG's financial results between 1997 and 2002.

Like many problems, this one started small, so small it didn't even catch the attention of our external auditors, Price Waterhouse. (If it did catch their attention, it wasn't viewed as material enough to red flag to the CFO or the chairman of the audit committee, let alone the CEO.) While I was CEO of Interpublic, I insisted on an annual meeting with the Price Waterhouse partner in charge of the audit before the books were closed in February. These meetings occurred after the audit had been reviewed by the CFO and the chairman of the audit committee. As we reviewed the books for both 1998 and 1999, the accounting issues that would create so much later trouble never came up. In fact, while we discussed some routine problems with the CFOs in some of the companies in some of the countries, nothing of any serious nature was raised and certainly not this subject.

Why was it missed?

The problem was strictly an internal one. No client funds were ever involved.

It stemmed from disagreements between agencies over the cross charging for services performed by one Interpublic agency on behalf of another. Cross charging of this kind was common in many multinational companies and the principle is a simple one: in every instance when a cross charge occurs, it has to be reconciled—i.e., what is booked as revenue for one company in the group must be offset by a matching expense for another. For example, if a London agency is doing creative work for Coca-Cola that will be used regionally, the work might be charged out to all the companies in Europe at 1% of the billings. In the case of L'Oreal, work produced in France would be charged out in a similar way. At the end of the year, these charges have to be balanced out.

When disputes arise—as they often do, especially in a company as fast growing and internally competitive as Interpublic was in the late '90s—they need to be arbitrated and resolved promptly. Within Interpublic, our process was to deal with these issues at the agency level, either regionally or globally. Only if a matter could not be resolved by the agency would it be escalated to the headquarters' office for a final decision. In cases that required arbitration between agency networks, the Interpublic Controller would be involved.

In 1998, however, a cross-charging dispute within McCann-Erickson Europe went unresolved. In 1999, a meeting was held with McCann-Erickson's top management where Interpublic's CFO Gene Beard informed them that up to $8 million in intercompany charges had not been settled within the European agency.

At the time, $8 million was little more than a rounding error to a multibillion global company such as Interpublic. McCann-Erickson management was asked to set up a reserve for the amount in the 1999 accounts and settle the allocation between agencies.

This was requested by the holding company. But it wasn't done by the agency. So the number kept growing. Despite this, it still wasn't picked up by Price Waterhouse in the external audit the following year.

It's also worth noting that, even after I left Interpublic, the chairman of IPG's audit committee has stated that, during the 2000 audit, he was never told by Price Waterhouse's senior partner nor was any member of the audit committee informed by Price Waterhouse that there were significant concerns related to intra-company accounts in McCann-Erickson Europe, let alone the possibility of problems in other parts of the world.

Left unresolved at the agency level, and with more clients adopting the practice of centralizing their advertising creative development, the number of internal disputes multiplied. Unresolved cross-charges ballooned to more than $100 million by 2002, when the issue was finally flagged to Interpublic by Price Waterhouse.

Gene Beard retired as CFO at the end of 1999 and I retired as CEO at the end of 2000. I guess no one was left at Interpublic who would have remembered the situation that took place in London with Price Waterhouse concerning due diligence work on Brands Hatch. If there was, they might have double checked the audits.

Why was Price Waterhouse kept on before and after the SEC investigation?

In the advertising industry, certainly the client would have fired the agency in circumstances such as these. Despite the problems associated with changing firms during an SEC investigation, one might have thought Interpublic should do just that. But following the demise of Arthur Andersen, there were only three possible alternatives, and one of these was deemed a conflict of interest. I'm sure Interpublic's new management was concerned about their relationship with Price Waterhouse. Most likely, they also thought that changing this late in the game would delay the outcome. So Interpublic didn't change accounting firms, even as Price Waterhouse's fees were escalating dramatically—some might say outrageously—along with Interpublic's perceived problems.

How to avoid a financial nightmare

1. **Start with a quality audit**: In a perfect world, Interpublic's auditors would have ensured that small accounting issues were not allowed to mushroom into major problems.

2. **Identify problems and spell out solutions**: Interpublic policy required the cross-charging issues to be arbitrated and resolved. Management also instructed the agency to set up the necessary reserves while this arbitration took place. These instructions were not adhered to by the agency.

3. **Follow through on execution**: To solve the problem, it must be monitored—a change in management is no excuse.

Interpublic: Management transitions and economic challenges

After 20 years as CEO—and more than 40 years at the company—I retired from Interpublic in December 2000. Gene Beard, my CFO, had retired the year before. After two decades of consistent management, continued growth and numerous acquisitions, Interpublic had grown to include 650 offices in 127 countries and was generating revenues of $5.6 billion, becoming number one worldwide.

Along with the rest of the world, Interpublic had survived the Y2K changeover without a hiccup. Now, in replacing a long-serving CEO, the Interpublic board was hoping for a similarly seamless transition.

The board approached the situation in a by-the-book fashion. Spencer Stuart, a leading global executive search firm, was hired to screen external candidates from both the advertising agency and the "client" side of the business. Corporate executives with relevant advertising experience were actively considered. A model for that kind of executive was at the time sitting on the Interpublic board: Michael Miles, the retired Chairman of Philip Morris, who had worked at KFC and Kraft, and before that at the Leo Burnett agency. Even as external candidates were reviewed, the board took a close look at all of the relevant internal contenders.

After an extensive and thorough search, the board promoted from within, selecting McCann-Erickson CEO John Dooner to become the new COO at Interpublic in April 2000, with a planned ascension to the CEO position following a final board review in November of that year. As part of the transition, it was agreed that Dooner and Sean Orr, the company's new CFO, recently hired from PepsiCo, would handle the majority of presentations to the board, giving Dooner as much exposure as possible to board members.

Dooner was promoted on schedule and assumed the role of Interpublic CEO in January 2001.

In any leadership transition, it's interesting to see how a new chief demonstrates his authority. Many new CEOs like to make a clean break with the past. My view is that it's perfectly appropriate for an incoming CEO to take full control of the business he's running. But any new CEO could listen to some advice and maybe even act on it from time to time, especially when making the leap from an operating company role to a corporate role, and when partnered with a CFO with little experience in a service business or hands-on experience in-market, except in Dallas ballroom dancing.

In stamping his authority as CEO, Dooner also faced another personnel challenge. While the former CEO was gone, Frank Lowe, his former internal rival for the CEO promotion was still around. Dooner thought he could handle that situation without considering outside advice. But it proved to be a major headache.

In addition to the external realities of a slowing economy, which were exacerbated by 9/11, Dooner's challenge in the CEO transition was making the switch from a McCann-Erickson mentality to an Interpublic (agency-agnostic) leadership role. The temptation was to push the other companies in the group to operate more in the way of the big, successful agency he knew so well, which didn't always sit well with the leaders of agencies that had a different culture and a competitive attitude toward McCann. This was something he adjusted to over time.

Beyond dealing with a tough business climate and growing internal problems, the new Interpublic management team was soon facing questions about its decision-making and execution. A good example of this was with respect to the IT challenges created by the 2002 Sarbanes-Oxley legislation (more on that below). The legislation was enacted three months after the SEC investigation into Interpublic's accounting practices had begun. Under the circumstances, it made sense to act swiftly to comply with Sarbox. Yet in trying to resolve these urgent IT issues, Interpublic management never got beyond the consulting stage.

The CEO and the board were alerted by previous management to the problems this delay might cause, with the suggestion that the hiring of the CFO should be reviewed. The suggestion was that mistakes, if made, should be addressed and rectified quickly.

Perhaps it's worth noting that the Interpublic board had seen several transitions of its own following my retirement. Two of the outstanding board members who retired early were Michael Miles and Allen Questrom, both of whom were excellent in their roles as directors and really understood the demands of a people-driven business. Miles, the former Philip Morris CEO, had a tremendous marketing and international background. Questrom, who had been responsible for taking Federated Department Stores out of bankruptcy, turning around Barneys and who became J.C. Penney CEO in 2001, taught me a great deal about retail and how it really allows you to take the pulse of the consumer. His influence had encouraged me to join the board of Woolworth's (now Foot Locker) back in 1997.

So, despite being alerted to problems in 2002, the board didn't act until 2003. John Dooner went back to his former role as McCann-Erickson CEO, a job in which he once again proved effective. David Bell became the third Interpublic CEO in three years. Soon after, Sean Orr departed and Christopher Coughlin, whom Bell had hired as COO earlier that year, assumed the additional responsibilities of CFO. Again, one wonders what due diligence was done. A couple of phone calls would've indicated the problem ahead. A year after joining Interpublic, Coughlin departed Interpublic to spend more time with his family and was replaced by Robert Thompson, who was senior vice president of finance and who himself spent less than a year in the CFO role.

When current CFO Frank Mergenthaler was appointed in July 2005, he found much to fix: Interpublic was already several months late in reporting its 2004 results.

Changing leaders in changing times

1. **Look for—and use—good judgment**: There's no perfect formula for selecting a new CEO—or any top manager. You're looking for someone with the right mix of experience and temperament. In the end, it's a judgment call.

2. **Embrace the future**: Look for someone who can manage the company and look to the future, anticipate, and execute.

3. **Don't close the door on the past**: Life's a lot easier when you take the advice—and learn from the mistakes—of those who have gone before.

4. **Reevaluate as needed**: No hiring decision—even at the CEO level—is guaranteed to succeed. No board should let a company head too far down the wrong path.

In the midst of the world's economic crisis, new CEOs are facing daunting challenges at companies as varied as AIG, AOL, General Motors and Yahoo.

McCann-Erickson: No longer singing in global harmony

After the rapid growth of the 1990s, Interpublic, its agencies, and McCann-Erickson in particular were in the process of integrating many newly acquired agencies into their worldwide systems as the new millennium began.

McCann especially had expanded geographically while simultaneously building out its integrated marketing capabilities. In addition to the main agency, McCann's networks included McCann Relationship Marketing for direct marketing; Momentum for promotion and events; Zentropy for digital and web marketing; plus the specialist McCann Healthcare agency and a coordinated global partnership with Weber Shandwick for PR.

In good times, propelled by client demand for these services, McCann had delivered strong growth and acceptable margins across disciplines. In addition, the specialist agencies had moved aggressively beyond McCann's international advertising client base to build their own, often local, client relationships. As the business expanded, with the perceived need to coordinate locally, regionally, and globally, each agency took on more people, more real estate and more management layers. It got to the point that, for example, nine "McCann" people from various agency disciplines would be sent to meet with a single Swiss client.

When the downturn hit, McCann could no longer support the overhead that had been created.

As global clients cut back, it was clear there were too many management layers at the local, regional and global levels. Rapid consolidation was essential to the health of the business. But the process was hampered by the fact that many of the "satellite" agencies had their own offices, geographically apart from the main agency.

Adding to the problems were the execution challenges McCann faced in integrating its newly acquired agencies. Through 2000, each of these acquisitions had been governed by Stage One and Two acquisition documents. But having the documents is one thing. Policing the execution after that is another.

Because of McCann's size, problems at acquired companies were happening in more places and more often than they were anywhere else in Interpublic.

Specifically, most acquisitions were based on five-year projections, with payouts to the management and contingent upon execution of approved succession plans.

Monitoring these transitions—and withholding payments if necessary—was crucial to the long-term heath of each acquired agency. But sometimes that didn't happen. And, even as the downturn was taking place, managers were collecting payouts and leaving McCann agencies after three years with no penalty. Worse, many of these executives would reappear a year or two later (having fulfilled the terms of their non-compete agreements), and begin stealing clients and personnel away to work at new local agencies.

Not only did many of McCann's acquired agencies face big voids at the management level, they were often soon in competition with their old bosses. It got to the point that McCann had to acquire some of these new agencies from the same people they had dealt with before, just to stay competitive in markets such as Germany, Mexico and Sweden.

The combination of too much overhead and poor execution on acquisitions weakened McCann over several years. The agency learned the hard way the importance of keeping costs low, emphasizing strategic and best practices coordination in place of management layers and the importance of paying attention to what happens within a company *after* an acquisition. By doing it, McCann became successful again.

What McCann Worldwide learned about managing in a slowdown

1. **Headcount matters:** In good times, it's easy to hire more people—and create more layers—than you need. In a service industry, too much headcount can sink you in a downturn.

2. **Succession plans matter:** Especially when you've acquired local companies—or expanded into new specialties—you need to be rigorous about executing management succession plans.

3. **Real estate matters:** When possible, consolidate real estate while you're growing—don't get stuck with leases for space you don't need and can't afford.

4. **Mix of business matters:** Within a global company, it's easy to be dependent on a few global clients. Local agencies are only self-sustaining

when they have a critical mass of local business.

5. **Execution matters. Drill-down and follow-up on an acquisition is not only important, it's a necessity.**

Don't get bloated. Plan ahead. And focus relentlessly on execution.

Lowe and lower

With all the challenges John Dooner faced at Interpublic and McCann, the last thing he needed was a problem at Lowe. But that's exactly what he got.

As I was retiring from Interpublic, Frank Lowe was offered the chance to retire for health reasons. But Frank decided to stay.

We knew in advance that Frank would not be a constructive presence working under John Dooner's management. Given the personalities involved, it was just a matter of time before problems arose. We suggested a way to handle it, but Dooner said he could deal with it. He planned to address the situation in due course. Six months later, more problems developed. Then an incident occurred that caused Frank to agree to move into retirement.

Despite this incident, Lowe was allowed to maintain an office in his London agency, with only a twelve-month non-compete beyond that.

So, even with very limited influence on the global agency he had helped create, Frank Lowe lingered in a major office and caused dissension before being asked to move out. Then, a year after his departure, he set up a new agency, Red Brick Road, that immediately walked off with two plum U.K. accounts—Tesco, the leading supermarket chain, and Heineken, the popular beer brand with which Lowe had long been associated.

As talented as he was and is, Frank was always a "management challenge." It's too bad an agreement wasn't put in place much earlier, including an office outside the agency. Many of the problems that ensued might have been avoided.

As an agency, Lowe struggled to position itself in the early years of the new millennium, going through four CEO changes in six years. Near the end of that time, an offer was made from the outside that Lowe be combined with Interpublic's marketing services agency Draft. Outside investors would control 51% of the new agency, endeavor to get it back on the right track and then give Interpublic the option to buy back the new entity at a reasonable multiple three years later. In addition to fixing problems at Lowe and Draft, the offer was intended to give Interpublic a much-needed cash infusion while allowing the holding company's management to focus on fixing Interpublic's other issues following yet another CEO transition.

Even though the offer was turned down, it did help Interpublic management to focus on considering other longer-term solutions for Lowe, as well as FCB. Soon after, Interpublic merged Draft and FCB, while trimming back Lowe Worldwide's global network in order to re-focus the agency on its core creative competency as others were doing.

Sarbanes-Oxley creates IT headaches

Two of the main aspects of the Sarbanes-Oxley legislation that passed in 2002 were transparency and accuracy of data.

The Sarbox act put demands on all industries, including the advertising industry. But these were demands that needed to be met. In many ways, the compliance regulations put the same kind of pressure on companies as the Y2K challenge had just a couple of years earlier.

Back then, Interpublic and other companies had risen to the challenge. Y2K was a worldwide issue that required different agencies and different offices to pull together. Cooperation was all but guaranteed. No one wanted to be the one who failed.

Within Interpublic, Sarbox failed to produce the same kind of response. Why?

One reason is that before 2002, Interpublic's financial systems had grown on different platforms and there had been no real imperative to ensure those systems were compatible. The important point was that financial data flowed through to home office in a timely manner. Even if, in some cases, data was still being entered manually.

Still, the need for efficiency, accuracy and automation had been recognized at least as far back as 1998. We had hired SAP in Germany to create a new platform for our financial systems within Germany with a view to expanding that platform throughout Europe. The project was intended to start within McCann-Erickson and then roll out through all our European agencies.

The project was progressing as Gene Beard and I retired. But Sean Orr, the new CFO decided to call in a consultant to consider the matter further, even if this slowed the planned rollout throughout Europe. At the same time, McCann's European chiefs balked at paying for the cost of the training that SAP recommended on the new system. The new Interpublic management apparently accepted McCann's decision. A few months later, I'm told, a second consultant was also brought on board to consider the matter further.

These delays exacerbated the cross-charging issues within McCann, which the SEC began investigating in 2002.

Then came Sarbox. Surely, one would think, the CFO would move quickly to a single-platform solution. But that didn't happen under Orr. And when Coughlin replaced him in 2003, he moved quickly to do one thing only: hire another consultant.

By now, other holding companies had responded to the challenges presented by Sarbox. WPP, for example, had already implemented a global accounting platform that was working smoothly. It was pointed out to Coughlin that the same team who had solved WPP's problems could do the same for Interpublic at a very reasonable cost.

That suggestion was rejected upon receipt.

By now, the rest of the world was operating in the "post-Sarbox" environment. Interpublic, meanwhile, was stuck with old systems and slower, outdated ways of doing business.

One of these issues was in regard to the local practices of "volume bonuses" that had existed for many years between media companies and advertising agencies in many local markets (described more fully in Chapter Five).

These kind of arrangements were not allowed in the U.S. because of the Robinson-Patman Act. In the post-Sarbox world, these agreements had to be contractually recognized by all parties, including the client. If not, you couldn't book the revenue.

The major impact of the change was in the contracts with big international clients. Omnicom heard of Interpublic's problem from a top person in IPG and immediately changed all their media contracts going forward. By moving quickly, Omnicom didn't lose any business over the issue. They also protected themselves from retroactive claims by global clients over past agreements between local agencies and clients that allowed for these "accepted local market practices" to take place.

Interpublic, meanwhile, implemented no coordinated response to Sarbox. In fact, many local offices fought the new rules. As a result, when the matter finally began to be addressed, the company was pressed to make longer term restitutions to clients, even in cases where local agreements between agency and client had been in place for several years.

None of this should have been surprising. The local market practices had been in place for years, even decades. Client companies were aware of these volume bonuses locally, regionally and also globally in some cases. Occasionally, the matter had been raised by a new manager moving into a market. That was the case in Brazil in the 1990s, where a new Unilever manager learned of the practice and insisted on receiving more of the agency's volume bonus in the form of an additional discount. The Chairman of Unilever contacted me personally to discuss the matter. Following that call, I flew to Brazil to meet with Roberto Marinho, the legendary head of Brazil's largest and most powerful media company, O Globo. At the time, O Globo controlled 80% of the Brazilian TV market, as well as many of the most influential print publications.

Marinho made it clear to me that his loyalty was to the local Brazilian agencies in his home market. He had no intention of changing the local market rules to help out an international agency. The way volume bonuses worked for both the agency and client in Brazil was that bonuses were paid to the agency, not the client, with the agency passing on their share of the bonus as a discount. If we insisted on passing our agency bonuses to our clients, he would simply stop honoring his existing agreements with Interpublic. Marinho wanted to make sure all the agencies in Brazil played by the same rules.

When this was communicated by letter to Unilever, that company's management agreed to accept the local market practice—after all, it was the only way to protect Unilever's existing media discounts. As was Interpublic's practice, we continued to apply the bulk of our agency discounts to additional services, such as research and sales promotion fees, to help benefit our clients in the local market.

At the time of these conversations, the cost of retroactively delivering additional discounts to Unilever in Brazil for 8-10 years would have been around $10 million.

Then Sarbox came along.

By not addressing the issue quickly, Interpublic allowed the issue of local volume discounts to become a thorn in its side for several years and, unlike Omnicom, the company opened itself to claims by several clients for restitution going back several years. It was a painful process and one that didn't have to happen.

Even worse, after Interpublic missed its first Sarbox deadline in 2002, the company and its agencies were still not making decisions and failing to institute the necessary changes.

Disappointingly, the company was not fully compliant with Sarbox for several years.

The perils of pausing

1. **Consultants vs. Compliance**: While consultants have a role to pay in advising on strategy, they shouldn't delay a company's ability to handle new regulatory imperatives.

2. **Thinking vs. Action**: Implementing a workable solution is often better than trying to devise a perfect one.

3. **Pay now vs. Pay later**: Not moving quickly on Sarbox compliance not only added costs, it also opened the door for clients to make retroactive claims that could have been avoided.

If you've got big problems, attack them with tremendous urgency.

True North: A major acquisition goes south

In 2001, shortly after WPP acquired Young & Rubicam to briefly become the #1 holding company, Interpublic reclaimed the top spot in global billings and revenues with the $1.6 billion, all-stock acquisition of True North Communications, a company whose holdings included FCB Worldwide, the Bozell Group, BSMG Worldwide and TN Media. Four decades after Marion Harper hired Emerson Foote, the founder of Foote, Cone and Belding to work for Interpublic, the FCB agency itself became part of the Interpublic family.

In the wake of the dot-com bust and the ensuing slowdown of the U.S. economy, *The New York Times* characterized the deal as a "major gamble" by Interpublic executives. Lauren Rich Fine, the famed Merrill Lynch analyst asked, "How smart will they look a year from now?"

True North was a holding company that Interpublic looked at acquiring in the late '90s after finding out that the company was looking to acquire a major agency. At the time, it was not known who they were talking to, but the company involved proved to be Bozell, Jacobs, Kenyon and Eckhardt, backed by Merrill Lynch. Interpublic was turned down after a request to open discussions, but a letter was sent to the Board that forced the nonexecutive Chairman and the CEO at that time to open up the process to Interpublic.

Negotiations took place with everyone involved knowing full well that the Chrysler account would most likely be in jeopardy because of Interpublic's broad relationship with General Motors in all its international agencies, a fact that was taken into account in our negotiations. We offered $28 per share for the company. True North's management was looking for $34, but we felt they would accept around $32.

Our offer was at a price we believed we could make work. As always, our belief was that if the target company couldn't accept our last best offer we should pass, which we did. True North went ahead with the BJK&E acquisition, in the process creating the world's sixth largest holding company.

By the fourth quarter of 2000, True North Communications had lost its most important client, the Chrysler Group. Its Chairman and CEO David Bell began shopping his company to the industry's biggest holding companies, including Interpublic, WPP and Havas.

John Dooner, who was due to succeed me as Interpublic CEO in a month's time, led the negotiations. In February 2001, Interpublic's new management team presented a final proposal to the Board of Directors. I was surprised to find that Goldman Sachs was hired to represent Interpublic, with Merrill Lynch on the True North side. No one who took part in the final negotiations for Interpublic had any background knowledge of our previous negotiations with True North, let alone the ability to analyze the differences between the two proposed deals.

At the last minute, I received a call from a lieutenant of John Dooner's to ask if I would participate in a phone call to the Board of Directors on the recommendation (John's way of asking for support). I reluctantly agreed but requested to see the documentation and the rationale. This was 24 hours before the meeting. I believe the documentation had gone to the Board maybe 48 hours before. When the call came through, I still had not received the documentation, but I listened in to the presentation via telephone. My comment was it seemed a reasonable proposal assuming the documentation, which I had not received, was correct and due diligence was carefully done. The acquisition—the largest and potentially riskiest in Interpublic's history—was approved.

I learned after the fact that not all the due diligence had taken place in regard to client conflicts. In 2000, Interpublic as a whole—not on a single-agency basis—had been named "brand steward" for the Coca-Cola brand. Meanwhile, FCB New York handled PepsiCo's Tropicana and FCB Chicago handled Gatorade, which PepsiCo was in the process of acquiring from Quaker Oats.

Among all global brand rivalries, there were none more sensitive than Coca-Cola and Pepsi. Dooner and Bell, along with FCB's CEO Brendan Ryan, thought that they could navigate the conflicts by keeping FCB Worldwide as an autonomous global agency while merging Bozell into the Lowe Lintas & Partners Worldwide network. Bozell's main account was Verizon, but most of their other business was not very profitable.

As CEO of Interpublic, Dooner got clearance from Coca-Cola to continue handling Gatorade for a year, since the PepsiCo-Quaker deal hadn't closed. Gatorade gave clearance at the Marketing Director level. This was a particularly sensitive account in 2001, as Coca-Cola was in the process of relaunching its PowerAde brand.

But these OKs weren't airtight. It didn't take long for Omnicom's John Wren to point out to PepsiCo's Chairman and CEO Steve Reinemund, "Don't worry, Coca-Cola may have okayed it at the time but it won't last. It's just a matter of time before they get rid of you."

Soon after, Gatorade moved.

In the case of SC Johnson, the biggest account at FCB, there was a question regarding McCann-Erickson Worldwide's handling of Reckitt Benckiser, the British-based multinational household products company, whose billings had grown to close to $300 million. Clearance from SC Johnson was obtained at the Marketing Director level in the U.S.—no higher. That didn't stop SC Johnson's European Regional Director from demanding his management insist that McCann resign Reckitt Benckiser, which McCann did in November, 2001. Another huge blow.

Given that the announcement was made in March and the deal closed in June, 2001, one wonders why Interpublic management didn't talk directly to the top management of all the clients most affected by True North acquisition and not doing so came back to haunt them. Even if account losses were unavoidable, at the very least, maybe the deal could have been adjusted to take into account these realities.

By the end of 2001, FCB alone had suffered $900 million in account losses related to the merger, including $350 million from PepsiCo, $100 million from Clairol and $400 million from AT&T Wireless. (This was in addition to losing the $800 million Chrysler account the previous year.) In January 2002, Lauren Rich Fine told *Advertising Age* that FCB was "a shadow of its former self." Throw in McCann's Reckitt Benckiser loss of $270 million-plus and it wasn't a pretty picture.

Having sold True North for $1.6 billion, David Bell became vice chairman of Interpublic. At the time of the acquisition, True North had reasonable revenues and profitability. But initial projections were missed by a wide margin. And problems persisted. By the third quarter of 2004, even as Omnicom and WPP were increasing profits by 17% and 12% respectively, acquisition troubles played a big part in Interpublic slumping to a $578 million quarterly loss.

Bell had sold at the right time and had negotiated well for his True North shareholders. After he became Chairman of Interpublic, Bell paid me a belated compliment by informing me he had worked hard to ensure I was not part of the Interpublic negotiating team, convincing John Dooner to let the two sides' investment bankers hammer out the deal. A brilliant move on his part, but one that reinforced the perfect storm that was engulfing Interpublic at that time.

By 2006, after several changes at FCB top management, the decision was made to combine FCB with Draft, a very strong direct marketing agency. As might be expected, merging two very different cultures took time and the idea had its detractors. But DraftFCB was created to bring together all the "total communications" elements offered by independent agencies, with the same approach to fee-based pricing. Even as questions about the marriage of cultures swirled, DraftFCB established itself as the first worldwide, totally integrated fee-based agency. In its first two years, the combined agency won 250 new pieces of business from around the world, growing into an operating agency that is now succeeding well in a difficult environment.

Making acquisitions in a downturn

1. **Get the valuation right**: In a slowing market, it's especially important to understand the true value and future potential of a business you are buying.

2. **Do the due diligence**: An economic downturn adds risk to any deal. In the case of True North, the risks were amplified by the lack of long-term certainty regarding client conflicts.

3. **Keep focused on execution**: Interpublic's perfect storm of business challenges made it hard for management to drill down and resolve the problems that arose from the True North acquisition.

Bargain hunting is fine. But buyer beware.

How personnel decisions can wreck a "people business"

In a service business, the Human Resources function always plays a key role in helping find, manage and develop the talent that will help a company execute its strategy effectively.

During Interpublic's perfect storm of business troubles, the company was more dependent than ever on the navigating skills of its Human Resources department. Yet time and again, crucial personnel decisions were made that steered the company right back onto the rocks.

What went wrong?

Clearly, many of Interpublic's problems were exacerbated by putting good (and sometimes not-so-good) people in the wrong jobs or in the right jobs, at the wrong time. This was a factor even within the Human Resources department itself.

Shortly after I left, I gave the Interpublic board and its key management copies of Larry Bossidy's book *Execution: The Discipline of Getting Things Done.* It was and still is a must-read for new managers in business. Unfortunately, Interpublic management didn't take the hint.

The book's main principles are:

- Dig down deep at every level of the company, not just yearly, but on a quarterly basis, or even a monthly if there is a problem.
- Spend time getting to know your customers from both the bottom up and the top down.
- Push innovation and reward it.
- Execute with accountability—with emphasis on growth and six-sigma accountability.

But most pertinent to Interpublic was the need for a company to:

- Put the right people in place to execute.

Especially when a company is looking outside to fill key roles, the head of HR can be as important as the CFO. Yet for four years, even as CEOs and CFOs came and went, Interpublic's HR department made a string of bad calls, including these:

- Hiring a new head of FCB who was not vetted properly and cost a fortune both coming in and going out. One call would have made a difference.
- The way in which the head of Lowe was fired needlessly upset the agency and a major client, then the hiring of the third replacement was bungled—again by not making a call or two.

Fixing the hiring problems at a company is never easy if you don't fix problems in the HR department. Sometimes, the fix is as easy as hiring an administrative deputy for the HR chief. You don't need a chief who just administrates, you need someone who knows the talent market and understands how to handle talent particularly in a service business.

Above all, it's important for the Chairman and/or CEO of a company to take an active role in evaluating major hires, from inside and outside the company. To truly know your own people, it's important to walk the halls and talk to your people.

Whenever I made a major hire from outside, I would interview not only the candidate himself, I would also talk to colleagues and clients. If we were hiring a top manager from a rival agency, I would make it my business to sound out one or two creatives from inside that agency to see how well he worked with creatives. If we were hiring a creative director, for example, I'd talk to account guys for their views on a variety of creative people just to understand how a specific creative candidate worked.

Management making time for an extra "background" phone call or interview on a senior candidate is a great way to confirm a good decision or avoid an expensive mistake.

Maximizing your human resources

1. **Staff the HR department right**: Finding, managing and developing the right talent is essential for a service business. Choosing the right person to run the HR function is one of the most crucial decisions a company makes.

2. **Get involved in the big decisions**: Putting the right people in the right jobs is crucial for successful execution. For major hires, C-level executives should get personally involved in the hiring process.

3. **Fix people problems fast**: If a good person's been put into the wrong job, make the change you need to put the right person in place.

Calmer waters, then new storms

After 20 years led by one leadership team, Interpublic began the new century with three new CEOs and four new CFOs in a little more than five years.

Amid all the other challenges that battered the company, turmoil in the top management suite only added to the uncertainty.

Could that management turmoil have been avoided?

In hindsight, it's easy to see how some of the problems arose. In bringing in two younger executives to replace me and Gene, the Interpublic board took a "generational change" approach. The downside to that, of course, was that both top executives began their new roles with steep learning curves, even as they faced a recession and a host of other problems. Questions about the credibility of the new CFO emerged early, but the SEC investigation that began in 2002 made it difficult for the board to act quickly in replacing him. As multiple problems swamped the company, John Dooner himself recognized the need for a different CEO to help Interpublic weather the storm. When a vacancy arose at McCann-Erickson because of its problems, he went back to a job he could do better than anyone and set about fixing the problems at the network that drove the bulk of Interpublic's revenues.

David Bell, who joined the company as a vice-chairman through the True North acquisition, had not been given an active role in directing the company. But his past experience and background made him the logical successor to Dooner. Bell was brought in to right the ship. But at a time when fast action was needed, Bell chose a CFO, Christopher Coughlin, who never met a consultant he didn't like and continued on a path of delaying and deferring crucial decisions. Coughlin was a big fan of McKinsey. He brought them in to help prolong the IT problems and also to assist in a plan for re-organizing the company. Meanwhile, the company failed to demonstrate the kind of leadership necessary to reassure clients and the financial community.

Michael Roth, who had joined the board in 2002, was named CEO of Interpublic in 2004 and some kind of stability was finally restored. Roth's background in the financial and insurance industries helped reassure clients and shareholders and he had the experience necessary to help see the company through its financial problems. He was not so immediately assuring in handling the emotional egos of the ad business, nor the demands of marketing and advertising clients. Over time, though, Roth is mastering the ability to relate to clients and the creative aspects of the industry.

Roth brought in as CFO Frank Mergenthaler, whose extensive media and entertainment industry experience made him the right kind of partner to help lead Interpublic forward.

As CEO, Roth's efforts have gained favorable attention in the trade and business media.

Unfortunately for him, just as he righted the Interpublic ship, the whole world was heading into the unprecedented financial storm of 2008. Today, enormous challenges are facing Interpublic, the advertising business and huge clients in many industries.

Only one thing is certain: The future will be more challenging than ever.

CHAPTER FOURTEEN

Stick to These 10 Principles in Good Times and Bad

How to deal with your current reality—while always keeping one eye on the future

"Genius is the ability to hold one's vision steady until it becomes a reality."
—*Benjamin Franklin*

The "Great Recession"

The recession that officially began in the U.S. in December 2007 is clearly more than your average recession. Comparisons to the Great Depression abound. But hopefully, America and the world will avoid the depths of the 1930s, when unemployment hit 25% and the stock market took 25 years to regain its September 1929, levels.

This is more like the Great Recession.

For many businesses, the first step will be simply to survive it. And not everyone will. Even before the Great Recession began, many industries, including advertising and media, were going through major structural changes. In the months ahead, we are sure to see more big changes in the automotive, entertainment, financial, pharmaceutical, real estate, and retail sectors, to name just a few. And as each of these industries gets reshaped—be it by bailouts, bankruptcies, mergers, or all of the above—the media economy will feel the impact.

The strong, of course, will find ways to survive. But surviving the Great Recession is only half the battle.

In the post-recession world, new challenges and new competitors will abound. Government programs and regulations will have transformed the business environment. Consumer brand preferences will have evolved, especially as pre-recession preferences have been adjusted to meet new pocketbook realities. The "garage economy" will have spawned a new generation of product innovation. Competition for capital, workers and resources will be intense.

Beyond simply surviving, thriving in the recovery will require smart planning, long-term vision, consistent innovation, excellent marketing communications and superb execution.

Everything that you and your company do now—in the midst of this recession—will affect your ability to compete successfully in the future. Staying true to a long-term vision is tough, especially as markets dry up, money becomes scarce and motivation gets depleted. But within the realities of a recession, it's important to think long-term and make the right moves to plan for the recovery.

But what exactly should you do? What budgets should you fight to preserve? How should you refine and integrate your marketing message? How do you remain a champion of creativity and product innovation? What's the most effective way to communicate to customers, employees, investors? What steps do you need to take now to build your career, strengthen your brand, inspire your people and lead your organization forward?

In this chapter, I'll describe 10 key principles for managing, marketing and motivating in a recession. Focusing on these principles will help structure your decision-making process and guide your execution. These principles are especially timely now. Stick with them and you'll discover they work equally well in good times as well as bad.

The 10 key principles are:

1. Adapt to your new reality
2. Motivate your people
3. Focus your efforts
4. Stay true to your vision
5. Communicate your strategy
6. Innovate your products

7. Seize new opportunities
8. Integrate your marketing
9. Retain your credibility
10. Inspire your customers

I've organized this list based on every company's need to think, adapt and execute internally, externally, or both.

Principles 1-4 help you strengthen your company's position from the inside out—making you more nimble, and helping build a solid group of dedicated employees and offerings. These are the principles that will provide you with the necessary tools to face the harsh realities of this recession.

Principles 5-7 build on the internal principles and will allow you to communicate to all your internal and external constituents—including employees, shareholders and consumers—explaining the changes you are making, the strengths you are reinforcing and your plans for the future.

Principles 8-10 guide you in delivering your message to your customers—letting them know that you understand the current environments and are working tirelessly to serve them.

The order I have laid out does not need to be followed in strict succession. But following all 10 principles will provide an excellent foundation for navigating through troubled times and emerging stronger.

1. Adapt to your new reality

A recession of this magnitude forces change upon everybody. In the case of the Automotive and Financial Services industries, change is coming in the form of government bailouts and new regulations.

But even without federal intervention, the Great Recession will force major changes in many industries. Don't hesitate to respond. This is the time to do whatever it takes to fix new and lingering problems, reinvent your product lines, adapt your way of doing business.

In good times, it's easy to put off addressing difficult problems. But those times are over. It's time to honestly assess your strengths and weaknesses. Confront the changes that you expect to be permanent. Respond quickly to the short-term realities.

In the case of Detroit, many of the Big Three's problems have been known for years, but the solutions were always too unpalatable to face. One example concerns General Motors. Back in the nineties, the company realized that their own Canadian manufacturing model, with fewer products under each logo and clear price differentiation between brands, would make sense in the U.S. market, too. With Cadillac at the top, Buick in the middle, and Chevrolet at the bottom, there would be less overlap between models and a more streamlined way to approach sales and marketing as well as combining and cutting back on dealerships. It didn't happen. Part of the problem was dealerships. State protections made it too difficult to adjust the dealer networks. Labor agreements made it impossible to efficiently cut back on models and production costs. Workers were paid whether they built the cars or not. These thorny issues were never addressed because all the constituencies involved were intent on protecting their own short-term interests, even at the cost of long-term viability for all. This kind of intransigence cost the whole U.S. auto industry greatly. Now, faced with extinction, the only hope is for everyone to solve their problems together. It's the only way to survive.

Other industries are facing similar existential challenges, none more so than print-based media. Newspapers in general, already greatly affected by the rise of the Internet, are being slammed by the advertising downturn. Bankruptcies and closures are inevitable. Even formidable titles are scrambling for new ways to cut costs. A couple of years ago, it was inconceivable that the *Washington Post* would combine news resources with the *Baltimore Sun* to cover local news in Maryland. But they are doing so now. In the magazine world, *Newsweek* has abandoned its mass-market approach and announced a substantial circulation drop as it repositions itself as a "thought leader" magazine along the *Economist* model.

Sometimes it takes the impact of a major external situation to force necessary changes through an industry or organization. But making the right changes now will make you stronger coming out of the recession.

2. Motivate your people

A recession takes its toll on your work force as much as it does on your bottom line. How do you deal realistically with morale issues as your business goes through wrenching changes? How do you ensure that you keep your best people? How do you maintain productivity even as you contend with layoffs?

In communicating with employees, honesty is always the best policy. Be upfront about the realities your company and industry are facing. Make sure employees hear the strategy and what it means for the company as a whole as well as their own individual prospects. Above all, make sure the strategy is clearly understood by people at every level of the organization. Vague-sounding slogans won't help if your people don't actually understand what it is they are being asked to execute.

Communicate. Communicate. Communicate.

As part of that communication, make sure that, if there have to be cuts, they are handled quickly and well. Don't just use a "last in, first out" approach. By clearly making the effort to keep the best people, morale can actually be enhanced despite downsizing. Using early retirement packages to ease the way for long-term employees will demonstrate your commitment to treating people well.

Cut deep—as deep as you possibly can in the first round. This makes it easier to say no future cuts unless you're faced with a real catastrophe. In most cases, a sudden, sharp shock to the organization is better than an endless series of layoffs, which will only increase the sense of impending doom among your remaining employees.

Under Jack Welch, GE was famous for its annual review policy—and for cutting its bottom 10% no matter what. When you have this kind of system in place and have established its practice during the good years, it's easier to use the same techniques to cut staff in a downturn, even when you need to cut beyond the normal 10%.

Once the cuts have been made, keep communicating. Try to be as reassuring as possible to those who still have their jobs. Let them know that their enthusiasm and hard work during this difficult period of time will pay off. Be upfront with and committed to them.

Above all, model the kind of behavior you want to see from your people. Put in the hours. Start early, walk the floors, and leave late.

Maintaining productivity with less manpower is not an easy concept. Communication is crucial. Setting the right example on a personal level also makes a difference.

3. Focus your efforts on your core strengths

The harsh realities of this recession mean that not all companies, products and brands will survive. This is the time to primarily focus on your core businesses and brands. What is essential? What should be abandoned? With a tighter focus, what can be done to strengthen your competitive situation in key segments? Now is the time to look for product lines and brands that tie into the major trends in your industry and offer both short and long-term potential.

General Electric introduced its "affordable" refrigerator costing $300 in 1927. By 1930, 15% of U.S. homes had a refrigerator and GE had succeeded in its goal of being the #1 refrigerator maker. But as the 1930s began, who could afford to keep buying such high-ticket items? GE responded with a new four-year service warranty. It was something no other manufacturer offered. Competitors responded with their own product and sales innovations. Refrigerator sales kept growing. By 1932, 20% of homes had one. By 1938, that number reached 50%.

In the recession of the 1970s, General Foods recognized the growing emphasis consumers were placing on value shopping, as well as the growing trend toward frozen foods. The era of economy-sized freezer foods was born. Freezer sales jumped 26%.

By understanding their consumers, recognizing the trends in the market and by adapting existing products to the new economic environment, both GE and General Foods increased sales in the harshest economic climates.

Hard times for consumers mean more time spent in the supermarket aisle and more attention paid to price differences. These consumers are also alert to companies who reduce the contents of a package but not the price. Today's consumers are well versed in comparing the "price per pound" data posted in the aisles, so price transparency will work far better than trying to fool the consumer. Lose your consumer's trust in a downturn and you could turn them off your brand for a long, long time. It's far better, if possible, to offer increased value through a larger, economy size.

Alternatively, look for an appropriate charitable tie-in for your brand. This kind of cause-related marketing becomes more effective in a downturn as people relate to others having needs. Research has proven that when a product is at the same price and has the same basic quality, a brand that donates a certain percentage of its purchase price to charity increases the intent to purchase by 60-70%. As well as doing good and helping your brand's image with consumers, this marketing technique has another clear benefit: It works.

Focusing pays off. By emphasizing the right products, at the right price, with the right marketing support, you will create an immediate and enduring competitive advantage, even in a difficult environment.

4. Stay true to your vision

Thriving beyond the current recession means knowing where you want your company to go when the recovery begins.

But in a time of prolonged crisis, how do you keep the perspective necessary to make the most successful long-term decisions?

Start by understanding how your company and your products fit into a changed world. Understand the position of your company, the position of your products, and the realities of the categories in which they are competing. In a manufacturing and retail situation, understand your competitive situation right down to the store level.

If you believe in a major undertaking that you're in the process of developing and executing, do not let the recession cause you to doubt your decision. Remember IBM's commitment to research in the Great Depression. Think how FedEx was born in the 70s recession. Look at the way Google expanded since the dot-com bust, moving beyond search to acquire the company responsible for Google Earth, as well as major players such as DoubleClick and YouTube.

It may be that the very act of a launch can make a real difference to your company and put your competitors on the defensive for not spending and not innovating. Henry Luce launched *Fortune* magazine after the crash in 1929 and his successors at Time Inc. launched *People* in the slumping ad market of the 1970s recession—it became the most successful magazine brand of the next 30 years. Bill Hewlett committed HP to developing the pocket calculator during the '69-'70 recession—today it's the largest technology company in the world. JetBlue achieved profitability in the airline slump after 9/11.

And look at Apple. It opened its first retail stores in the recession of 2001. That same year it introduced the iPod—a product that transformed the company, the MP3-player market, and the entire music industry.

5. Communicate your strategy

In times of rapid change, consolidation, and reinvention, effective communications are more necessary than ever. Make sure your key constituencies—customers, employees, business partners, and investors—understand what you are changing and why. Is this the time to re-emphasize your heritage and enduring principles? Or announce a new approach to how you run your company and promote your products? Either way, communicate.

For a company like Wal-Mart, reinforcing an everyday low prices philosophy, as the company does with its "Save Money, Live Better" campaign, plays into core attributes that resonate strongly with today's consumers.

Simply communicating what your company is doing in the face of the recession can have a powerful effect on long-term perception. In the recession of the 1970s, Mobil began a 30-year communications campaign to ensure its corporate position was understood by all key constituents. GE has a history of maintaining its visibility during downturns with campaigns particularly emphasizing innovation for innovative products.

From an overall communications perspective, now is the time to emphasize your corporate values and showcase major brands. The goal is to create a halo effect around your entire business and allow your lead brands to do more of the heavy lifting. If budget cuts are essential, it's more important to maintain share of voice for an umbrella brand, keeping spending at least at your share-of-market level, and allowing that brand to carry others.

Effective communication with all your stakeholders will make a difference for your company as we emerge from recession.

6. Innovate your products

A recession may delay the introduction of new products but it cannot stop innovation. If big companies cut back on R&D now, they risk being blindsided by an onslaught of products created within the downturn-fueled "garage economy." The little guy has a real chance when the big spenders cut back.

The eighteen-month recession of the mid-70s saw the birth of transformational companies such as FedEx, Microsoft, Charles Schwab and Vanguard.

Expect more of the same this time around. When the recovery begins, the landscape will be different in ways that were unimaginable before the recession began.

Existing companies must be prepared and that's why research and development matters more than ever. DuPont invented nylon in the Great Depression and revolutionized the clothing industry. In the same era, Douglas Aircraft built the DC-3 and soon captured 90% of the commercial airline market.

Ad agencies must find ways to innovate, too. For themselves and their clients.

Interestingly, just before the launch of *People* magazine was announced in 1974, McCann-Erickson Europe approached Time Inc. with a big new idea. Europe had also been hard hit by recession and we saw another likely development: governments were looking at banning television advertising for liquor and cigarettes. We developed a prototype magazine, one with great appeal to liquor and tobacco advertisers. It was a celebrity and entertainment monthly. I flew over to New York and went to Time Inc. management with the possibility of publishing such a magazine in Europe. I couldn't understand the icy stares we got at the presentation.

Three months later, they launched *People* in the U.S. I was asked to the launch event. "How did you know what we were doing?" one of their top managers asked me.

If nothing else, this story illustrates how, if you are not thinking about revolutionizing your business, someone else will be.

Remember: Recessions don't stop innovation. Make sure this one doesn't kill innovation within your company.

7. Seize new opportunities

In the midst of a recession, strong companies are often presented with new opportunities to acquire weakened competitors. We saw it happen in the financial services industry in 2008, as JP Morgan Chase swooped in to acquire the remnants of Bear Stearns in May. Just four months later, Bank of America moved to acquire the venerable Merrill Lynch brokerage firm for $44 billion. These deals were done at a speed that allowed little time for due diligence. There is still a question as to how the first will turn out; the second ran into big problems almost immediately.

During and after the downturn, companies that survive—and plan to thrive—will need to seize new opportunities as they arise: opportunities to acquire new brands, new technologies, startup companies and even established competitors.

Having cash on hand helps greatly. Just ask Warren Buffett. In addition, companies that have maintained their borrowing power, with long-term, overlapping commitments from their banks, will have the most flexibility.

In a recession, just as venture capital dries up, the "garage economy" begins to take hold. New companies are created. New technologies developed.

This creates occasions when companies can make smart acquisitions that help them position themselves for the long term. But even if the price seems right, due diligence has to be done even more thoroughly. Before making any acquisitions in a recession, ask yourself: How essential is this? What do we gain that we couldn't do ourselves? Are the products truly innovative? Does the company have the right management? How efficiently can we integrate this acquisition?

Warren Buffett is the master at bargain-hunting in a downturn. In the 1970s he did very well buying Interpublic and General Foods. In 2002, he made a very opportunistic move to acquire Dynergy's Northern Natural Gas pipeline, which quickly generated tremendous cash results. His one big mistake was in 1987, when he bought Salomon Brothers. Soon after, the firm got involved in a trading scandal that forced Buffett to personally step in and run the company for nine months. His more recent $5 billion investment in Goldman Sachs created fewer headaches and better results.

Before making any acquisitions in a recession, make sure you are clear on your own long-term strategy and your reasons for buying. Buy wisely and you will position yourself to be even more competitive in the recovery.

8. Integrate your marketing

Even in bad times, smart marketers know how to increase market share and position themselves for the recovery. And the benefits of continued marketing activity are well documented. In "Should Firms Increase Advertising Expenditures During Recessions?"—a report available from the 4A's—Kristina D. Frankenberger and Roger C. Graham analyze the available data. Their conclusion? That John O'Toole, President of the 4A's had it right when he said in 1991, "in a recession, the most productive decision for most companies is to increase rather than decrease advertising spending."

Marketers who are able to maintain or increase ad spending gain real upside during and after a downturn. The upside begins with negotiating power. Simply in terms of media buying, it's easier than ever to drive deals as both new and established media compete for dollars. Even a small amount of increased spending can deliver tremendous additional visibility. The studies analyzed by Frankenberger and Graham show the value of continued advertising through a recession, not just on sales and market share but on long-term stock performance.

Having the data to justify spending is one thing. Hanging onto the budget is another.

Depending on your corporate realities, preserving marketing budgets is not always possible. Even if you fight hard for your marketing budget, you won't always win the battle. If you do find yourself working with a smaller budget, you will still need to connect with consumers as powerfully as ever and maybe even more so.

Getting the message and the mix right is crucial. Integrate your campaigns to connect with consumers on TV, online, in print, and out-of-home. My advice is always to build campaigns around one, big central idea and push the same message through all the "pipes," or media platforms. As the old saying goes: Repetition builds reputation.

Remember, too, that the brand, not the technology, should drive the message. Make sure you are communicating on an emotional level with your flesh-and-blood customers. Especially when using highly targeted mobile and location-based media, look for ways not simply to be intrusive, but to deliver messages that reinforce the consumer's perception of—or relationship with—your brand. Where possible, get consumers to opt-in for specific brand communications rather than generalized offers within your category.

In tough times, of course, it pays to deliver real value. In the last three months of 2008, coupon usage expanded over 15% and companies increased their coupon issuance. And we're certainly living in the age when deep discounts are expected at the retail level. But simply cutting prices is not the answer. Take this opportunity to let your customers know that you are offering additional value.

Don't forget the power of effective sales promotions. When executed right, they will help you maintain a price point, drive consumer behavior and increase market share.

One example: In the recessions and oil crises of the 1970s, McCann-Erickson worked with Esso in Europe to develop a series of special sports-related collectible coins. Timed for the World Cup and other major soccer events, these limited edition collections became must-haves for a generation of British schoolchildren. Kids clamored for the coins. For parents, filling up the car at the Esso station became an easy way to give the kids a treat (at no extra cost to the parent).

Lesson: In tough times, adding value is sometimes as important as lowering price.

As consumers pull back in some categories, other areas benefit. Soup consumption usually goes up in a recession. And that's a time for leading brands to reinforce their position in the market. Campbell's Soup, for example, has used downturns to increase marketing of key products and has emphasized its all-natural and organic lines—in contrast to competitors who might still use, for example, MSG. By combining its traditional "value" pitch with an emphasis on "nourishment," Campbell's drives short-term sales and positions itself effectively for the long-term at a time when more consumers than usual are paying close attention to the company's products.

Package goods manufacturers in general have discovered that, during downturns, it pays to focus on their highest share of markets brands and target their advertising in those markets where those brands sell best. By focusing on present users and aiming to increase volume among them, they get the biggest return on investment, especially with TV advertising. Ancillary brands may suffer in the short-term. But by heavying up on lead brands, these marketers maintain revenue and position their overall business for the recovery.

Bottom line: Keep your budget intact if possible. Play to your strengths. And keep your messaging consistent across multiple platforms.

9. Retain your credibility

When the news is bad, it's tempting to try to sugar-coat it. Don't.

Reliability is essential in times of chaos. Dealing honestly with all your constituencies—customers, employees, investors, and business partners— during and after a recession will have a big impact on the prospects during recovery.

Make sure your people are reminded time and time again: "I want to know about any bad news right away. I can wait on the good news for a day or two."

Retaining credibility with investors is essential in a downturn. If results are down, communicate why and what you are doing about it. Many companies will be reporting declines in earnings and making downward adjustments to forecasts. Missing Wall Street's quarterly earnings forecasts can have a really damaging effect on a stock. So keep surprises to a minimum. If you lack the visibility to make quarterly forecasts, don't make them.

The best approach is to make an annual forecast and update it as needed. Use each quarterly call to offer commentary and explain how the quarter just passed fits within the annual forecast. If you need to adjust the forecast, adjust for the year, not the coming quarter. Above all, communicate to Wall Street that you have a plan, including the parts you are sticking with and those you are adapting to changing circumstances.

Swiss-based Nestlé—a company with $16.6 billion in 2008 revenues— believes in six-month reports and focuses their communications to analysts on internal growth metrics and how well they are meeting their own margin targets. Maybe that's not exactly possible for a stock traded on the NYSE or Nasdaq, where missing targets can take you on a rollercoaster ride from quarter to quarter. But try to change the focus of the conversation. If you can't avoid making quarterly estimates, always try to underestimate and overdeliver. In talking to investors, keep the focus on the quality of your strategy, execution and full-year results.

Remember: retaining your credibility is crucial. Don't promise when you can't deliver. Don't fail to communicate when the news is bad.

10. Inspire your customers

Along with innovation, optimism has been a key ingredient in inspiring consumers and building great brands through the last ten recessions. But in troubled times, striking the right note is crucial. What is the appropriate creative strategy? What brand attributes should you emphasize? How do you connect with your consumers in a positive way despite the hard times?

As the Great Depression began, Eastman-Kodak celebrated its 50th anniversary by giving away 500,000 cameras to children across the country. Parents and grandparents—already Kodak's best customers—loved it. The entire supply of cameras was given out on a single day. And Kodak inspired a whole new generation of amateur photographers to go out and take pictures, cementing its place as the photography brand for a whole new generation.

That same year, the McCann and Erickson agencies merged. Throughout the Great Depression, the new McCann-Erickson embraced new media innovations as a way to showcase their clients' brands and inspire consumers. Innovations included the first shortwave broadcasts from a ship in mid-ocean, a live radio show from a transcontinental flight to help inaugurate new Boeing planes, the first advertiser-sponsored sound motion pictures, including *Neath the Bababa Tree*, which used animation by Dr Seuss in a movie for Flit insecticide. It debuted at the Strand Theater in New York on June 24, 1931.

In the days of severe rationing in post-war Britain, Unilever kept advertising its top margarine brand, even when branded products were not allowed on the shelves. The advertising helped communicate that better times were coming and that Unilever would be there when they arrived. The company's margarine re-emerged as the #1 brand.

Coca-Cola's history of optimistic messaging is legendary. The brand epitomized American optimism as it expanded globally during WWII. During the recession of 1980, consumers were reminded to "Have a *Coke and a Smile*." Amid the funk of the mid-70s, when a recession was accompanied by the Watergate scandal and the last days of the Vietnam War, Coca-Cola famously announced it was time to "Look Up, America!"

Never underestimate the power of optimistic marketing to bolster people's mood and drive sales at the same time.

What we are living through today may be a once-in-a-lifetime economic downturn. It's a time when tough, short-term decisions may need to be made. But always keep one eye on the future. Don't forget what it is you want to create for yourself and your company. Don't shy away from the innovation and risk-taking that, especially in a recession, can make a real difference. Use your marketing communications to promote key brands and, wherever possible, communicate optimism about the future. Look to solve problems. Nurture and promote creativity. Keep your focus on your customers and your clients and maintain a frequent dialogue with both.

And finally, whatever your business, never forget to have some fun doing it.

Life Beyond Business

Some closing thoughts on matters close to—and concerning—my heart

On gratitude

I'm WRITING THESE words almost three years since I collapsed and died on a tennis court in midtown Manhattan.

The date was February 1, 2006, just three weeks before my seventy-first birthday. I had already lived three score years and ten and I had lived those years well. Notwithstanding a long and successful career in business, my finest achievements were undoubtedly my then-45-year marriage to my vivacious wife Faith, and my two beautiful and accomplished daughters, Hope and Johanna. I took great delight in being a grandfather to four unstoppable beings named Briell, Teddy (Spike), Ashby, and Gillen.

At the moment my heart stopped beating, I was engaged in an activity I loved: playing tennis with friends.

This wasn't my first instance of heart trouble. I had already been equipped with a pacemaker and had recently required the use of a defibrillator following an electrical heart problem.

The bad news: the club had no defibrillator.

As I lay lifeless on the clay surface, my friends were unable to revive me. Seconds turned into minutes. Panic turned into prayer. The situation looked increasingly dire.

The good news: the famed cardiac surgeon Dr. Karl Krieger just happened to be working out at the club that day.

Karl Krieger saved my life. After four minutes, he got my heart beating. And I discovered that, as charmed as my life had been up till that point, my luck hadn't quite run out.

Getting my old heart beating again wasn't the end of the story. As my condition went downhill in the ensuing weeks, my cardiac doctors, Theodore Tyberg and Karl Krieger, decided I needed a new one. They recommended I go in for a heart transplant, since I could barely walk half a city block.

I was added to the bottom of a long list of patients in need of new hearts. But again I was lucky. My B-negative blood type is shared by just 1.5% of the population. It means the chances of a compatible donor heart are small. But when one appears, you automatically go to the top of the list.

After just an eight-week wait, I was told that a suitable heart had become available. Normally, a patient my age receives a heart that's 55-60 years old, which can usually be relied upon for a good 10-15 years or more. The heart I received came from a 39-year-old woman in West Virginia. A liberal Democrat, no less. Some have noted that the arrival of her heart in my body has coincided with a new sensitivity in my nature.

I'm not sure if that's exactly true. But I hope my donor would be pleased to see the use to which her heart is being put. Her willingness to serve as an organ donor has allowed me not simply to extend my life, but to approach each day with a deeper level of gratitude for everything life offers. The period after a transplant and possible rejection is difficult. The retired Senate majority leader Dr. William Frist (who incidentally, has done approximately 100 transplants) and Dr. Donna Mancini and Dr. Yoshifumu Naka, both from Columbia-Presbyterian, were a great help.

Amid a nationwide shortage of organ donors, it's a shame that states don't require citizens to donate unless they indicate otherwise when applying for driving licenses. "Opt-out" systems like this are already in place in some European countries. You donate unless you say no.

On family

I was born in Cleveland, Ohio, in the middle of the Great Depression, the first of six boys born to my parents Philip and Jane. My father ran the Royal Vacuum Cleaner Company. But it was my mom who was the leader of the family. She was a great skier, tennis player, dancer and flirt. She always got us to do everything together. The way my family worked and played together taught me a lot about teamwork, listening to others and recognizing when other people in the room came up with ideas that were equally good as (occasionally even better than) my own. All great attributes for the advertising business.

Though my dad was running a business, he held only a third of the voting shares, along with his two sisters. When his sisters insisted on their husbands getting involved with the business, dad moved on at a very low price. He got involved selling insurance, but he also began working with small companies, helping to build and package a variety of new business ventures.

I admired my dad's entrepreneurial spirit and willingness to take risks. But when he passed away I was worried that there wouldn't be enough money to support my mother. As it turned out, some of dad's ventures (a lot were losing propositions) were bought out by a public company and went from 10¢ to $30 a share. My mom's financial security was assured and I learned another valuable lesson about investing in ideas.

The best M&A deal I ever made was marrying my wife, Faith. We first met in 1960 when I had just moved to New York and was living in an 8' x 10' room at the Pickwick Arms. I was with a friend who was a model, and she suggested we go to P.J. Clarke's to meet up with a friend of hers, also a model. That's where I met the beautiful and amusing Faith Power. (I found out later she was a hat model.)

Our courtship was a little bumpy. Every time I tried to invite her to a Broadway show, she seemed to have already seen it. But I finally found one she hadn't seen and the romance began. (Interestingly, a hobby I have now taken up is co-producing Broadway shows through Bill Haber. I became the first first-time producer to win a Tony with the revival of the World War I drama *Journey's End*. I lost the investment, but it was worth it.)

Faith's family had seats on the 50-yard line at the New York Giants games, which convinced me to switch my allegiance from the Browns. Even better, she also had a place at Sea Girt at the Jersey Shore for the summer.

We married the following February and have been together through thick and thin ever since.

Faith has been a great partner in business as well as life. Without her support, strength and engaging personality in the early days I would have been unable to take advantage of—or truly enjoy—all the opportunities my career at Interpublic offered. When we moved to London in the late 1960s, Faith flew over with a five-year-old and an three-month-old baby. We had just thirty days in which to get our life in order, including finding a new home and a school for Hope but it was worth it.

London was a terrific place to live. In the late '60s and '70s the ad business was creative and dynamic, with a heavy emphasis on social interaction. Faith was always great with clients. At the same time, as our daughters grew, Faith ensured they created some cherished early memories.

And Faith did a lot of childrearing without much help from me. As my responsibilities grew, especially when I took over McCann-Erickson Europe, I began traveling on business up to 80% of the time. I was home on weekends and every couple of weeks for a week at a time. It wasn't easy on my wife and children. But Faith, even with a bad back, made it work.

One thing we were able to do as a family in Europe was ski. We lived next door to the U.K. ski club and took advantage of their special packages to visit a different ski resort during the holidays each year. It was great to watch the girls, who are both good athletes, enjoy themselves on the slopes. Pretty soon they were out-skiing their parents—just like their grandmother!

My one regret concerning my children is that I didn't see enough of them in their earliest years. Since returning to New York, I have been proud to watch Hope and Jody finish college and build lives of their own. Thanks to them I have two great sons-in-law and four grandchildren, two on each side.

Today, I try to make up for lost time. I visit as much as possible with my daughters and their families. Hope and Jody have brought up great children and passed on their sporting genes. Two of my grandkids are playing tennis in the USTA, and the two youngest are already big on skiing.

On loyalty

Growing up with a fiery Irish mother, a good-humored father and five younger brothers, I had a strong sense of loyalty bred into me. I married an equally strong-willed Irishwoman and somehow built a partnership for life.

Throughout my life, I've defined loyalty as being part of a team, working together and caring for one another. In my case, people have told me, I'm definitely an enabler.

When you're part of a team, whether or not you are the leader makes no difference. What matters most is working towards a common goal, maximizing the strengths of each individual and all being committed to a successful result.

Demonstrating your loyalty to others also has a way of paying you back just when you need it most.

On retirement

When I retired from Interpublic at the end of 2000, I wasn't ready to completely switch off my business brain. I started a marketing communications group, primarily focused on helping smaller companies develop effective strategies. The Geier Group soon evolved beyond marketing into the venture capital area, supporting young people starting new businesses. Like my father before me, I had left a large and successful company to discover great satisfaction in working with entrepreneurs. My daughter pointed out that I often found myself not asking for money for my services, but what I found most intriguing was the opportunity to help others succeed.

Simultaneously, after talking to three other investment banks, I went to work with Lazard as a Senior Advisor. Lazard was an independent company, primarily an advisory service, so it was not like the investment banks that sold both their own loans and client equity to themselves and to the market. Because I could operate on a straight fee arrangement without a success fee, I was free to offer advice on behalf of Lazard but in a way that clients could feel I was really putting their interests first. The relationship has been very rewarding.

On political involvement

On a personal level, I'm a lifelong Republican. But I always felt that in business you should try to help whenever possible, no matter what party was in power, to support programs that could make a difference and were part of your own beliefs.

At Interpublic, I pushed the idea of acquiring two lobbying organizations, one for the Democrats and one for the Republicans. Having a voice in Washington not only gave us clout for ourselves regarding advertising issues, but also allowed us to provide additional services for our clients. It proved very worthwhile.

One major issue we faced was a proposal to apply a five-percent service tax to advertising by the Florida legislature in 1987. We put together a group that brought together the broadcasters, magazine publishers, and the advertising community. Each group had a representative at the table, and I worked with Bob Wright, Chairman of NBC to organize the various advertising associations.

The tax had passed in Florida in July 1987 and other states were salivating at the prospect of enacting similar legislation.

But the efforts put forth by our entire group—including clients—made a difference. We put together a great amount of data to communicate why the tax was a bad idea. The broadcast and print media ran ads condemning the tax. And we applied economic pressure, too, as industry members cancelled a slew of conferences previously scheduled in Florida.

Six months later, the tax was repealed. Other states backed away from their plans. In 2008, when the idea of a similar tax was floated again, one former state Senate leader from Florida said the idea had "a snowball's chance in hell because of the effective job the ad community did in 1987."

After I retired, I got involved in another lobbying effort—this time focused on energy conservation, following the major blackout that hit the East Coast and Canada in 2003.

I had been in London in 1975 when, in the midst of the energy crisis, a national "Save It" advertising campaign had reduced electrical consumption by 10% within six months. (Also, getting the bath-loving Brits to switch to showers saved 20% on water heating costs.)

In 2005, a proposal was developed and presented to Energy Secretary Samuel Bodman and his committee. The plan called for a coordinated communications campaign targeting consumers, industry and government. With the backing of the Ad Council, the cost to develop the campaign would be about $850,000 with millions of dollars in free media to support it.

While Bodman liked the idea and suggested his people move forward on it, he was told that the Continuance Budget rules that were in effect at that time would not allow him to increase budgets or shift budgets. He even offered to pay for the program out of his own pocket, but the counselor in the meeting said, "no, you're not allowed to. It's a conflict of interest."

So the Energy Secretary wasn't allowed to act on his own for the good of the country and the plan died. Still, his department did take a major portion of the ideas to major industries, which made a difference. Simply making sure lights are turned out in offices and businesses has a big impact on a national level.

On a more partisan level, I was pleased to consult with Senator Bill Frist who was the GOP's National Senatorial Committee Chairman for the 2002 elections. Haley Barbour, the former RNC Chairman who went on to become Governor of Mississippi, was at the time heading up a powerful Republican lobbying firm. He suggested I get to know the Senator and look at the plan he was working on.

Back in '02, the Republican Party and its committees were way ahead of the Democrats in how they used advertising, particularly TV, to get out their message and reach highly defined voter segments. From a marketing communications standpoint, I was surprised at how detailed and sophisticated Frist's plan was. Every aspect of the strategy had been thoroughly reviewed, from the choice of candidates, to the content of advertising, to the targeted nature of the advertising spending. Efforts were primarily focused on 12 key states with messaging and spending executed down to a local level. Getting the right people to run was one thing. Secondly, to communicate their strengths against the issues that were most predominant in the minds of most consumers in those states was another.

The plan was as comprehensive as anything P&G or Unilever could have put together. It was superbly packaged and I was happy to be a slight part of it, especially when the Republican Party won the Senate back in 2002.

In the last presidential election, of course, the Democrats did a far better job of understanding and controlling the media and taking advantage of the targeting and social networking possibilities of the Internet. They not only knew how to use the technology but how to create a fully integrated marketing campaign with messages selectively delivered to their relevant targets. Packaging a candidate like a brand, and connecting emotionally in every medium, including email, makes a real difference.

On giving back

Even before I got my new heart, I had discovered the value of giving back. I had chaired the Ad Council, the non-profit organization that brings together media, clients and agencies to create public service advertising programs in areas such as improving the quality of life for children, preventative health, education, community well being, environmental preservation and strengthening families. And I was a Trustee already working with organizations such as Autism Speaks, Columbia Business School, Memorial Sloan-Kettering Cancer Center, Save the Children and the Whitney Museum.

Since my transplant, I have intensified my involvement by working on a major ongoing effort with each of these groups, as well as developing projects with the Presbyterian Hospitals—New York and Columbia—where I spent so much time.

More than ever, I'm giving my time to help shape projects and following through to get them implemented. There's no greater satisfaction than when one's efforts contribute to something truly important getting done.

In the case of Autism Speaks, I have been involved from the outset, in the company of such luminaries as Bob Wright (Chairman of NBC) and his wife Suzanne, who had an autistic grandson, and Bernie Marcus of Home Depot fame. Here, I was pleased to work with the Ad Council to develop a major national communications program designed to build awareness among parents and doctors of the symptoms connected to a disorder that affects one in 150 children. More children will be diagnosed with autism this year than with AIDS, cancer and diabetes combined. For more information, I encourage you to visit www.autismspeaks.org.

As an alumnus of the Columbia Business School, I have been pleased to be involved in their communications and looking forward to marketing the new location they are developing uptown.

I joined both the Memorial Sloan-Kettering Cancer Center board and the management board in the 1990s. Having also chaired the Joint Organizational Policy Committee, I am continuing to stay active on two committees of the board.

The art world connections that led me to the Whitney Museum's Board of Trustees began with my wife Faith. Because of her back problem, she could not participate in tennis and got me hooked on art. She took great delight in visiting the art galleries of Soho and her interest rubbed off on me. Ultimately, I proposed decorating the gray walls of Interpublic's HQ with some contemporary art. My good partner and CFO criticized my extravagance at several board meetings, but I was able to set aside a small allocation. Three years later, after enduring much criticism, it was not amusing anymore. I finally suggested we have the company's collection independently appraised. To my CFO's surprise, the art we had purchased had compounded at 35%, even as the company as a whole was growing at 22-25%. After that, he started to invest personally, as we traded up bit by bit. Displaying art in a business like advertising also has a good impact on the creative people who visit your office. I've kept my hand in modern art ever since. And working with chairman Leonard Lauder at the Whitney, I was pleased to get involved with every operational aspect of the museum.

With Save the Children, I worked at first primarily on the U.S. side of the organization. More recently, I have expanded my efforts to more global programs. To help the effort, I encouraged retired Senator, Dr. Bill Frist to join the Save the Children Board. In 2007, we launched "Survive to 5," a major new effort that focuses on saving the lives of millions of children who die each year—at the rate of 27,000 per day—from treatable or preventable causes in developing countries. The program invests in low-cost solutions that make lifesaving medicines and treatments available to newborns and their mothers through educating the caregivers in the field. For more information, I encourage you to visit: www.savethechildren.org.

On faith

Having married a woman called Faith Power in 1961, it's easy to say I've always believed in the power of faith.

While I can't claim that it was divine intervention that has brought me this far, I can say I'm more of a religious person today than I was before my heart transplant.

Above all, I know that I am lucky to be here. I'm lucky for the life I've had, with all its vicissitudes. And I'm lucky for the family I have and that I'm still here to enjoy it all.

Mr. and Mrs. Phil Geier on their way to the United Kingdom.

Now in the United Kingdon.

While being honored by the Whitney Museum of American Art, the author is joined by his daughters and sons-in-law: Hope and Ted Smith and Jodie and Peter Ashby Howard.

Christopher Plummer, Actor, Elaine Plummer, his wife, Bob Wright, retired Chairman of NBC, and Paul Newman, Actor – they all couldn't believe I won a Tony for producing Journey's End on my first time out! (Bill Haber, head producer, took the picture)

Faith's new best friend.

Colgate DKE roomates meetng every year for 30 years; Rocky Stoner, author, Larry Bossidy, Charles Garivaltis.

Acknowledgements

I AM DEEPLY indebted to the people of Interpublic Group and all its agencies—and the many hundreds of exceptional clients—with whom I worked for more than 40 years. Only a few of you appear in the pages of this book. Nevertheless, all of you helped build a superb global organization, created some of the world's finest brand advertising, and navigated an unforgettable period in the history of globalization with tremendous skill and good humor.

Among the many past and present Interpublic people who assisted in the preparation of this book, I would especially like to thank: Barry Linsky, whose fact-checking and memory-jogging were invaluable in maintaining its accuracy; Stewart Alter, who was an ever-willing sounding board – and whose excellent book Truth Well Told: McCann-Erickson and The Pioneering of Global Advertising provided a rich source of historical detail; and Juliana Mardones, whose regular advice, suggestions, and frequent bursts of telepathy helped keep the project on track. I'd also like to thank Gene Beard, who was a great partner and Chief Financial Officer through all the good and bad times we had together.

Writing this book gave me a great excuse to relive old times and (once again) benefit from the input of retired agency talents and clients. Richard Hine, my writing partner on this book, played the doubly essential role of organizing my thoughts and energizing my language.

Finally, I would like to thank Faith, my wife of 48+ years, my two incredible daughters Hope and Johanna, my sons-in-law Ted Smith and Peter Ashby Howard, and my four grandchildren—Briell, Teddy (Spike), Ashby, and Gillen. My family sustained me throughout my life in business and continues to inspire me in the business of life.